Praise for *Smart Schools, Smart Kids:*

"A lively, informative tour of the why's, what's, who's, and where's of the public-school restructuring movement. Ted Fiske, a seasoned observer of the school scene, is an able guide to some of the most significant educational developments of the day."

—Albert Shanker, President, American Federation of Teachers

"Describes many schools that work—schools that will help make responsible citizens and good thinkers. And that is a small but significant contribution to the transformation of a basic American institution."

—The New York Times

"Must reading for anyone ready to give up on public education. Fiske shows that the new American School is already being created in school districts across the country."

—Keith Geiger, President, National Education Association

"The most important work on education to be published since *A Nation at Risk*."

—Terrell H. Bell, U.S. Secretary of Education, 1981–1985

"American education is in the grip of powerful changes. How are educators and citizens to understand these complex forces? This book . . . makes plain what is actually meant by the new concepts . . . Even better, it provides carefully researched examples of how these have been worked out in real schools by real people."

—Frank Newman, President, Education Commission of the States

"Cogent and insightful . . . important for everyone from the 'education president' to parents of preschoolers who are facing years of difficult choices about their children's learning."

—Kirkus Reviews

Also by Edward B. Fiske

The Fiske Guide to Colleges
How to Get into the Right College
The Best Buys in College Education
Get Organized!

Smart Schools, Smart Kids

EDWARD B. FISKE

with Sally Reed and R. Craig Sautter

WHY DO SOME SCHOOLS WORK?

The nation's leading education correspondent reports on the grass-roots revolution that is transforming America's classrooms.

A TOUCHSTONE BOOK
Published by Simon & Schuster
NEW YORK   LONDON   TORONTO   SYDNEY   TOKYO   SINGAPORE

TOUCHSTONE
Simon & Schuster Building
Rockefeller Center
1230 Avenue of the Americas
New York, New York 10020

First Touchstone Edition 1992

TOUCHSTONE and colophon are registered
trademarks of Simon & Schuster Inc.

Designed by Laurie Jewell
Manufactured in the United States of America

10   9   8   7   6   5   4   3   2   1

Library of Congress Cataloging-in-Publication Data

Fiske, Edward B.
    Smart schools, smart kids : why do some schools work? / by Edward
B. Fiske.
        p.   c.m.
    "The nation's leading education correspondent reports on the
grassroots revolution that is transforming America's classrooms."
    Includes bibliographical references (p. 279) and index.
    1. Public schools—United States. 2. School improvement pro-
grams—United States. 3. Educational innovations—United States.
4. School management and organization—United States. I. Title.
LA217.2.F57   1991
371.'01'0973—dc20   91-19530
                                                                 CIP

ISBN: 0-671-69063-9
ISBN: 0-671-79212-1 (pbk)

ACKNOWLEDGMENTS

SMART SCHOOLS, SMART KIDS is a product of the time, energy, ideas, and talents of many people. I am indebted to all those who played a role in its creation, in big ways and small.

At the top of the list are my two collaborators, Sally Reed and R. Craig Sautter. Sally is a skilled reporter and editor with a deep commitment to education. Craig is a thoughtful observer and critic of educational trends. I was fortunate indeed to have had them as my colleagues.

Special thanks are in order to Ernest L. Boyer, president of the Carnegie Foundation for the Advancement of Teaching, who provided both moral and financial support for this book starting when it was still in the planning stages. Peter Stanley, formerly of the Ford Foundation, who recently became president of Pomona College, was also most generous, and I am grateful to Vartan Gregorian, Artemis A. W. Joukowsky, and all my other friends at Brown University, where I had the opportunity to serve as the first Joukowsky-Wolynsky Fellow. Thanks also to the Lilly Endowment, Inc., the Joyce Foundation, and DePaul University for their financial assistance to Craig Sautter's research.

My appreciation goes to *The New York Times* for a leave of absence to complete the project, as well as to numerous journalistic colleagues who were good enough to serve as additional eyes and ears. These included Ellis Berger, Catherine Carey, Susan Chira, Karen De Witt, Dorothy E. Dubia, Robert A. Frahm of *The Hartford Courant*, Charisse Grant, Bruce Hammond, April Hattori, Erin Hoover, Mary Jane Smetanka, Jennifer Stoffel, Mary Tabor, and Amy Stuart Wells. Other generous people read parts of the manuscript and offered suggestions. These include Michael J. Alves, Joseph Fernandez, Louis V. Gerstner, Jr., Albert Giroux, Jr., David

Hornbeck, Tom James, Joe Nathan, Frank Newman, Warren Olson, Hugh Price, Diane Ravitch, Roger Semerad, Theodore Sizer, Marc Tucker, and Grant Wiggins. While grateful for their wisdom, I, of course, accept responsibility for the final text.

Alice Mayhew, my editor, and Ari Hoogenboom of Simon & Schuster kept me moving along the straight and narrow. Thanks, too, to Sterling Lord, my agent. Others who provided help of various kinds along the way were Terry Brooks, Pat Todd, and Debbie Riggs of the Gheens Professional Development Academy; Frank Dobisky, Marilyn Cookson, and Judy Paradis of Dobisky Associates; Pam Callahan; Gary Cosimini; Cathie Hardie; Pat Kok; and Robert Tolles.

The real heroes of *Smart Schools, Smart Kids* are the principals, teachers, students, scholars, and political leaders who are carrying out the transformation of American public education that is the subject of the book. I am grateful to all of them, especially those who welcomed us into their classrooms and were so generous with their time and thoughts. In a few cases—for reasons that are obvious—we have changed the names of students in the interest of confidentiality and respect.

Finally, thanks to my wife, Dale, and to my two daughters, Julie and Suzanna, for their love and support. I hope that *Smart Schools, Smart Kids* will serve to make this country's schools a better place for my daughters' children.

Greens Farms, Connecticut
May 1991

To my first writing teacher,
my father, Edward R. Fiske, Jr.

CONTENTS

PREFACE

IT'S NO SECRET that America's public schools are failing. Since the early 1980s Americans have been deluged with reports and studies, backed by abundant anecdotes, documenting the academic deficiencies of our young people. One survey of high school juniors discovered that only one in three could put the Civil War in the correct half century. The National Assessment of Educational Progress found that only one in five young adults between the ages of twenty-one and twenty-five could read a bus timetable or draft a simple letter asking for a job in a supermarket. In the nation that first landed a man on the moon, a full quarter of adults cannot say whether the earth goes around the sun or vice versa. In 1987 the New York Telephone Company had to screen 57,000 applicants to find 2,000 with the skills to become entry-level operators and repair technicians.

Nor has there been any shortage of advice on how to improve the situation. Allan Bloom, author of the best-selling *The Closing of the American Mind* (Simon and Schuster, 1987), wants to recover a lost age when schools and colleges concentrated on basics. Other reformers point wistfully to Japanese schools and wish that our students, like theirs, would go to school on Saturdays, do more homework, and cram for tests. Still others hold out the prospect of some silver bullet that, all by itself, will get public schools back on the right track. The National Education Association sees salvation in more federal money. The Bush administration asserts that allowing parents to choose among several schools will do the job. Others put their faith in cultural literacy, more math and science, or new rules that will make it easier to get rid of incompetent teachers.

Such discussions are, for the most part, wishful thinking. The

Golden Age for which Bloom and others long never existed in the first place. There may have been a time when American schools had higher standards for those who completed high school, but it was also a time when the overwhelming majority of students, especially those who were poor, handicapped, or otherwise difficult to teach, dropped out of the system long before they got that chance. Japanese culture differs from ours in such fundamental respects that even if we could import Japanese-style schools, they would never take root in our heterogeneous society. Pouring more money into—or making kids log more time in—a system that has already demonstrated its ineffectiveness is patently foolish. Most important, while ideas such as parental choice have merit, the problems facing American public education are too complex to be solved by any single elixir.

It's now time to put both hand wringing and wishful thinking behind us. Louis V. Gerstner, Jr., the chairman of RJR Nabisco, Inc., has what he calls the Noah Principle: "No more prizes for predicting rain. Prizes only for building arks." If Americans are serious about rebuilding their schools we must look to the present and the future rather than to some mythical past. We must seek distinctly American solutions, and we must avoid the temptation to grasp at gimmicks. That's what this book is all about.

Smart Schools, Smart Kids takes its title from the technological concept of the "smart machine" and it differs from most previous discussions of schools in two ways.

First, this book argues that the time for tinkering with the current system of public education is over. After a decade of trying to make the system work better by such means as more testing, higher salaries, and tighter curriculums, we must now face up to the fact that anything short of fundamental structural change is futile. We are trying to use a nineteenth-century institution to prepare young people for life in the twenty-first century. American public schools grew up around an early industrial model that has outlived its usefulness in education as well as in the industry that created it. The renewal of public education in this country requires nothing less than a frontal assault on *every* aspect of schooling—the way we run districts, organize classrooms, use time, measure achievement, assign students, relate schools to their surroundings, and hold people accountable. Trying to get more learning out of the current system is like trying to get the Pony Express to compete with the telegraph by breeding faster ponies.

Second, *Smart Schools, Smart Kids* argues that the radical transformation of an institution as complicated as the American public school system may sound like a fantasy, but the creation of a system of smart schools is already underway. We know how to fix American schools, and they are being fixed. This book is descriptive, not homiletic. It does not focus on what *ought* to happen; it tells what *is* happening. It's just that until now hardly anyone has been in a position to notice.

As we begin, some warnings are in order. For one thing, we are still in the early stages of this revolution, and full-blown smart schools do not yet exist. Most of the changes thus far have taken place in bits and pieces, and it's not yet clear how they will fit together. Some people are attempting to decentralize the management of school districts and individual schools, while others have focused on new teacher-student relationships. Still others are looking at new ways to organize time, test students, build bridges to the local community, or hold teachers and principals accountable for student learning. Most of these educational pioneers have little, if any, idea of what others are doing or how their own work fits into the bigger picture.

So don't expect a neat and tidy blueprint for the school of the future. Indeed, such expectations are part of the problem. The last thing we need is some modern-day managerial guru laying out another "single best system" for overhauling public schools. *Smart Schools, Smart Kids* lays out a vision that it is possible—indeed inevitable—to have a very different system of public education in this country. The first nine chapters will take you into classrooms around the country where the building blocks of smart schools are being developed. No one ever said that overhauling a $200-billion-a-year enterprise is easy, so chapter 10 looks at some of the political problems involved in bringing these elements together. But in the final analysis it is up to every school district, every school, every reader to decide which blend of the available elements is best for particular circumstances. That's what it means to be "smart."

The United States has entered a new era—one marked by a global economy in which countries will prosper or fail not on the basis of geographical location or the availability of natural resources but on the capacity of their citizens to think. "When resources came out of the ground, the United States was a rich country," said John Sculley, chairman of Apple Computer Inc. "Now that resources come out of people's heads, we are a developing country." The strength of the United States has always been its capacity to innovate in the face of new situations and new threats. That is exactly what has begun to happen in public schools across the country. Smart schools are being built—piece by piece. That's what *Smart Schools, Smart Kids* is all about.

1.

THE LEARNING CRISIS

MORRIS JEFFERSON was an academic failure in a school where academic failure was commonplace. A sprawling one-story brick building in a barrio on the northwestern outskirts of Houston, the Hollibrook Elementary School sits across the street from a run-down public housing project where the roofs leak and the potholes in the street are large enough to swallow a tricycle. Almost all of the school's one thousand students are poor members of minority groups who live in homes where a language other than English is spoken. The typical Hollibrook student entered kindergarten ill prepared for academic work and, year by year, slipped farther and farther below grade level. When it came to standardized test scores, Hollibrook was the caboose of the Spring Branch School District.

As a second-grader, Morris was traveling the familiar route. Tall and skinny, with olive skin, big brown eyes, and dark hair cut in bangs over his forehead, he showed a wry sense of humor and a talent for goofy drawings but little enthusiasm for sitting quietly and listening to teachers talk. He neglected his homework assignments and picked fights with classmates. A standardized reading test put him at only the 8th percentile nationally, and by the end of the 1989 school year he had failed to master the full list of "competencies" that the state of Texas requires for promotion to third grade. Morris was, as educators like to put it, "retained."

By September, though, just as Morris was gearing up for his second shot at second grade, major changes were taking place at Hollibrook. The school had a new principal, Suzanne Still, a former special-education teacher whose years of working with struggling young people had convinced her that *all* students, including the Morris Jeffersons of the world, could learn more than most public schools either encourage or expect. One of her first acts was to tack a small sign above the door to her office: "A good principal always remembers what it was like." She then set out to overhaul Hollibrook around principles that were the exact opposite of most of those held dear by the state of Texas, the Spring Branch School District, and a century of American public school tradition.

Instead of putting every student in a class with peers of like ability, as had been the practice for years, she grouped them randomly, even allowing children in various grades to work together in a multiage "pod." Two second-grade teachers got the go-ahead to combine their classes and do team teaching, while three others took on a group of second-graders and agreed to stay with them until they graduate in 1993. Spanish-speaking students worked side by side with Anglos. The school day was no longer divided into regular forty-five- or seventy-two-minute periods, and teachers were encouraged to disregard artificial distinctions between the various academic areas. Students wrote while they were doing math, learned spelling from the social studies teacher, and read for the first half hour of every school day.

Whereas Texas expects its teachers to take their state-approved basal readers and textbooks in hand, start on page one, and work their way through to the last chapter, Still told her faculty to use whatever teaching resources they wanted. Gone, too, was the requirement that teachers file the educational equivalent of flight plans (otherwise known as planning books) so that the principal or a visiting inspector from the State Education Department in Austin could quickly ascertain that on Thursday at 10:15 A.M. "Miss Burpee in 5B" is doing simple division. As a teacher, Still recalls, she "always preferred to work for someone who thought that I had a brain and could think." So at Hollibrook decisions on everything from the hiring of new teachers to the choosing of curriculum materials are now made by committees dominated by teachers. Perhaps most important, Hollibrook adopted the principle of "accelerated learning," which asserts that if students are having difficulty, teachers should give them *more* academic stimulation, not plunk them in "remedial" classes, slow down the learning process, and condemn them to perpetual failure.

Cumulatively the changes at Hollibrook constituted a frontal assault on just about every aspect of traditional school management—how to manage a school, treat teachers, deal with students, organize instruction, and manage time. It was also politically risky. To deal with the threat that some inspector from the state or local school district might show up and call teachers on some technicality, Hollibrook set up an early warning system. Whenever such a visitor showed up at the front office, one of the secretaries unobtrusively meandered over to the nearest classroom, stuck her head in the door and spoke the code word, "Bluebird." The teacher immediately dropped what she was doing and sent a student on the rounds of the other classrooms, like a modern-day Paul Revere, spreading word of the impending danger.

"Bluebird."

"OK."

"Bluebird."

"Thanks."

"Bluebird."

"Got it."

Within minutes, students who were reading on their own in the halls would be recalled to their desks. Officially sanctioned textbooks were pulled from their hiding places in closets and opened prominently on the teachers' desks. To the untrained eye, Hollibrook had become a model of educational orthodoxy.

The turnaround at Hollibrook was virtually immediate. By the fall of 1990 students at Hollibrook were performing at the national and district average, and in math they were even higher. Vandalism and fights in the halls became a rarity. Attendance reached a lofty 96 percent, and more than 1,000 parents show up for regular conferences with their children's teachers. Most significant, the average student in Hollibrook is now making *more* than a full year's progress in basic academic subjects—this in a school where two-thirds of a year's progress would be considered respectable.

The success stories included Morris Jefferson, who was assigned to the team-taught second grade. The two teachers, Joy Campbell and Marylou Bland, tried everything they could think of to get Morris and the other students actively involved in their own learning. Instead of having students simply read stories about the circus and answer questions, they had them do research on elephants and clowns, give reports, and make costumes. The teachers also noticed that Morris became engaged whenever the topic under discussion involved science, so they began building on this strength.

Soon he was introducing fourth-grade words such as *predator* and *camouflage* to his classmates. One night at the end of the school year Bland was sitting at home thumbing through a report on the reading-test scores of her students. She was dumbfounded to see that Morris's had jumped from the 8th to the 86th percentile. "I was so excited that I called his mother at ten P.M. to tell her the news," she said. "We cried."

The story of what Hollibrook calls its renaissance is dramatic but by no means unique. In recent years a growing number of farsighted and courageous educators like Suzanne Still have become alarmed at the way public schools are failing America's children. They have begun to question traditional theories of learning and notions of how to run schools and to put their ideas into action. In many cases their ideas have been embraced by entire districts and even states. They have become the pioneers in a transformation of virtually all of the fundamental structures of American public education.

The failures of the current system are well documented. The 1983 federal report by the National Commission on Excellence in Education, "A Nation at Risk," warned of a "rising tide of mediocrity that threatens our very future as a nation and a people." Since then our national senses have been numbed by one horror story after another about the abysmal ignorance of our young people. It would be comforting to say that such findings resulted from the well-publicized problems of inner-city and rural schools, but we would be kidding ourselves. Even our *best* schools are failing to meet minimal international standards. Extrapolation of data from the National Assessment of Educational Progress shows that only 5 percent of the graduates of American high schools can read at a level that would qualify them for a spot in a university in Europe. And when they get to a college in this country, the overwhelming majority of these graduates start off studying what their European counterparts learned in high school. Some high schools never graduate 50 percent of their students. By some estimates, 50 percent of those who enroll in college never get degrees.

The country is paying a terrible price for the failure of its public schools—economically and socially. Study after study has described the "mismatch" that exists between the needs of employers and the skills of available workers. The head of the Federal Reserve Bank of Boston once observed that New England's so-called economic miracle came to a grinding halt not because employers were not ready to invest in new factories but because they feared that they would not be able to find workers to run them. Yet he spoke from a city where thousands of persons are unemployed. American companies spend an estimated $20 billion a year—and colleges and universities spend billions more—on remedial education programs to teach what should have been learned years before. "Business is having to do the schools' product-recall work for them," grumbled David Kearns, the former chairman of the Xerox Corporation who joined the Bush administration as deputy secretary of education earlier this year. Louis V. Gerstner, Jr., of RJR Nabisco, Inc., was equally blunt. "Every corporate chief in the country now faces an annual crop of entrants to the labor force that every year contains a higher proportion of functional illiterates," he said. "The results of this educational drought go straight to the bottom line— lost customers, poor product quality, lost shipments, garbled paperwork."

The social cost is equally devastating. More than a quarter of students who start out in American high schools fail to graduate with their classes. (Given the job prospects for high school dropouts, that's the equivalent of driving 7,800 school buses a year, or 43 buses every school day—with a different group of passengers each—up to the welfare office.) Economically the 1980s was a decade when the rich got richer and the poor got poorer. Study after study has documented the widening earnings gap between the well educated and poorly educated. The Economic Policy Institute, for example, found that between 1979 and 1987 the wages of working male college graduates rose by 7 percent in real dollars while the wages of those with only a high school diploma fell by a comparable amount. We are moving toward becoming a nation of educational haves and have-nots. Such a situation may be tolerable in England or other countries where rigid class structures are the norm, but in this country it is not only morally wrong but tantamount to planting a social time bomb.

We live in an increasingly competitive global economy, one where information is power and where, as Shoshana Zuboff of the Harvard Business School put it, "learning is the new form of labor."

Samuel M. Ehrenhalt, the regional commissioner of the United States Bureau of Labor Statistics in New York, noted the "historic moment in American economic development" that occurred in the late 1980s when the number of professional, managerial, and technical workers exceeded the number of blue-collar workers for the first time. The shift ended an era that began in the early days of the twentieth century, when manual workers succeeded farm workers as the largest group of employees. "Now, three-quarters of a century later, the blue-collar preeminence is giving way to the quintessential workers of the new economy," he said. "Their stock in trade is knowledge, their working tools, above all, ideas. With the changes in the industrial structure of the 1980s, these occupations comprise the prime growth field of the American labor force."

Gone are the days when a young person could drop out of school and get a job with his father at the local meat-packing plant. Jobs of the future will require higher levels of mathematics, better reading skills, and a greater capacity for high-level thinking. Paul O'Neill, the chief executive officer of Alcoa, argues that American industry is, in effect, rolling back one of the fundamentals of the Industrial Revolution. "Instead of dumbing-down production, business is evolving a high-tech version of preindustrial craftsmanship," he said. "This time the artisans are using their heads, not their hands." Consider, for example, the task of repairing textile machinery. In the past a semiliterate worker could look inside a loom, see how the parts fit together, diagnose the problem, and fix it. Today the comparable machine is full of nonobservable microprocessors and other electronic equipment. To diagnose and fix the new machines, technicians must be able to represent the workings symbolically in their minds through the use of complicated manuals, diagrams, and updates provided by the manufacturer. The entire process has been moved to a higher level of abstraction—one that requires a whole different level of educational preparation.

In its report "A Nation Prepared: Teachers for the 21st Century," the Carnegie Forum on Education and the Economy, based in Rochester, New York, described what goes on at the Samsung Electronics plant outside of Seoul, Korea, which produces home video recorders for sale in the United States. The line workers at that plant, who are better educated than their American counterparts, work twelve hours a day, 363 days a year, for $3,000 a year.

American firms cannot compete with the Samsungs of the world in their terms. American industry must shift its focus from rote, low-wage operations to those requiring a better-educated workforce. The choice is either to transform ourselves into a high-skill, high-wage economy or see a rapid deterioration of our standard of living. "America must leave the routine work of the world to others," says Marc Tucker, president of the National Center on Education and the Economy. "We must become a nation that thinks for a living. We must become smarter than the rest of the world."

The consequences of becoming a learning society are enormous, for it means that for the first time schools have been given the job of producing the *capital* on which the country depends. Yet unless drastic changes are made, American public schools are going to get worse. The fastest-growing segments of the school population are precisely those students with whom schools have been least successful in the past. Between 1970 and 1980 the proportion of minority students in American public schools rose from 21 to 27 percent, and by the year 2020 it is expected that such students will represent almost half of all students—something that has already happened in California and Texas. Between 1979 and 1983 the proportion of students living in poverty rose from 16 to 22 percent, and this, too, is projected to increase.

Outside pressures are making it increasingly difficult for schools even to hold their own. In its new report, "The Condition of Teaching, 1990," the Carnegie Foundation for the Advancement of Teaching provided vivid firsthand documentation of the difficulties that teachers confront. "Today's children are living with many more stresses than children of a decade or even five years ago," wrote one teacher. "Single-parent families, dual-employed parents, unemployment and teen parents have produced children with little or no coping skills, and parents are too busy, too uneducated themselves, to help." Another commented that "the quality of life for my students" is her biggest problem. "Divorce, substance abuse and plain loneliness leave students with very little curiosity, very little interest in learning," she said. "The biggest battle I have as a teacher is getting my kids to care about their own intellect." Ernest L. Boyer, president of the foundation, drew the inevitable conclusion. "The problems of society are washing over schools, dramatically distracting and even damaging the children and reducing their motivation and capacity to learn," he said. "Unless prospects for success improve, not only the schools but the very future of our nation is imperiled."

The failure of our public schools has, of course, not gone unnoticed. Largely because of the political impact of "A Nation at Risk," the 1980s was an era of feverish educational reform efforts. Legislatures and state boards of education in every state moved aggressively to tighten the course requirements for a high school diploma, raise teacher salaries, and set new standards for those entering the teaching profession. Tennessee enacted merit pay for teachers. New Jersey allowed liberal arts graduates without education degrees to become teachers. Everyone had new standardized tests—for teachers as well as students. Over the decade spending for elementary and secondary education rose by one-third. But then a funny thing happened. In April 1988, five years after "A Nation at Risk," President Reagan hosted a ceremony in the East Room of the White House to celebrate this flurry of school-reform efforts. Leading politicians and educators, as well as those in the national media who cover education, used the occasion to reflect on the accomplishments of school reform. And we came to a startling conclusion:

There *weren't* any.

To be sure, standardized reading and math scores were up slightly—but mostly in the lower grades and in the most primitive academic skills. In November 1990 the Policy Information Center of the Educational Testing Service issued a report summarizing the results of what it termed the "education reform decade" of the 1980s. The report looked at achievement test results ranging across all major curriculum areas, starting with reading, where it found "no gains in average reading proficiency." The researchers identified "some improvement" in average math proficiency, but "none at the higher level we associate with having taken several years of high school math." Not surprisingly, American students were still "bringing up the rear in science achievement." As for writing, the study concluded: "Our students are poor writers, and they are not improving. They don't much like to write, and they like it less as they go through school." The only big increase, the study found, came in time in front of the tube. "Television watching increased substantially in the 1980s," the researchers said. Some good news came in the form of a narrowing of the gap between seventeen-year-old black and white students. But even this good news was tempered, for the gains came "more at the basic and middle ranges . . . than at the top." At the academic level required for moving on to college, the black-white gap widened, and there was no narrowing of the chasm between whites and Hispanics. "A Nation at Risk" and the reforms associated with it had done little if anything to help the Morris Jeffersons of the world, who themselves were "at risk."

With the wisdom of hindsight, the reason became clear: The reforms inspired by "A Nation at Risk" contained no new ideas! They called for more of the same: more core academic courses, more standardized tests, a longer school year, more money for teachers. By the end of the 1980s it was evident that the existing system of public education had been pushed to its limits and that more of the same would not make any difference. School reformers in the 1980s tried to squeeze more juice out of the orange. It took five years to realize that we were not dealing with an orange. We were holding a lemon.

The reforms of the 1980s were doomed from the outset because they asked American public schools to do something they were never designed to do, never did do, and never could do. We have been asking schools to prepare students—*all* students—for demanding, fast-changing jobs of the future with rigid structures and teaching methods designed for the factories of the early industrial age. We have been asking a nineteenth-century institution to educate people for life in the twenty-first century. Public schools as currently organized are as archaic as a turn-of-the-century Model T Ford rattling down a thruway.

Public schools are nineteenth-century institutions because they were organized around an industrial model that prevailed at the turn of the century. Mass production sought to reduce as many elements of the manufacturing process as possible to simple, repetitive tasks that could be handled by workers who were easily trained and, for all practical purposes, interchangeable. A relatively small group of people—perhaps 20 percent—did the thinking for the entire enterprise. Industry embraced the principles of managerial theorists of the day such as Frederick Winslow Taylor, who spoke of "scientific management" and the "one best system" to solve any organizational problem. He called for a centralized, hierarchical style of management and preached the value of standardization, a rigid sense of time, and an accountability system based on loyalty to the system. As agents of the state, public schools did their part to reinforce these values. They organized themselves to turn out a few well-trained "thinkers" and large numbers of ordinary workers with the knowledge and skills to do their own jobs. In their own functioning as educational institutions, schools also embraced the values of centralization, standardization, and bureaucratic accountability.

In recent years many of the same American companies that gave birth to this old industrial model have been abandoning it. Corporations such as Ford, Xerox, and Motorola have recognized that, given the complexity of new production processes and the need to introduce new products more frequently, they must abandon the old hierarchical structures. They have decentralized and trimmed their management structures and reorganized their workplaces around teams of workers, each given responsibility for organizing and carrying out their assignments, whether they be assembling lawn mowers or processing insurance claims. They have adopted more flexible work schedules and developed new standards of quality control. To pull this off, they have poured billions of dollars into educational programs aimed at equipping workers to learn new skills, solve problems, and take a more active role in promoting the economic and other goals of the enterprise.

It is now time for schools to do the same. It is no longer possible to run an effective system of public education under the old values of centralized authority, standardization, and bureaucratic accountability any more than it is possible to run *any* large institution effectively in this fashion. Moreover, the "product" that schools must turn out is changing, and the traditional structures are as ill suited to meeting the new market demands as a buggy factory would be to turning out jet aircraft. The "thinking society" of the twenty-first century can no longer be content with graduates trained to take in and recycle information handed out by teachers and other authority figures. Today's students must be taught to think for themselves and to generate new information. But you cannot say: "We will lecture to you about how to be creative, and then we will measure your creativity with this multiple-choice test." We need a whole new approach to designing and running schools.

Technology has given us the concept of the "smart machine"—one that, instead of simply repeating the same operation over and over in rote fashion, is capable of receiving new information and altering its actions accordingly. The emerging global economy requires workers who are "smart" in the same sense: workers who can analyze new situations, come up with creative solutions, and take responsibility for decisions relating to the performance of their jobs. The functioning of a modern democracy requires citizens with similar skills, and to produce "smart" workers and "smart" citizens, we need "smart" schools and "smart" kids.

This transformation of American public schools from nineteenth-century institutions into schools that reflect the values of twenty-first-century economic, political, and social life is well under way. Teachers, administrators, parents, and political leaders are questioning the old way of doing things. Although full-fledged smart schools do not yet exist, every one of the ingredients for creating them—new ways of managing school systems, running schools, organizing classrooms, using time, measuring results, and so forth—exists somewhere in the United States. Somewhere, some public school or group of teachers within a school is turning every one of the elements of the factory-model school on its head. Thus far, most of these modern-day Horace Manns are working in isolation, and by themselves none of their new ideas is powerful enough to transform American public schools. But put together, these bold experiments can bring about the smart schools that American students need if they are to be prepared for the twenty-first century. The situation is a bit like the proverbial story of the blind men with the elephant. Each touches a part, but no one has a grasp of the whole elephant.

The purpose of this book is to outline the elephant. The chapters that follow constitute a journey through the quiet revolution that is slowly transforming American education. Our journey will take us to Miami, where teachers, parents, and even students have taken over most of the important decisions previously reserved for high-ranking administrators. We will visit Louisville, where historian James Streible and his colleagues are getting students to take charge of their own learning. We will visit Hannibal, Missouri, and other sites where teachers are resetting the academic clock to fit the differing needs of students, including those judged to be "slow" learners. Our journey will take us to Cambridge, Massachusetts, where parents are now free to choose which school their child will attend, and Indianapolis, Indiana, where teachers have scrapped multiple-choice tests and measure students on a broad range of intelligences. We will stop in Silverdale, Washington, where educators have rethought the relationship between technology and learning, and Prince Georges County, Maryland, where schools are redefining the relationship between schools and the community that surrounds them. We will look at the obstacles these educational pioneers faced, how they overcame them, what they achieved, and what still remains to be accomplished. Along the way we will begin to realize that what we are seeing is not only a redesigning of the fundamental structures of American public schools but a cultural transformation of one of the most basic institutions in our society.

When we have completed our journey, we will look back on what we have seen, make some connections, and speculate on what a smart school—an elephant, if you will—might look like if the parts were put together and these prototypes became the norm. We will also discuss what it will take politically to create whole systems of smart schools.

These are exciting times. It's an exciting journey.

First stop: Miami.

2.

SMART SCHOOLS

TEACHERS at the Myrtle Grove Elementary School in the Opa-Locka section of Miami were uneasy. Students were getting a full hour of reading instruction every day, but with twenty-four students in a classroom teachers were spending more time than they liked standing in front of the blackboard and lecturing to the whole class. "It was hard to find more than a few minutes a week to work one-on-one with any given child," recalled Patti Bartels, who teaches third grade. "You didn't have a chance to spot individual problems."

Then one day, while thumbing through a professional journal, Cecil Daniels, Myrtle Grove's principal, came upon an intriguing idea. Why not extend the reading period to two hours and then divide each class into two groups of a dozen students? Give the first group an hour of personalized reading instruction and send the other twelve students out to some other activity where lecturing was OK and another dozen students would not make any difference. "That way everyone got at least an hour of pretty intensive teaching," said Daniels. "It seemed so obvious you wondered why you hadn't thought of it yourself."

Daniels stuck copies of the article into each teacher's mailbox, and soon the teachers began bouncing the idea around in the teachers lounge. They liked the thought of having two hours a day when they only had to deal with a dozen students. The problem, of course, was logistical—how to blend the scheme with the rest of the school schedule. A magnetic board was set up in the teachers lounge with pieces of metal representing each class that had to be scheduled. Teachers started playing around with it during their spare time, and one of them solved the puzzle of how to organize what came to be known as the Wheel. Teachers of five lecture-oriented subjects—career education, media skills, computer literacy, expressive language, and counseling—agreed to let a dozen extra students rotate through their classes during the first two periods of the day. A committee of teachers came in over the summer to work out the details, and in September 1989 Myrtle Grove opened with the Wheel in full operation. "It's been fantastic," said Bartels. "Having that time with only a dozen students means that I can catch every move they make and really understand why they may not be learning something. Our class is about to finish reading a whole book. Before the Wheel that never happened."

The Wheel came to Myrtle Grove Elementary School because of shared decision making, a new, decentralized approach to the running of schools and school systems that within a few years promises to transform the management of American public education. Scores of school districts have already implemented some form of shared decision making, and the number is growing geometrically. Two states—Washington and Tennessee—have begun encouraging districts to adopt decentralized approaches, and eight—California, Florida, Hawaii, Kansas, Kentucky, New York, Texas, and West Virginia—are making it mandatory. Illinois mandated it for Chicago.

The premise of shared decision making is simple: Those closest to the action should have the authority and responsibility to make most of the decisions. This principle applies both to the relationship between central school districts and individual schools and to the relationships within schools among principals, teachers, parents, and others. Thus in Dade County, Florida, if two-thirds of faculty members in a local school vote to do so, that school becomes part of the "school-based management" program, and authority to make decisions on everything from budgets and hiring to curriculums and textbooks is automatically transferred from the central board of education to people in the local school. At the same time, in what is known as shared decision making, management of the school is transferred from the principal to a team, or cadre, as they call it, that includes the principal but is dominated by teachers and frequently includes parents, clerical and custodial workers, and, in some high schools, students.

Locating the authority to make instructional decisions closer to the students may sound like common sense, but it is far from the way American public schools have traditionally operated. Americans are proud that we do not have a national ministry of education and that public schools are in the hands of sixteen thousand local school boards. Yet, for all this emphasis on local control, public schools are one of the most authoritative and top-heavy institutions in American society.

The inspiration for school management as it exists today came from the industrial models that prevailed at the turn of the twentieth century. Large American companies developed around those ideals—top-down management, a single best system—articulated by Frederick Winslow Taylor, the managerial guru mentioned in chapter 1. American industry sought to break as many jobs as possible down into the most simple rote tasks, each of which was assigned to a single low-skilled worker or group of workers who repeated these tasks over and over with machinelike efficiency. Indeed, the workers themselves were viewed as little more than interchangeable parts. Directing and motivating these workers, of course, required an elaborate network of better-trained middle managers, who also served as the conduits by which decisions were made by top administrators, who did the thinking for the organization. At every level the emphasis was on standardization, uniformity, and efficiency. Time was rigidly fixed, and management became the art of getting as much production as possible out of an eight-hour shift.

Such an approach to management reflected the social climate of the time. Late nineteenth-century America was a society in flux. The country was absorbing perhaps the largest influx of immigrants ever to descend on a single nation. Between 1880 and 1920 alone, over 23 million newcomers crowded onto America's shores, more than the entire population in 1850. The breakdown of agrarian society and the unplanned expansion of cities created a yawning social void, and labor unrest intensified the fears of middle-class Americans that their stable life was threatened. Taylor's values of hierarchical management, standardization, and ordered scheduling provided a welcome affirmation of order and predictability, values that Americans also sought in their schools. Rigidly controlled public schools were the first line of defense against anarchy and the destruction of democratic values. "The first requisite of the school is Order," asserted William T. Harris, one of the leading superintendents of the day. "Each pupil must be taught first and foremost to conform his behavior to the general standard."

To carry out this mission, schools, too, followed the principles of scientific management. Public education was to be a rational enterprise, run by dispassionate professionals free from political influence. Security lay in the stability and predictability of bureaucratic procedures. Decisions on everything from teacher credentials and graduation requirements to curriculums and textbooks were made at the top by state boards of education and flowed down through each layer of the educational ziggurat to local school boards, superintendents, and principals. Eventually they reached teachers who, like factory workers, were viewed as interchangeable parts and had little control over what they did in their own classrooms. For their part, students were seen as products moving along an assembly line. Put them in a room, do something to them, ring a bell, put them in another room, do something to them, ring a bell, and so on.

The ultimate—and all-pervasive—symbol of the factory-model school is the public address system, which allows the principal to interrupt anything going on in a classroom and sends an unmistakable message about whose concerns are paramount. Never mind that Miss Smith's class is just getting into a heated discussion about King Lear's misplaced sense of loyalty. Just make sure you bring your money to reserve a yearbook. Instruction within the classroom put heavy emphasis on standardization, for it went without saying that there was a "one best way" to teach any given subject or lesson. Student progress of course was measured by "standardized tests" built around the same values. Just as Henry Ford mass-produced the Model T, so, too, school administrators set out to mass-produce the largest generation of students the nation had ever taught. Indeed, every one of the fundamental building blocks of public school grew out of an attempt to make schools every bit as efficient as the factories of the time.

Contemporary accounts testify to the accuracy of the factory metaphor. "Our schools are, in a sense, factories in which the raw materials (children) are to be shaped and fashioned into products to meet the various demands of life," said Harris. "The specifications for manufacturing come from the demands of twentieth century civilization, and it is the business of the school to build its pupils according to the specifications laid down." In *Middletown*, their classic 1925 study of Muncie, Indiana, Robert and Helen Lynd used the same analogy: "The school, like the factory, is a thoroughly regimented world. Immovable seats in orderly rows fix the sphere of activity of each child. For all, from the timid six-year-old entering for the first time to the most assured high school senior, the general routine is much the same. Bells divide the day into periods. . . . For nearly an hour a teacher asks questions and pupils answer, then a bell rings, on the instant books bang, powder and mirrors come out, there is a buzz of talk and laughter as all the urgent business of living resumes momentarily for the children, minutes pass, another bell, gradual sliding into seats, a final giggle, a last vanity case snapped shut. 'In our last lesson we had just finished'—another class is begun." Such extremes have been tempered in recent decades, and there has always been a diversity of teaching styles among individual teachers. Yet the principles of the factory-model school still provide the basic organizing structure under which all educators function. Few have ever questioned its underlying assumptions. As Suzanne Still and her colleagues at Hollibrook in Houston will be quick to tell you, Texas still has a law on its books spelling out precisely how many minutes each teacher must spend teaching each subject to each student every day!

By and large the factory-model school accomplished the mission it was given. It integrated millions of immigrants into a democratic society. It helped stabilize the new urban culture and turned out the kind of workers needed by the industry of the day—millions of workers with enough knowledge to perform routinized jobs as well as thousands of well-educated leaders and managers to do the thinking for the system as a whole. There were, to be sure, millions of casualties. The number of high school dropouts in this country exceeded the number of graduates until 1950, and if you happened to be poor, handicapped, or a troublemaker in the classroom, it was likely that some way would be found to ease you out of the system. But even that, at the time, was not necessarily a catastrophe; for without a high school diploma one could get a job, raise a family, and live a decent life. The factory-model school succeeded because no one ever asked it to educate large numbers of students to a high level. No one ever asked it to teach most American students to *think*.

Starting in the late 1970s the same American industry that had fostered the Taylor model for the better part of a century began to have serious doubts about it. Americans were threatened by a new industrial model from the Japanese that created teams to solve production problems. Likewise they realized that production requirements had become too complex, and markets too diverse, for strategies to be decided solely at the top and filtered down through a pyramid that in many cases had to span the globe. No one today can be that *smart*. The rapid flow of information and the need for adaptability and versatility means that workers must be brought into the decision-making process. For the first time American industry is seeking a substantial nucleus of workers who can accept some responsibility for organizing their work, not simply take orders. The old tool was machinery; the new tool is the minds of workers. "The old smokestack division of a firm into 'heads' and 'hands' no longer works," says Alvin Toffler in his new book *Powershift* (Bantam, 1990). "Just as owners once became dependent on managers for knowledge, today's managers are becoming dependent on their employees for knowledge."

This realization came the hard way. Donald E. Petersen, who recently retired as chairman of Ford Motor Company, recalled that in 1980, his first year as president, Ford lost $1.5 billion. "By any measure, Ford Motor Company was in trouble, the likes of which we had never seen before," he recalled. "The experience, in a word, was harrowing, and after a fair amount of soul-searching and bullet-biting—and many hard decisions—we determined that the only real solution was a total transformation of the company." Ford's solution was to decentralize its management so that as many decisions as possible were made not in Detroit but by people as close to the markets as possible. It hired Edwards Deming, the American management consultant credited with guiding Japanese industry to its remarkable postwar recovery, and Ford implemented his concept of "quality circles," in which workers collaborate in small groups to plan and carry out their work. To equip workers for these new responsibilities, Ford and the United Auto Workers collaborated on a massive education program that, among other things, put thousands of workers through courses on problem solving.

Ford's story is one that can be told, with minor variations, about dozens of other corporations.

The same forces cited by Petersen are now having an impact on public education, starting with the sheer complexity of managing a large enterprise in today's world. Primary and secondary education in this country is a $200-billion-a-year industry that cannot be managed without the empowering of those in direct contact with students. We can no longer tolerate a system that has two and a half administrators for every classroom teacher. Demographic and socioeconomic changes in the student population mean that public schools, like private industry, face increasingly diverse "markets." Even the school's "product" has changed. Schools can no longer function as filling stations to which young people drive up, receive the knowledge they need for a working lifetime, and then drive away. Students must be taught to think and to solve problems. The new goal of education is to "learn to learn." It took Ford until the late 1970s, with the very real prospect that it might soon be forced out of business, to figure out that it had to make some fundamental structural changes. It is hardly surprising that public schools, lacking a profit motive and not threatened with extinction, might take a little longer. But the urgency is just as great. Schools, too, must radically overhaul the way they run themselves. And that is exactly what they are beginning to do.

The first school system to decentralize on a large scale was Dade County, Florida, which includes the city of Miami and 25 other municipalities. With 300,000 students and 18,000 teachers in 271 schools, it is the fourth largest school system in the country—and getting even bigger. By 1996 the district will build or redesign 51 schools to handle Dade's exploding population, due in part to waves of immigrants from the Caribbean, Central America, and Asia, many with little or no formal education. The student body, which comes from 118 countries, is 46 percent Hispanic, 33 percent black, and 20 percent white. In March 1988 citizens passed the largest school bond referendum in the nation's history—$980 million—to finance the construction of the new schools and the renovation and expansion of 260 existing facilities that have fallen victim to old age and severe overcrowding.

Considering the challenges they faced, Dade County's schools were doing reasonably well. But the leaders of the school system and United Teachers of Dade, the teachers union, thought that they could do even better. They decided that the key to better schools was the "professionalization" of teaching. The concept of the professional—a worker who is highly trained, defines his or her job in terms of responsibility to a client, and accepts collective responsibility for defining and maintaining standards in a field—is one that has only recently been applied to teaching. Indeed it is the polar opposite of the role of the teacher in the factory school. But officials in Dade County argued that this must change. The best place to start raising student achievement, they argued, was by treating teachers as respected professionals, not as interchangeable parts of a machine.

Dade County has a strong tradition of union-management cooperation that dates to 1974, when the Florida legislature passed a collective-bargaining law for state employees that cleared the way for teachers to begin to play a role in educational policy-making. The two sides set up task forces to work out as many problems as they could before they reached the bargaining stage, and faculty councils were set up in each school to advise principals. In 1984 the legislature approved a "merit schools" program offering financial incentives to improve schools, and in Dade County the school board and the union set up a cooperative program to oversee the program and allocate the rewards. Finally, in 1985, the two sides created a Professionalization of Teaching Task Force cochaired by Leonard Britton, the school superintendent at the time, and Pat Tornillo, Jr., president of the teachers union. The task force's job was to monitor "A Nation at Risk" and the other national reports that were coming out and to suggest ways of improving the professional status and working conditions of teachers. A new contract moved in this direction by offering expanded training opportunities for teachers, giving them time and money to attend conferences and establishing a career ladder that permitted superior teachers to diversify their careers by taking on additional tasks, such as serving as mentors to younger teachers. From there it was a short leap to giving teachers a role in making decisions on educational policy.

An important factor in the decentralization of Dade County schools was strong leadership on both sides. Tornillo, who led a bitter statewide teachers' strike in 1968, has been on the scene for nearly three decades not only as leader of United Teachers of Dade but as head of the statewide Florida Education Association. On the administration side was Joseph Fernandez, a former mathematics teacher and union steward who had risen to the post of deputy superintendent under Britton and has since moved on to become schools chancellor in New York City. Tornillo and Fernandez are two peas out of the same pod, able to size up situations quickly and to make decisions. The idea for shared decision making was first suggested to the superintendent by Tornillo over breakfast. Britton, a capable but cautious administrator, was sympathetic to the idea, but it was his deputy, Fernandez, who decided to run with it.

Fernandez and Tornillo struck a two-part deal to experiment with a new system of governance for Dade County schools. The school-based management component redefined the relationship between the district and the local schools, starting with finances. Traditionally each school was given its budget in terms of "units"— so many teachers, so many support staff, so much for plant maintenance, and so forth. The only discretionary funds were for teaching supplies and equipment, which typically amounted to no more than 10 percent of a school's expenses. Under decentralization each school was given a total dollar figure, based on an allotment of $3,400 per student. Starting with this lump sum, schools were free to devise budgets as they saw fit. They could, for example, trade in an assistant-principal position and use the savings for hourly aides, additional supplies, or any other item. Schools were also given more discretion over educational and other decisions, and the board and union agreed to seek waivers from state law when required for purposes such as class size, the length of school day or class periods, and "balanced curriculum" requirements spelling out how much time students must spend on each subject. The second part of the plan, shared decision making, reformed the governing structures *within* each school. Decisions on educational matters were no longer the sole prerogative of the principal. Instead they would be made by an elected cadre, or governing team, that included teachers and in many cases parents, community representatives, and members of clerical, cafeteria, and custodial staffs. "It's the classroom teachers who know what kids need," said Fernandez. "It's time to let them try things that they think will work."

Schools could buy into what Dade County called, somewhat

infelicitously, school-based management/shared decision making by a two-thirds vote of the faculty and sign-off by the principal. The only rule was that the new, more democratic approach could not cost more than regular schools. "If we'd thrown a few million dollars into this, we wouldn't be proving the point: that the type of management makes a real impact," said Gerald O. Dreyfuss, the assistant superintendent who was put in charge of the program. Fernandez and Tornillo took to the road to promote their plan, plugging it with teachers, parents, business people, and legislators. Their presentation came to be known as the Joe and Pat Show, and the sessions frequently ended up sounding like revival meetings. "Joe is Puerto Rican and I'm Italian," said Tornillo. "We both can get emotional."

The first problem the pair faced was selling it to teachers, many of whom viewed it as just the latest new gimmick to save the schools—and one that, like teaching machines, management by objective, and all the others, would soon pass. The Odd Couple visited the faculty at one school at the end of the school day. As they entered the room, the assembled teachers were reading papers, talking, and writing. Clearly the last thing they wanted to do was listen to them. But when Tornillo told the teachers that in the future *they* would be the ones making the decisions in the schools, they were suddenly energized. One teacher stood up and said, "Are you telling us that we are going to make the decision on such things as class size?" "Yes," he said. Suddenly the pencils went down. The newspapers went down. Now the teachers were not just listening, they were spellbound. A teacher at the side of the room, surprised and somewhat horrified at the implications of this new responsibility, was heard to say, "Oh no!"

In 1987 a formal agreement was signed, and schools were invited to take a crack at doing things differently. Sixty schools indicated interest, and thirty-two were given the go-ahead. They were regrouped for administrative purposes under a separate administrative structure, headed by Dreyfuss, one that allowed schools to communicate directly with the superintendent's office rather than going through one of the six regional offices.

One of the pioneers was Myrtle Grove Elementary School, located in a blue-collar residential section of Opa-Locka, which was ranked in a 1987 study by Roosevelt University in Chicago as the seventh poorest city in the nation. Most of the school's 725 students are black, with 465 of them qualifying for subsidized lunch. Like most Dade County elementary schools, Myrtle Grove occupies a one-story building with open courtyards and a light, airy feeling. The school motto is "Eagles Fly High," and a wall near the entrance displays a picture of an eagle and a sign that reads, "Every Child a Winner, Every Day."

Cecil Daniels, the principal, is a forty-eight-year-old educator who bristles with energy and quickly wins over visitors with his candid manner. Daniels grew up in the Coconut Grove section of Miami and graduated from the nearby George Washington Carver High School. His father was a construction worker and gardener whose formal schooling stopped in the fifth grade. His mother, who worked as a maid, had a high school diploma. There was strong emphasis on education and discipline in the Danielses' home. "Mom required us to be in the home by seven P.M. to hit the books," he recalled. Daniels went to Florida A&M University intending to be a lawyer, but he soon found himself majoring in elementary education, a career that his sister has also pursued. He got his first job as a fifth-grade teacher in the predominantly white Ludlum Elementary School in 1967, where he was the first black on the faculty. The principal, Edna Curry, "took a chance on me," he said. Daniels was eager to make a name for himself and, after several other short posts, set his sights on an assistant principal's job, a position that traditionally had not gone to blacks. He was successful, and he went on to run the William Jennings Bryan Elementary School and the Highland Oaks Elementary School. By then Daniels had become known as an effective troubleshooter, one who could take on tough situations. In 1975 he was assigned to Myrtle Grove, which at the time was more than 90 percent white but was about to undergo rapid demographic changes.

In many ways Myrtle Grove was an unlikely choice for shared decision making. Daniels is the first to admit that, in keeping with his own family upbringing and training, he was a "militaristic and authoritarian" administrator—a style that is the antithesis of the new approach. "At the university I was taught that the principal is the most important person in the school," Daniels said. "His word is the only word. I was comfortable with that because in our home

Daddy was the king. Right or wrong was not a question." Daniels's authoritarian style seemed to be working, for the school was designated as a meritorious school for four years out of five. But Daniels also found that he was chafing at his superiors in the area office, and when he began hearing about school-based management on the grapevine, it occurred to him that this might be his ticket to more independence. "I went into it for the wrong reasons—to do an end run around middle managers in my district," he confides. "I wanted to get the regional people off my back."

Ironically, the teachers at Myrtle Grove were experiencing similar frustration, but in their case the problem was Daniels! They saw reform as a way of getting out from under the heavy thumb of his militaristic style—a fact of life that Daniels readily concedes. "I was well aware that my staff did not trust me," he said. "It seemed that a change would be in the best interest of Myrtle Grove Elementary School. Shared decision making scared me to death, but I was a risk taker."

So Myrtle Grove voted to take part in the experiment. In the spring of 1987 the faculty elected an eleven-member steering committee consisting of Daniels, the assistant principal, eight teachers, and one parent in a nonvoting capacity. The cadre set up committees of teachers to deal with curriculum, budget, discipline, peer assistance, and parent involvement and decided that teachers would be involved in hiring decisions. If the open job was in the first grade, interviews started with the other first-grade teachers. The steering committee got off to a good start by resolving some nagging problems, such as giving teachers greater access to the photocopy machine.

But shared decision making soon hit some rocky shoals. For one thing, steering-committee meetings seemed to go on longer than Monday night football games, primarily because two of the teacher members talked far too much, the others felt, and the principal felt compelled to give his thoughts on every issue, however minor. "We would spend from three to six P.M. deciding on the time of the next meeting," recalled Carla Rippingill, a member of the original steering committee. She compared shared decision making to having a committee driving the principal's car. "We got our driver's license, but no one told us how to drive," she said. "We were all sitting behind the wheel, driving all over, and bumping into things. We didn't have a common goal. Instead, some people who had their own personal agenda got what *they* wanted. 'I think all teachers should clean out the closets and be neat.' 'I'd like an aide, so everyone should have one.' We made decisions about music without consulting the music teacher. We were using the word *should* a lot." Sharon Beck, another original member, recalled, "I look back at the first meetings and I just laugh."

After several months of this, members of the steering committee decided that they needed help. Using the $6,000 that had been allocated to them by the district for training purposes, they called in a consultant to guide them through the minefields of democratic policy making, starting with basics such as how to run a meeting and moving on to such skills as how to reach consensus with a group of people. The steering committee approved a gag rule limiting speeches to two minutes, and Rippingill was given a stopwatch and a gavel to enforce it. "We changed real fast," she recalled. "People began to realize that they didn't always have to be a winner. If someone has a better idea than yours, so be it." The makeup of the steering committee was modified to include at least one teacher from each grade and each special area, such as music. Perhaps most important, an agenda committee, consisting of the principal and two teachers, was created to serve as a traffic cop for meetings, and criteria were established for appropriate topics. A sign was posted in the school office with a drawing of a light bulb and the words "Your idea may be all right if it's board approved, legal, ethical, and good for Myrtle Grove students."

Soon the steering committee began to move beyond issues such as photocopying and started to deal with serious instructional matters. A Saturday School was established to offer tutoring and enrichment, and small groups of teachers were authorized to explore new ventures in cooperative learning and critical thinking skills. Concerned that students were not receiving enough training at home in table manners, several teachers proposed that, instead of eating in the cafeteria, they would have their children bring their lunches to their homerooms and dine under the supervision—with gentle nudging about eating habits—of the teachers. This required teachers to waive their contractual right to thirty minutes of duty-free lunch time; in return, though, they would be allowed to leave school earlier each day. The plan was tried for nine weeks, then eighteen, and then it became permanent. A side benefit has been that, since lunch does not take the full thirty minutes, teachers have used the time for reading a story or other pleasurable exercises. "If I had tried to get teachers to eat with the children, the union would have come down on me," commented Daniels.

The teachers used their new decision-making authority to scuttle a state-mandated reading exercise that involved rote teaching from piles of cards but was known among faculty members as "teaching for morons." Another change had to do with the process of winding down the school year. Teachers who dealt with special areas such as art, physical education, or Spanish were entitled to up to two weeks in order to close down their operations and make sure that they had the supplies necessary for the following fall. This meant, however, that they were no longer available to cover for the teachers in specific subject areas during the planning period to which they were entitled each day. It occurred to teacher Patti Bartels and other members of the steering committee that some of the special-area teachers might not need the full two weeks, so the committee developed a questionnaire and approached the special-area teachers to ask about their real needs. As a result some of these teachers surrendered some of the time that they did not really need, and a new schedule was drawn up that minimized the disruption for regular teachers. "This would never have happened without shared decision making," said Bartels.

Three years after its bumpy start, shared decision making at Myrtle Grove has been a success. Teachers like it because they feel more professional. "They have to listen to what we have to say," said Bartels. "Cecil still gets what he wants most of the time, but he has to ask. Also, it gives us a sense of accomplishment. For years I was looking for ways to show that what I did had direct effect on test scores. Now, with things like the Wheel, where I work with my children and plan with teachers, I can show my contribution. When the scores come back, I can say I am part of the success." Shared decision making is a safety valve, she added. "No one can complain that no one listened to them."

Daniels agrees that the atmosphere of the school has improved. "My blood pressure has gone down, and attendance is up, even among the staff," he said. "Teachers are happy, so they come to work, and grievances filed with the teachers union have dropped to zero. Some previously borderline teachers became the leaders of the school, and people who would not traditionally have come to me began to deal with me directly rather than complain in the lounge. There's a lot more trust and feeling of ownership."

The principal is still frustrated about the time-consuming nature of shared decision making. "It can take us a month to make decisions that the assistant principal and I could make in one concentrated day," he said. He also concedes that he found the transition rough. "I had the uneasy feeling that I was giving up my ship," he said. "I now had to share decisions that traditionally belonged to the assistant principal and the principal, such as the opening of school procedures, scheduling, movement of teachers from grade level to grade level, budget decisions, curriculum, and instruction decisions. I really believed that teachers were not capable of making such schoolwide decisions. I have since been proved wrong." In a symbolic gesture of his transformation from Little Napoleon to King Arthur, Daniels scrapped the desk in his office and replaced it with a round table.

Daniels is not *always* on the winning side of steering-committee votes. Several months after the Wheel went into effect, teachers began to complain that they did not have enough time to work with the children on handwriting and spelling, which lent themselves to whole-group instruction. So the committee—over the opposition of Daniels—voted to trim the time for the small-group teaching from sixty to forty-five minutes. But in what may be the ultimate irony, Daniels, the erstwhile military commander, thinks shared decision making has enhanced his *own* power and effectiveness. "I no longer have to justify budget decisions on my own because we are making decisions together and building bridges on a daily basis," he said. "Sharing authority is a small price to pay for the development of trust. Words like *team building, consensus management,* and *shared decision making* are catchwords that have become a part of the new vocabulary at Myrtle Grove Elementary School. Of course I have days when I revert to the old style of leadership that once brought me comfort. But I now have friends on the staff who will nudge me and say, 'Mr. Daniels, is that shared decision making?' "

Shared decision making at the high school level is more complex than in elementary schools, mainly because the schools themselves are more complex. High school teachers tend to identify with their departments, not with the school as a whole. The community is larger, which means that the cadres themselves tend to be bigger. At Palmetto Senior High School, located in Dade's southwestern suburbs, where the neighborhoods range from middle class to affluent, the faculty voted to set up a cadre with thirty-two members, including the principal and his top aides, teachers, parents, a student, and representatives of the school's clerical, custodial, and cafeteria staffs. To facilitate the work of such a large group, a nine-member coordination council was set up to do fact finding on items proposed for cadre consideration. The cadre also decided to devote the first ten minutes of every meeting to what it calls Open Forum—an open-microphone period during which any teacher, parent, or student can address the cadre on any subject. On one occasion a teacher pointed out that relatively few minority students were enrolling in advanced-placement courses. As a result the cadre voted to free a teacher for two periods a day to look over school records, identify minority students who were qualified for such courses, and encourage these students to pursue them.

As with most new governing bodies, the Palmetto management team's first steps were small. "You start with things that really bug the teachers," said Roseanne Sidener, a music teacher who served as chairperson. The cadre allocated $50 to each teacher to buy supplies and responded favorably to student requests for a new soda machine. Like its counterpart at Myrtle Grove, it also confronted that most universal symbol of the factory-model school: control of the photocopy machine. As ridiculous as it sounds, prior to shared decision making teachers at Palmetto had to get the permission of their department head to do photocopying and then wait up to three *weeks* to get the work done by office personnel. The cadre gave teachers the authority to authorize their own copying, added more clerical help, and insisted that every job turn around within forty-eight hours. One machine was also set aside and made available to teachers during their free time, including lunch, if they wanted to do the photocopying themselves. Once this plan was in operation, the cadre moved to get an exhaust fan installed in the photocopying room. "I've been trying for sixteen years to get that fan," said Rosalie Moore, the principal's secretary. "When the teachers discovered how hot it was, I finally got it."

It may seem to the reader that the biggest achievement of decentralization has been to free up the photocopy machines. This may, indeed, be true, for such machines are symbolic of the level of control exercised over individuals in the factory-model school. Societies like the Soviet Union have gone to elaborate lengths to keep photocopy machines under lock and key. Similarly, in a system where teachers have little control over their environment, even the freedom to accomplish routine tasks quickly and easily becomes a cherished victory.

At Palmetto, as in most shared-decision-making schools, the big issue was control of the budget, or, to be more specific, control of the discretionary funds that remain once negotiated items such as teacher salaries are taken care of. In the past, Peter Buckholtz, the principal, decided on how discretionary funds would be allocated, and teachers lobbied him vigorously for their pet projects. Resentment abounded when requests were turned down. Moreover, teachers did not even know how much money was available. Under shared decision making, the budget-making process was opened up for all to see, and the changed atmosphere was immediately apparent. Because teacher complaints about lack of supplies were so strong, the cadre voted to eliminate a teaching position and use the funds saved to increase the supply budget. When the needs of the various departments were put on the table, it became clear to all that the science department badly needed additional textbooks, so everyone agreed to move in that direction. This made Bill McCreary, head of the science department, a happy man, and the following year he asked for a lot less money. "I got my textbooks, and I know that this year Roseanne Sidener in the music department needs a little more for instruments. Everyone helps each other out. That sure never happened before because in the past you worked in your department and did not know much of what was going on elsewhere. We went from being little building units to being a school."

Decentralized management has now moved far beyond the experimental stage in Dade County. Over half of its schools—151 of 260—now operate under the system, and new ones can sign up for it every nine weeks. Though Fernandez has moved on to New York City, the Dade County school board has made it clear that it favors the concept and eventually expects to see the entire system run in this way. To speed up the process, the central office has designed a computerized accounting system to help schools run their finances. The district suggests that schools concentrate their shared decision making in four areas: curriculum, budget, scheduling, and personnel and hiring. But schools pick and choose what they want—which is, of course, the whole point!

The directions in which schools in Miami and the rest of Dade County have taken shared decision making are as varied as the schools themselves. When the parents of students at Palmetto Elementary School complained that their children were not learning enough Spanish, the management team decided to hire the local Berlitz language school to instruct students. The cadre at the Charles Drew Elementary School, also responding to pressure from parents, made Drew the first public school in the nation to adopt voluntary uniforms. Boys wear blue pants, white shirts with the school's initials on the pocket, and blue clip-on ties; girls wear white blouses and blue skirts. Not only have the uniforms cut down on sartorial competitiveness and lowered the cost of dressing for school, but teachers say that the fighting among students has been reduced. Drew's test scores were among the lowest in the system. To combat it, teachers volunteered their own time to tutor students on Saturday morning, with community groups taking turns providing everyone with lunch. This led to a community school next door where parents could work on their high school equivalency degrees. At the Charles Hadley Elementary School cabinet representatives interviewed the applicants for a kindergarten spot that became vacant. Mariana O. Beraja, a first-grade teacher and chairperson of the cadre, said that peer selection is more effective because, since teachers make the selection, "we make sure that person is successful." Also, the cadre of eight teachers and three administrators was concerned that children were doing too little writing and too many rote exercises filling in work sheets. So it set a limit of twelve copies per teacher per month.

At South Miami Junior High, which has a program for artistically talented students, the management team decided to cut eight full-time salaried positions, mostly teachers, and use the money to hire outside instructors by the hour to teach dancing, cello, and other specialized subjects. The Nautilus Junior High School voted to replace an assistant principal with two faculty members who divide their day between teaching and such tasks as discipline and counseling. These "teacher deans" each receive $1,200 more a year in salary. Similarly, Horace Mann Junior High School turned responsibility for curriculum development over to teachers and agreed to pay them an extra $3,500 for their services. Miami Sunset Senior High School added a thirty-five-minute "teacher as adviser" program in the middle of the school day so that teachers can counsel small groups of students about drug abuse, suicide, and stress-related problems. To make time, they have reduced most classes from fifty to forty-five minutes.

Management teams at various schools take strikingly different philosophical approaches to some issues, such as whether they want to involve teachers in evaluating each other's performance on the job. The union contract authorizes only principals and assistant principals to make formal evaluations, but at least ten of the participating schools have obtained waivers to permit teachers to do so after receiving training from the district. At the Coconut Grove Elementary School, for example, Joe Carbia, the principal, wrote 90 percent of his evaluations on the basis of written reports from four teachers who were specially trained for this task. The other 10 percent involved teachers who were having difficulty of one kind or another. "One thing we agreed on at the beginning was that if a teacher is having problems, teachers will not do the observation," said one teacher. By contrast, teachers at Myrtle Grove Elementary School have shied away from any peer evaluation because they feared it would be disruptive. "Teachers fear each other more than they fear administrators," said Harriet Berkowitz. "Peers are harder on each other."

Another issue over which cadres have gone in different directions is the role of parents. At some schools, including Coconut Grove and Palmetto High School, parents have been full voting members of the cadres from the outset. At Myrtle Grove, on the other hand, parents were initially involved only as nonvoting observers. This soon changed, though, when parents pressed to be included. As David Faison, the current parent representative, put it, "They seemed to think that the only role of parents in the school was to sell Snowballs and come to PTA meetings."

In January 1991 the Office of Educational Accountability of the Dade County Public Schools issued a long-awaited report on the results of the first three years of school-based management/shared decision making in Miami. It made use of interviews and questionnaires and compared data from the thirty-three original schools that began the program in 1986 with comparable figures from all 260 Dade schools. The report was generally upbeat, concluding that decentralization had improved teacher morale, cut high school dropout rates, and improved the overall climate of schools. "Teacher status has improved, and there is evidence that the school environment is perceived as being more collegial and less autocratic," the report said.

Specifically, the report found that whereas student suspensions climbed as a whole for Dade County schools over the three-year period, they declined significantly at the thirty-three school-based-management schools. Similarly, the overall dropout rate for the twenty-four Dade County high schools rose slightly, from 8.1 to 8.2 percent, but the percentage of students dropping out of the four decentralized high schools fell from 7.0 to 5.7 percent. School-based-management schools also showed slightly higher attendance rates than Dade County schools as a whole. On the other hand, students in school-based-management schools did no better than others on standardized reading and mathematics tests. Skeptics have pounced on the latter as evidence that shared decision making is a misguided policy, but their criticism is, at best, premature. For one thing, overall scores in the district have been declining because the system has been absorbing 15,000 children a year from South and Central America, most of whom do not speak English. School-based-management schools have no special solution to this problem. Moreover, it is far from clear that standardized tests—the ultimate symbol of the factory-model school—are accurate barometers of the creativity and new approaches to learning that shared decision making fosters.

William R. Renuart, principal of the South Miami Middle School Center for the Arts, said that school-based management helped his school maintain test scores above the national average during four years of what he called "massive" changes, including a 40 percent growth in the school's overall size, an increase in minority students from 65 percent to 75 percent of the population, and transformation from a junior high school to a middle school. He credited shared decision making with improving not only student performance but attendance, parental involvement, and teacher morale. "We would never go back to the old authoritarian ways of doing things," he said. "Just like Eastern Europe, we have tasted the exhilaration of freedom and the creative urge that goes with it. It takes time to learn to make freedom improve your life, but after four years of school-based management, life is better. We will never go back."

Why does shared decision making work? The answer you hear is that teachers, parents, and others who were at the bottom of the hierarchy of the old system now have a sense of "ownership." "Everyone is swimming in the same direction and working for the same goals," said Sue Austin, a teacher at Drew Elementary School. "That's because these are the goals that everyone decided upon. Shared decision making is democratization. Everyone is involved now and is enthused. We are building self-esteem and saying to ourselves: There is nothing we can't do."

There is, however, nothing about decentralized management that comes naturally, especially to educators trained in the factory-model school. Shared decision making institutes a major cultural change in the way schools function and think about themselves. "You're talking about changing patterns that have been in place for one hundred years," said Frank Petruzielo, who heads the Bureau of Professionalization that Fernandez created to oversee the district's burgeoning efforts to upgrade the teaching profession. Bringing about changes of this magnitude requires tolerance of mistakes, something that Fernandez, to his credit, articulated early on. "We have told people that there are going to be some failures," he said. "We wanted that, because we didn't want to deter them from thinking, from creating. We wanted to remove that threat from hanging over their heads. What we have said is that we're not leaving anything to chance. If we see something that is not working, we can go in and try to correct it. Let's not continue like we often do in education: We put things in, and we leave them there whether they're good or not."

For the superintendent and other top administrators this means, as Cecil Daniels discovered, a very different style of leadership. "To survive, I had to learn to network better with the faculty," said Peter Buckholtz of Palmetto High School. "I've been forced to explain, sell, and develop support for ideas. That is time-consuming, and not always comfortable. The payoff, though, is that when a decision is made, it already has the support of the staff."

Some principals, such as Joe Carbia, had this driven home to them the hard way. The Coconut Grove Elementary School, which started as a one-room schoolhouse in 1877, is the oldest school in Miami and is one of the country's few naturally integrated elementary schools. For its first half century the school was all-white. After court-ordered desegregation in 1970, it became half minority, half white, and stayed that way. Symbolically, the school is located in an area of small shops close to the line that divides the "black Grove" from the "white Grove," with its chic retail village that makes it one of Miami's trendiest neighborhoods. There is a court-yard in the middle of the school where teachers eat lunch and alumni stop by to chat.

When decentralization came along, the faculty of Coconut Grove signed up quickly and elected a cadre that included not only teachers but parents with voting privileges. The cadre took some bold steps, such as cashing in the part-time assistant principal post to which the school was entitled and using the money for other purposes, such as hiring teaching assistants. Faculty members felt that the school's program for teaching Spanish as a second language was weak, and the cadre voted to increase the amount of time that English-speaking students spend on the subject from thirty to forty-five minutes a day. The big trauma in Coconut Grove's march into shared decision making, though, came over the issue of whether the school should operate a magnet program for gifted students. The idea was first proposed by the central school board, and Carbia liked the idea. "I thought it would fill up the empty spaces we had in the school and bring good public relations to the school," he said. "I also thought that if any school could do something like this properly, we could. I told this to the board but added that, since we were a school-based-management school, I would have to run it by the cadre." Much to his surprise, the cadre turned it down flatly. "We didn't like the idea of having gifted kids in one area and regular kids in another," said Miriam Mades, a first-grade teacher. "The two groups should benefit from each other. Otherwise you have a false sense of reality. Besides, we have always been open to everyone who walked through the gate, whether you are from Timbuktu or Haiti or Cuba." The school district sent in a speaker to try to convince the faculty members to go along with the program, but they did not budge. In retrospect, Carbia agrees that the cadre was probably right. "What I did not realize was that the idea ran counter to the culture of the school—a school available to everyone," he said. "Coconut Grove had always been a showcase of people from different groups getting together. This would have created a school within a school."

Likewise, for teachers trained under the factory model, decentralization brings a sea change. One day they are being told to be quiet like children, to be seen and not heard, to take orders, and to keep their ideas to themselves. The next day someone announces that their ideas are important and that they—individually and collectively—are responsible for managing a budget, setting instructional policies, and guaranteeing student performance. This requires a major shift in teachers' attitudes, self-image, and skills. "You have to become skilled in conflict management," said Barbara Reker of Coconut Grove. Everyone agrees that shared decision making can be time-consuming. It takes extra thought and effort, and teachers invariably end up devoting some of their own time. They come to school early for meetings and stay late. Many also sacrifice their professional planning periods to address schoolwide business. Participation can be difficult for teachers who, because of young children of their own or other reasons, must leave school promptly at the end of the day. When only five teachers expressed interest in running for its governing board, South Dade High School had to draft four others to fill the spots. Rosemary Hildebrandt, a South Dade teacher, said that time was a factor. "It would be nice to have eight days a week," she said.

Several Dade County schools even came close to abandoning shared decision making. The governing council at South Miami High School encountered one frustration after another. One of its original goals was to cut five minutes off each sixty-minute period in order to add a twenty-minute schoolwide reading period every day. That plan bit the dust, however, when the school board decided to add a seventh period in high schools by reducing periods to fifty minutes. Now the school only has the reading period once a week. "Out went all our glorious plans," said Betty Gibson, a former council member. Another council plan called for a detention study hall, but this died under the mountain of paperwork it required. "It just got to be such a cumbersome thing that the teachers decided they couldn't sustain it," said Warren Burchell, the principal. The teachers took a nonbinding straw vote on whether to continue in shared decision making, and while the vote was 89 to 86 in favor of scrapping the idea, the school has hung in.

It is by no means clear that all teachers *want* this new kind of responsibility. While it is certainly true that good teachers understand what's best for their students and know how to go about achieving it, it does not follow that good teachers want to be managers or take the time required to add that role to their others. They certainly don't want to have to worry about whether there is enough toilet paper in the bathrooms. What most teachers want is to be left alone to do their job as teachers. The trick, then, is to not overload teachers with a lot of extraneous responsibilities that really have nothing to do with what's taking place in the classroom—and at the same time keep them involved in the decisions of how the school is to be run. The late Paul Bell, who succeeded Fernandez as superintendent, observed that, as with principals, decentralization is likely to alter the type of person attracted to the teaching profession. "Most educators are not risk takers," he said. "It's a conservative profession that promises high levels of security. Historically, if you do a job appropriately, you will complete your career in it. Shared decision making, though, requires a different mix of people. We have to attract more risk takers."

In the meantime, the need to train teachers and administrators in the subtleties of shared decision making quickly became apparent. District officials had assumed that schools would figure out how to get training on their own—though not much thought was given to where they would find it—but they soon found themselves inundated with calls for assistance from faculties that needed help learning how to set up the new governments. Rather than add to the administrative overhead to meet the demands, the district drafted experts from the district's finance office to train faculties in how to manage their budgets. It also set up a Teacher Education Center, run by a group of nine teachers on special assignment. They set up courses on topics such as team building, conflict resolution, and problem solving. The district also developed a network of consultants from local universities whom schools could engage with their discretionary funds. "When we went into school-based management, we underestimated how difficult it was going to be," said Karen Dreyfuss, director of the Teacher Education Center. "If we had been able to do training ahead of time, particularly in the areas of problem solving, conflict resolution, and time management, it would have helped tremendously. When you go in retroactively, it's always more difficult."

There is virtually no active opposition to school decentralization in Dade County, if only because the school board has made it clear that this is the wave of the future and that outward opposition would constitute professional suicide. In Rochester, New York, though, the supervisors union went to court to block a new plan under which, as part of shared decision making, teachers would serve as mentors to younger colleagues. The suit, which was thrown out of court, argued that the plan usurped managerial prerogatives. Such an event would be unlikely in Dade County because Florida law does not permit school administrators to organize unions. Thus the principals had no choice but to surrender their traditional roles to the alliance of the teachers union and the central board. The opposition is passive: from teachers who simply do not join the process and from middle managers who drag their feet.

Bureaucratically the major losers in shared decision making are midlevel administrators whose jobs become superfluous. This has been the story in every large organization that has sought to decentralize, from the political structure of the Soviet Union to major American corporations. Within the Dade County school system the most vulnerable jobs are those having to do with the six regional offices, each of which is in charge of fifty to sixty schools and has a staff of twenty to twenty-five persons headed by a regional assistant superintendent. Their job is to make sure that decisions coming out of the superintendent's office are communicated to each of their schools and to monitor what these schools do in areas of curriculum, hiring, physical plant, student discipline, budgets—just about everything they do. When the principal of a school needs to communicate with downtown, he or she must go through the regional office. Parents also turn to the regional offices if they have a complaint about something going on in their school.

Gerald Dreyfuss, the Dade County assistant superintendent, estimates that under a decentralized system the role of approximately half of the 150 persons working in the regional offices will change. "Since schools are making more decisions on their own, there is no need for all that monitoring and reporting," he said. "The reporting that does go on can go directly to the people in the central office who make decisions. Since they are handling fewer problems, they can handle more schools." Regional offices are likely to remain as a support mechanism for making the school system accessible to parents and others, but even this function is likely to change. "Parents must get accustomed to taking up their problems with the local schools," he said. "The region will help them do this."

Converting to school-based management poses some temporary problems. How do you simultaneously run two different kinds of structures, one traditional and centralized, the other innovative and decentralized? Miami's interim solution was to group all of the school-based-management schools together under Dreyfuss and to eliminate the administrative layers in between. But now that more than half of the system has been converted to school-based management, the system has returned to a unified structure. This means that area superintendents are responsible for both types of schools, a condition that can cause problems. For example, Cecil Daniels was told by his area superintendent that all of the schools that feed into a particular junior high school must use the same basal readers. "I'm caught in the middle," said Daniels. "I can't go to the cadre and say we have to use these textbooks."

Dade County has discovered that eternal vigilance is the price of shared decision making. In practice, this means that someone must be put in charge of maintaining the integrity of the system. Dade County's approach was to create a joint board-union "SWAT team" to monitor progress and investigate complaints. John Birk, representing the union, and Dreyfuss, representing the board, visit each school-based-management school at least once a year, meet with the cadre, offer technical assistance, and try to spot problems as they develop. One elementary school in North Miami got a new principal who indicated at the outset that he was committed to shared decision making but then asserted that he held what he called a "heavy vote." By this he meant that, despite a guideline saying that no cadre member could sit on any subcommittee, he, as principal, had the right not only to attend all meetings but to vote. He also started overruling the cadre on such issues as how teachers should spend their "professional time." The SWAT team was called in, and, after some protracted negotiations and false starts, the principal agreed to change his style. At least five other principals have been transferred because they could not operate under the new conditions.

Shared decision making spread to New York City, where Fernandez is now the schools chancellor. Because it has thirty-two "local community school districts" with boards that hire elementary and middle-school principals and shape education policy, many people think of the New York school system as already decentralized. In reality, many of these "local" districts have more students than the school systems of some small cities—and they are just as top heavy and authoritarian. More than two hundred New York City schools have now taken decentralization to the next step and adopted school-based management. In Memphis the local affiliate of the National Education Association initiated localized decision making in seven schools. RJR Nabisco has given $2.4 million to nine Washington, D.C., schools to implement the approach. In Kentucky, 133 schools in the Louisville area have opted for the new management style as part of a collective bargaining agreement, and a new statewide school reform package requires each of the 177 school districts to designate at least one such school by 1991.

Just as schools within Dade County differ in their approach to shared decision making, so do school districts elsewhere come at it from many directions. Dade County's plan took the form it did because leaders of the school system and the teachers union came to a philosophical agreement and struck a deal. In Los Angeles, by contrast, the decentralization was imposed on the board by the union as a condition of settling a bitter eleven-day strike in 1989. Under the contract all schools must move to shared decision making through the formation of school leadership councils, half of whose members are teachers, that will be empowered to address five limited areas: staff development, student discipline, scheduling, use of school equipment, and some discretionary spending. In August 1990 seventy schools were picked to embark on an even more ambitious program that would require waivers from the union contract and various state and federal rules and regulations. Thus far, forty schools have begun to decentralize.

Whereas teachers in Dade County wax eloquent about the need for trust, the rhetoric in Los Angeles takes a different tone. No sooner had the first part of the plan begun operating than conflicts erupted over such issues as whether "school equipment" includes telephones and public address systems. "Somewhere out there there's this feeling that to have this work, you've got to trust and love each other," said Wayne Johnson, president of United Teachers of Los Angeles at the time the contract was negotiated. "That's hogwash. Power sharing is about power. Teachers and administrators can hate each other and still share power."

One of the first districts in the country to decentralize its operations and learn this lesson was Hammond, Indiana, an industrial working-class harbor town on Lake Michigan, between Gary and Chicago, known for its specialty steel and gas companies. What Miami did with a dream of better schools, Hammond did out of desperation. In 1981 its school system was in deep trouble. Hammond High, once one of the academic jewels in Indiana's crown, had low achievement on standardized tests, soaring dropout rates, and a high level of apathy on the part of students and teachers alike. Police were frequently called to break up racial confrontations that spilled from the classrooms and halls into the parking lot, and middle-class parents were pulling their children out of the schools and sending them to private ones. It was obvious that big changes were necessary. Raymond J. Golarz, a burly school administrator, had an idea. The way he saw it, Hammond's schools were as outmoded as the nearly silent steel mills in northwestern Indiana, where workers watched as business went to competitors overseas. The same rigid factory-management mentality that was leading to economic decline in the Midwestern Rust Belt was also failing in the schools. To him the solution seemed obvious. Why not involve everyone—all of the teachers and all of the managers—in improving the schools?

Working with the superintendent of schools, the president of the school board, and the teachers union, Golarz began pushing a team-based approach analogous to the quality circles then being introduced into industry. At Eggers Middle School, with a high percentage of poor and non-English-speaking students, the governing council decided to divide students into three "schools within the school." Students stay with the same ten teachers for all three years, thus permitting more continuity in student-teacher relationships. At Hammond High School the school-improvement team set up a series of smaller "design teams" to tackle problems. The new approach worked. By 1988 enrollment began to rise, largely because students came flocking back from private and parochial schools. For the first time in fourteen years every grade level in the Hammond system tested above average on national examinations. The dropout rate dropped to 7 percent—low for an urban high school—and is still declining. "There is no graffiti, and there are no broken windows in any of our buildings," said Thomas Knarr, the assistant superintendent. "Parental involvement is up. Teacher morale is up. We think it is the result of site-based management. We used to be like a lot of schools with unions in urban smokestack areas. But we don't have confrontations anymore, and that is directly related to how teachers feel about site-based management. The trust factor is extremely high between management and the teachers today." Perhaps the policeman in charge of the parking lot put it best. "I don't want to lose my part-time job," he said, "but there isn't anything going on out here anymore."

But shared decision making still poses some big unanswered questions. Dade County has clearly taken a giant step toward what is described in political terms as teacher empowerment. That is to say, it has moved to rectify teachers' long-standing complaint that they have little control over their professional lives. In some Dade County schools the initial reaction of teachers was to see shared decision making as a power grab. At last the animals have gotten control of the farmhouse. Then, after commandeering the photocopy machine and getting rid of that hated green paint on the walls of the lunch room, the management team starts to think in broader terms, assuming an overall sense of responsibility for the school. "Eventually, teachers become more comfortable with their new role and begin to understand the difference between power and leadership. To do this, you need a willingness to take risks, to change, to let go of old antiquated ways," said Shirley Hekimian, who was cadre chairman during the first year of shared decision making at

Palmetto High School. "You need what Rollo May called 'the courage to create.' You also need a tremendous amount of patience. To
be a manager, you have to know the grapevine and be willing to
stand back and allow people to catch up. You have to let go of a lot
of ego, to learn to teach and coach. But you end up in a greater role
in terms of prestige. Power and control is not something that is
acquired and earned. You don't really have it until you share it."

But while teacher "empowerment" and teacher "professionalism" are no doubt worthy objectives, they are, from the point of view
of the system as a whole, limited ones. Do happy cooks make better
soup? Do happy teachers make smarter kids? Common sense says
that this follows, but the connection has yet to be demonstrated. Perhaps Joe Carbia of Coconut Grove put it best. "I don't know if happy
cooks will make better soup," he observed. "What I do know is that
happy cooks will *try* to make better soup." He then went on to speak
of his own personal educational odyssey. "When I was a young
teacher, I found it hard to accept the fact that society did not value
what I was doing and loving. My friends were making four or five
times what I was, and I hated this. I thought my job was more important. I went into administration because of the economics, but I
love teaching and look forward to going back to it. Professionalization is very important to me. Attracting good people to teaching is
important to me. That's why shared decision making is important."

Where does decentralization stop? If the underlying premise is
that "stakeholders" in the educational enterprise should have a
voice in running the system, then why not include parents? Students? Members of the community? Some management teams embrace all of these. Others, such as Myrtle Grove, tried to draw the
line at teachers but found that this was untenable. Two years ago,
in response to organized parent groups in Dade County, the school
board sent out a directive that every cadre must include at least one
parent as a voting member. Once the first seat was guaranteed,
though, parent groups began to make it clear that a sliver of power
was not enough. They wanted parity. In keeping with the cooperative tenor of Dade County's reform movement, these calls were
viewed by both sides as mere suggestions—suggestions from groups
that still lack formal clout in school politics—and they were vehe-
mently attacked by Tornillo, the union chief. Teachers argue that
while parents have a legitimate role to play in what is happening

to their children, teachers have an even greater stake. This is their life, their career, and giving parents an equal voice is going too far.

Chicago has taken a very different approach to decentralization, by turning the governance of local schools over to councils dominated by parents. This drastic action grew out of a nasty teacher strike in the fall of 1987, after which the late Mayor Harold Washington organized an "Education Summit" that brought together representatives from business, community organizations, parents, and teachers. This citywide coalition hammered out a reform agenda that convinced the Illinois State Legislature to dismantle the authority of the mammoth central board and to transfer significant decision making and budget power to local councils at each school. Initially each local school council, or LSC, has been composed of two teachers, two community representatives, the school principal, and six parents. Since the reform movement was fueled by parents, they held the majority vote. A state supreme court ruling struck down the election method, but backed the reform agenda. Now principals can be hired and fired—not by the central administration but by individual councils.

Within a year of passage of the Chicago School Reform Act, a school-based-management system was in place in all 542 Chicago schools. After a massive information drive coordinated by community groups, roughly 17,000 parents, community members, and teachers put their names up for election to the councils. More than 330,000 votes were cast, representing 35 percent of eligible parents. Another 65,000 high school students voted for their student-advisory representatives on the high school councils.

The new system has already allowed some schools to begin solving nagging problems. One school went to a year-round schedule to relieve overcrowding; another became a computer academy. Some schools began to emphasize ethnocentric curriculums. Progress seems to be made, problems seem less overwhelming. But political squabbles within councils and a shortage of funds have hampered efforts to give council members the training they need for a very different style of running schools.

Two years into the Chicago reform experiment, some indications of success are emerging. One survey by Northwestern University found that at the end of the first year "the majority of Chicago parents—regardless of race, or their children's grade, or enrollment in public or private schools—are satisfied with their children's education." More than 85 percent expressed a high degree of satisfaction with the quality of teaching, 88 percent with the treatment of their children, and more than 80 percent with the time devoted to reading or math and the amount of discipline.

According to Dan A. Lewis, professor of education and social policy at Northwestern, "More than half of the parents strongly agreed that they understood more about what their children were being taught in their schools than they did a year earlier, while another twenty-three percent 'somewhat agreed' that they knew more." That's a considerable turnaround from the year before reform, when thousands of parents marched in the streets, organized protest meetings, and engineered the political forces to demand systemwide reform. Professor Lewis concluded that "after the first year of reform, the situation could have been very discouraging, but from the parents' perspective it is not discouraging at all."

Other benefits of the new governance system are also becoming apparent. According to the research advocacy group Designs for Change, the Chicago reform experiment has nearly doubled the number of African Americans and Hispanics making educational policy decisions in the United States. Nationwide 4,500 African American and 1,400 Hispanic school-board members are empowered to make decisions. In Chicago 3,200 African American and 1,000 Hispanic parents and educators have been elected to local school councils and are shaping school policy.

Teachers have been very much a part of the reform process. The Chicago Teachers Union, which was one of the major activist forces at the Mayor's Education Summit that created the blueprint for reform, lobbied strongly for the legislation. With automatic representation on the local school councils, teachers have been given a meaningful voice in local school decision making. The reform law also created a Professional Personnel Advisory Committee at each school to tackle problems of curriculum and education. One poll conducted by Leadership for Quality Education, a business support group, found that about half of the teacher members were "very satisfied" with how their principals and local councils "had solicited and accepted" their recommendations.

On the other hand, there are some concerns about the "unevenness" of reform progress around the city. Fred Hess, executive director of the Chicago Panel on Public School Policy and Finance, found that the councils are operating in just over half of the schools. But some schools are networking with one another to share their innovations and help schools that may be lagging.

Since as many as 80 percent of Chicago public school children come from impoverished homes, it is unrealistic to expect instant improvement on academic test scores and other standardized measures. But there can be little doubt that the Chicago reform experiment has infused energy and enthusiasm in schools across the city. Far from being "chaotic" or a "dismal failure," as cynics had predicted, this massive exercise in educational democracy and decentralization has raised the hopes of thousands of parents and teachers that they can find workable solutions to their problems. After two years of activity, politicians, parents, and teachers stand strongly behind the reform movement.

Shared decision making is clearly no panacea. As the three-year report on Dade County made clear, its significance for the overhauling of American public education lies not in what it guarantees but in what it makes possible. "School-based management gives teachers a convenient way to deal with problems," says Patti Bartels of Myrtle Grove. "It doesn't guarantee that anything will happen, because you're changing a whole mentality. We're coming from an attitude that 'they don't care what I think.' And it's hard. It's like living with your parents after you're twenty years old. You still do what they say even though you don't have to."

Pat Tornillo thinks the risks are worth taking. "Without shared decision making at local schools, America won't be able to give kids the kind of education they need to survive economically in the twenty-first century," he says. "They need a better and a different kind of education. And the only way they will get it is if there is a cooperative effort on the part of teachers, administrators, parents, and business. You have to turn the schools back to these people, because they are closest to the educational problems. They will come up with ideas that work for their particular school."

But it does no good to redesign the governance of schools and school systems unless we also redesign the classes inside those schools. Smart schools require smart classrooms. To see what they look like, let's move on to Louisville.

3.

SMART CLASSROOMS

JIM STREIBLE'S eleventh-grade American history classroom at Fairdale High School in Louisville was a mess. The school building was being renovated for the first time since it opened in the late 1950s, and the windows of his second-floor room were covered with plywood. The wiring for the neon lights hanging from the ceiling lay bare, and holes had been drilled in the floor in preparation for the laying of computer cables. "Please excuse the disarray," he says as he introduces a visitor to his twenty-eight first-period students.

Even under the best of circumstances Jim Streible's classroom is not the sort that most readers have ever known. There is, to be sure, the classic three-section blackboard on the front wall. A small portable lectern sits on a table. At the rear are some metal shelves and two beat-up lockers. A Martin Luther King, Jr., poster and a bulletin board pasted with clippings from current events hang on the side wall. But there are no rows of desks. Instead students sit in clusters of four or five desks spaced around the room like satellites. One group of students is having an animated discussion about a short play they are writing about life in the 1920s and 1930s. Across the room another cluster of students is putting the final touches on a video documentary on the life of D. W. Griffith, who is buried a few miles away. They have divided up the research, the writing, and the actual production and seem proud, even a bit awed, of their work. A third group of students is over near the lockers trying on period costumes to wear when they will dance the Charleston and show their fellow students how to do it, while a fourth group is finishing up a gigantic Hooverville house constructed from cardboard, not dissimilar to the rows of shacks that once stood on the banks of the nearby Ohio River during the Great Depression. As they work, they discuss the life of the homeless of yesterday and today.

Streible keeps track of all this independent activity, unobtrusively moving from group to group, observing and listening, answering questions, prodding, chiding. "I don't see myself as someone who should stand in the front of the classroom and give out information," he explains. "That's something that students can and should get for themselves. I see myself as their academic coach. I float around making sure that everyone stays on target. They are the ones who do the teaching and learning. They teach themselves, and they teach each other. They learn a lot more than they would if I were just talking to them."

Jim Streible is part of a growing movement to turn the traditional way of organizing classrooms on its head. In the factory-model school, teachers exercise the same authority over students that school boards, superintendents, and principals do over the teachers themselves. American public education is built on the premise that students will not learn something unless a teacher teaches it. Teaching—not learning—is the central activity. John Goodlad, a professor at the University of Washington, estimates that as much as 90 percent of the activity that goes on in America's classrooms consists of what he calls "teacher talk." His research shows that in most American classrooms students sit in rows of seats, hour after hour, year after year, listening to adults talk—just like cars lining up at the gasoline pump to have their tanks filled. The role of the students in such a setting is passive. They are the raw materials, passed from station to station to be molded, stamped, and fabricated by various skilled craftsmen. In a study for the National Association of Secondary School Principals, John H. Lounsbury and Donald C. Clark "shadowed" 162 eighth-graders in 161 schools across the country in March 1989. They found that all too many students were little more than "sponges"—soaking up lessons with little opportunity to discuss or analyze them. "Most eighth-graders," they found, "spent their day as passive learners—listening to teachers, copying from chalkboards, reading assignments, filling in worksheets, and taking tests."

Such an arrangement—the authoritarian teacher and passive student—may or may not have worked in the past, but it is certainly not working now. For one thing, teacher talk is boring. Several years ago, in an effort to increase their understanding of students, a group of Fairdale teachers agreed to follow a student schedule for a whole school day. "Some of them didn't last till noon," said Marilyn Hohmann, the principal. "They said: Nobody ever asks what we think about anything." Students who grow up watching MTV and are accustomed to television commercials that raise and solve pressing personal problems, such as eliminating acne in twenty seconds, are unlikely to find much stimulation in a fifty-minute lecture on transitive verbs or five reasons for the Civil War. For example, between 1985 and 1989 the New York City school system poured more than $120 million into new attendance and guidance services in a futile effort to reduce the dropout rate. But a major study of the program concluded that the real problem was a need to make teaching "more appealing to students."

Today's students can be excused if they see little or no connection between what they are doing in school and their own futures. Lauren B. Resnick, a psychologist at the University of Pittsburgh and former president of the American Educational Research Association, speaks of the "striking discontinuity" between the culture of schools and that of the real world. Schoolwork centers on individuals, while real work, personal life, and recreation almost always involve other people. School instruction focuses on "pure thought," whereas most productive activities outside school involve what she calls "cognitive tools" such as books, notes, calculators, and computers. School instruction focuses on a relatively narrow range of verbal, mathematical, and other forms of abstract thinking, yet success in life is often based on artistic, mechanical, or interpersonal abilities.

Teacher talk violates everything we know about how students learn and the diversity of learning styles. Everyone knows that some students take in information best through listening, some through seeing. Some learn quickly, some slowly. Some have learning disabilities. Some study best while working alone, others thrive in seminars or group discussions. Some learn best with trial and error, others are more intuitive. And so on. Yet despite this rich diversity, we impose a single style on the captive schoolchildren who fill our nation's schools. "Think about what it takes to succeed in a typical American classroom," said Albert Shanker of the American Federation of Teachers. "Students who do well in school are those who can sit still for long periods of time, learn by listening to someone talk, think abstractly, and not talk to anybody around them. It's a style that may come naturally to fifteen percent of the population. Can you imagine organizing an adult workplace this way? In an office, if you are having a problem, the first thing that your boss asks you is 'Did you ask anyone for help?' This is common sense in the workplace. Schools call it 'cheating.' "

Not only are educational researchers learning more and more about differing learning styles, but students in American elementary and secondary schools are becoming increasingly diverse. As noted in our first chapter, almost all of the expected growth in the elementary and secondary school population in the foreseeable future will come from students from minority and low-income families—exactly the students that schools serve least well now.

Finally, authoritarian teaching is incompatible with the new demand for thinking and problem-solving skills. At the turn of the century 30 percent of the labor force worked as agricultural or nonfarm laborers, and 10 percent in professional, technical, or managerial occupations. By 1980 these percentages had roughly reversed, with 6 percent as laborers and 26 percent as professionals, technicians, or managers. The concept of the strong back, weak mind—"check your mind at the plant door"—no longer applies, even if it ever did. Today's information society requires more than the accumulation of knowledge and recitation of facts. As a matter of fact, much of today's "knowledge" will soon be out of date, and no one can predict what knowledge and skills will be needed in the future. The most important attribute that schools can give students is the ability to learn on their own. You simply cannot give students the coping skills they need for a complex, changing society by teaching them in a rigid, authoritarian style. Ernest L. Boyer, president of the Carnegie Foundation for the Advancement of Teaching, points out that the key to problem solving today is not to figure out the answer to a question that someone else hands you but to define the right problem. "An educated person today," he says, "is someone who knows the right questions to ask." The most destructive characteristic of the factory-model classroom was not that the teachers had the answers but that they controlled the questions!

Clearly the factory model of the classroom must go. Just as the goal of shared decision making is to unleash the untapped power and abilities of teachers, parents, and others, so the goal of smart classrooms is to unleash the untapped learning power of students by redefining the teacher-student relationship. Smart schools are learning-oriented, not teaching-oriented. The operative metaphor that is emerging for this new relationship is "teacher as coach, student as worker." In the factory-model classroom the "work" that went on was the delivery of information. This was something that the teacher did. Smart classrooms shift the emphasis from teaching to learning. Education is what takes place in the mind of the students. In smart schools the teacher does not *do* the learning any more than a coach scores goals or shoots baskets. He or she is the facilitator, the manager of instruction, who creates the proper learning context and helps the student to take responsibility for his or her own learning. It is the student who does the real "work" of the classroom.

The best-known proponent of this new relationship between student and teacher is Theodore R. Sizer, a lanky, boyish-looking fifty-nine-year-old professor of education at Brown University. Despite his penchant for tweedy sport coats and credentials that include serving as dean of the Harvard Graduate School of Education and headmaster of the prestigious Phillips Academy at Andover, Sizer is at the core an educational populist who believes that every student can—and has the right to—learn. His views were shaped by the five years he spent studying American high schools for the National Association of Secondary School Principals and the National Association of Independent Schools. The results were summarized in his 1984 book, *Horace's Compromise* (Houghton Mifflin). He has formed a nonprofit organization known as the Coalition of Essential Schools, headquartered at Brown University, to develop and promote his ideas. Its principles have been taken up by half a dozen state departments of education and a geographic assortment of schools.

Sizer starts with the assumption that the best way to improve education is to understand fully the proper relationship between student and teacher. He also assumes at the outset that the purpose of education is not to transfer information from the brain of the teacher to the brain of the student but to make students think.

"Education," he says, "is about habits of the mind." To promote this goal, he says, schools should concentrate on teaching a few "essential" subjects well, not on covering the intellectual waterfront. His battle cry is "less is more." High school schedules should be arranged so that no teacher must know and work with more than eighty students. Doing this might require English teachers to help out with social studies, math teachers with science, and so forth. Teachers and administrators should think of themselves as generalists first, specialists second, and they should expect to play multiple roles in the learning enterprise. Educational decisions should unquestionably rest with the principal and teachers, but learning is primarily the responsibility of the student. Diplomas should be awarded not on the basis of accumulated credits—that is, seat time—but of "exhibitions," in which students demonstrate and defend what they have learned.

Readers familiar with the history of American education are already asking themselves, What's new about all this? And they're right. The thrust of Sizer's ideas has a long history. Ralph Waldo Emerson talked about "respect for the child," and John Dewey wrote eloquently about the need to involve students actively in their own learning. He, too, viewed the good teacher as one who guided the student on a voyage of self-discovery. When he used the word *authority* in reference to teachers, he usually put the word in quotation marks. Sizer stations himself squarely in this Progressive tradition. What makes him significant is that he has also set in motion a program to translate these ideas into practice on a massive scale.

Several years ago, Sizer's ideas came to the attention of Jim Streible at Fairdale, who is, perhaps not coincidentally, a former coach and athletic director. His school, Fairdale High School, is by any definition a tough place to teach. It is located in a blue-collar area, half-rural and half-suburban, on the outskirts of Louisville. Few of the parents have college educations, and there are not many who aspire to this for their children. Many of the juniors and virtually all of the seniors hold after-school jobs. Many of them have kinfolk in the hills of rural Kentucky. In 1976, when Louisville faced court-ordered busing, Fairdale became a symbol of white resistance, and National Guardsmen patrolled the school and rode the buses. Today a third of the students are bused in from Louisville's predominantly black West End. Four out of five of Fairdale students qualify for free lunches, and 62 percent meet the state definition of "at risk," meaning that they are at least two grades behind in reading.

Ever since he was a teenager in West Point, Kentucky, Jim Streible knew that he wanted to be a teacher. He went to Georgetown College in Georgetown, Kentucky, where he studied physical education and history, and in 1955 returned to his hometown to start teaching for the lofty salary of $2,350 a year. "The extra three hundred fifty dollars was because I was coaching baseball and basketball," he explains. Streible first set foot in Fairdale in 1958, when it was a brand-new building, and except for a year with the Parks and Recreation Department and another at Valley High School, he has been there ever since. For ten years he was the athletic director, but eventually he found his way back to his first love, the classroom. His fields were history and geography, but he was ready to do anything. "One year I even taught beginning Spanish," he recalls. "I was, quite literally, one page ahead of them in the book."

Streible was, by his own admission, a traditional teacher. "I used to be able to lecture with the best of them. I could tell stories and little anecdotes, and students would take notes, and I'd give them a test every other Friday, and they would regurgitate it all back. Two weeks after that I would ask them about something I had filled them up with before, and they wouldn't remember. Eventually I got bored with the whole thing. I decided I just wasn't the person to pump facts into kids' heads." One day Phillip Schlechty, a teacher trainer who is now director of the Center for Leadership in School Reform in Louisville, came to talk to the Fairdale faculty. "He talked about taking chances and asked us to imagine what our classes could be like if no holds were barred," Streible recalls. "He said that teachers ought to think in terms of 'what if,' not 'we can't.' I had never heard anyone with a top salary saying those things." Streible began to change from his lecture approach to coaching students, and while he was doing this Ted Sizer visited Louisville. Sizer encouraged Streible, telling him he was moving in the right direction. At first Streible was skeptical. "I'd seen a number of education trends come and go over twenty-five years," he says. Still, he liked what Sizer and Schlechty were saying and decided to give it a try. "I got involved in planning strategy for the second year with other teachers, and a lot of good ideas came up. Educationally speaking, Ted Sizer raised me from the dead."

These days Jim Streible is raising students, if not from the dead, then at least from deadly apathy. In his teaching, Streible's overarching purpose is to show students how to take responsibility for their own learning. "My goal is to make them think," he says, "and the way you teach students to think is by forcing them to make decisions." Getting students to take a more active role in their own learning, though, is no easy task, for it collides head-on with everything they have experienced since they first walked into kindergarten years before. So Streible starts out slowly. At the beginning of the year he randomly assigns students to working groups and gives every group the same assignment. If the topic is why different immigrant groups came to the United States, he will ask the group to divide up the textbook chapters among themselves. Each student must master the material on a particular set of immigrants and then teach it to the rest of the group. Then the group will be asked to organize dramatic readings or write a skit about the material they discover.

Then he begins asking the groups to design short presentations for the rest of the class. Students know that the focus of the presentations is to help them gain confidence and poise so that they can successfully become the true workers in the class. Streible doesn't give them a lot of direction on how to do this. He simply tells them what is required—what concepts they are to stress—and suggests that they use props. Students must decide how to divide the work and group themselves. "It seems the kids today don't have any confidence in themselves," says Streible.

As "coach," Streible uses his expertise to suggest where students can find the resources they need. He is the architect of activities that generate student interest, creating an agenda that unlocks the students' curiosity to find answers and to share their discoveries. The students look to him for guidance, but they are also anxious to show him just how much they are learning. In his room learning is organic and natural. "I tell them very early in the year that my main goal is to teach them to think and that I want them to be the workers," he says. "At first kids like it and think it is easy.

After ten years of teacher talk most of them at first say, 'Boy, this is good. I don't have to take a lot of notes and take tests.' Then, as the year goes on, they begin to see that they are masters of their own destiny, and they start to ask themselves, 'Am I doing what I ought to be doing?' As I keep them under my method of instruction, they teach themselves, perk up again, and then they start thinking, 'Hey, this is serious stuff.' "

Streible asks his students to do a lot of reading and a lot of research. He will point them in the right direction, but he refuses to help them process the information they uncover. "It's up to them to decide what is important," he says. "I want to give them practice in processing information." He makes extensive use of repetition. "I coached for fourteen years," he says, "and when I wanted a kid to learn to sacrifice bunt in baseball, I would have kids repeat it until they got it down real well. I do the same in the classroom. When students have done their own particular version of a chapter, they'll hear somebody else's version and have to make comparisons. They work on teams, go through material, discover information by themselves, and teach someone else. That's the whole key—teaching someone else—and it sinks in. I want kids to understand. I want them to understand the leadership of the Washingtons and Hamiltons and people like that. I want them to understand the Civil War and how we became an industrial giant. I want them to understand our competition with the Pacific Rim, why the Vietnam War was unpopular, and the concepts about the world wars we fought in and why we did."

Streible also wants that information coming at them in different forms—not just books and discussions but drama, songs, satires, essay writing, and other modes of communication. "I have them on their feet, talking to other people, the center of attention, all eyes focused on them," he says. "They have to make things happen, and this builds self-confidence in kids."

Typical of Streible's approach was an assignment given to his fourth-period American history class one day last fall. The topic was "America's Wars Against Communism," and five students— Shannon Hughes, Rick Buchanan, Amanda Weston, Jason Stinson, and Kelley Brooks—volunteered to work together to do research on Korea and Vietnam and make a presentation to the class. They had a week of class and homework time to complete the assignment.

Their first step was to huddle in a corner of the classroom and divide up the work. Rick, whose father had served in Vietnam, volunteered to work on the military side of that conflict. "I was interested in the planes and soldiers," he explained. Amanda and Kelley also worked on Vietnam, while Jason and Shannon took Korea. They asked Streible for some leads and then headed for the library. When they had completed their research, they roughed out their presentations to the class and did a trial run to fellow members of the team. When the day came to perform, the team spent about five minutes putting up posters they had prepared on items such as the major events of the Korean War and statistics on military casualties. Shannon then led off with a talk on the political background of the Korean conflict before turning to Jason, who, leaning against the lectern with his feet crossed, went through his note cards telling the class about the military side of the conflict. He described the dogfights between American fighters and the Russian-built MiGs and recalled how helicopters, first used only for the evacuation of the wounded, were eventually used as a means of delivering troops. As Jason talked, Jim Streible sat quietly in the back of the room making notes about the student's performance on a checklist. He notes that the student consistently mispronounced *repatriation* and at one point writes, "You all certainly presented a lot of facts. How are we going to use these facts?" Another note says, "Shannon, go slow."

Streible explains to his visitor that he takes these presentations very seriously. "One of the goals I selected for myself was to try to help the kids learn to talk on their feet in front of people," he says. "When I first asked them to do this at the beginning of the year, it was like telling them they were going to the woodshed. 'Mr. Streible, I've never done anything like that!' I grade them not only on the material they develop and organize but on things like eye contact. And everyone gets a grade based not only on what they do themselves but on the performance of their group."

When Shannon and Jason wind up their presentations on Korea, the other three take over to tell about Vietnam. Kelley talks about the Tet offensive and the "huge mental victory" that it represented for the Viet Cong. He also points out that "this was the first time that America went somewhere with goals that it could not accomplish" and discusses some of the terrible side effects of the war, including drug problems, the high suicide rate among veterans, and the feeling on the part of many veterans that they were ostracized by their own countrymen. All the while Streible is taking systematic notes. "Amanda, bless you for carrying on with that bad cold and cough." "Rick, you have developed some good speaking skills—eye contact, good voice, gesturing." At the end of each presentation students are required to pose and then answer a question that will then become part of the final examination for the course. Rick's question was: Why were we not able to beat the Vietnamese? The main reason, he said, was that while the United States usually won particular battles, North Vietnam could always replace its losses with fresh soldiers.

In a discussion after the class students say that they like the idea of taking responsibility for their own learning and working in groups. "It keeps the class from being boring," says Jason. "Kids can explain things to each other in ways that teachers can't. And the higher-up kids don't get bored. They have something to do." Kelley agrees. "In any class some students will be faster, some slower," he says. "Instead of the teacher taking the whole class at one pace, those who get it quicker can help others. The best way to learn something is to teach it." It is also a way of turning peer pressure into a positive force. "If Rick doesn't do his part of the assignment, he will look like an idiot, and it will affect us," says Kelley. "If he doesn't have the information, neither do we." Jason sees the whole thing as good preparation for the future. "In college you don't rely on teachers," he says. "You rely on yourself and your friends."

Streible has dozens of other arrows in his pedagogical quiver. On one occasion two groups of students were asked to compare the governing philosophies of Herbert Hoover and Franklin Roosevelt. The school librarian brought some materials to class and arranged for the students to rummage through the stacks of the University of Louisville library. Once the facts were gathered, the class held a debate and voted on which chief executive was the most effective. Such exercises force these once-apathetic students to think, argue, reason, and express themselves more clearly. No one is slumped down in a desk hiding from a teacher. The normal classroom lethargy, so pervasive in America's failing classrooms, is gone. It's replaced by plenty of noise, and plenty of learning too. Peer pressure to perform is present for student and teacher alike, and so is freedom to explore for themselves.

One day the class was working on immigration patterns, and a group of students wrote a skit in which the daughter of an immigrant family complains about going to America, where she doesn't know anyone, where it's cold and filled with nothing but trees. Her parents explain they need the religious freedom of a new place. The skit ends with "The Plymouth Rap," written by a budding poet who said she hadn't had much chance to write poetry in her previous schooling. "I was hoping we'd get to do it in English," she said. "But we never did." Streible's class gave her a chance to do her first love. It went as follows:

In 1620, a time of the past,
when times were rough, and the ocean was vast
We jumped on a ship and we sailed away
to a brand-new land we're happy to say.
Back in England we had no rights,
no religious freedom, so we had to fight.
It took everything, our heart and soul,
but before too long we reached our goal.
When we arrived in America everything was new,
the trees were blooming, and the sky was blue.
One hundred two passengers came for the ride,
nothing to fear and nothing to hide.
We discovered this wonderful place,
come one, come all, come any race.
Without the Pilgrims to open the gates,
Today there would be no United States.

As students perform, Streible laughs at their jokes or their clever plays on words. He genuinely enjoys teenagers. He listens closely to the words they use, and corrects them when a word is mispronounced. He confronts the students individually as he walks around the room. While students are working in groups, he may take a student to the side of the room and talk with him or her seriously, individually. There is no room for humiliation in Streible's class. To Streible the skit demonstrated that the students understood the sections of their reading and the concepts stressed in the textbook. He quibbles with the line in their rap song—a home for all races wasn't the early motivation to come to the United States, he notes, though he agrees that the settlers opened the gates. The class breaks out into applause when the skits are finished. Students videotape each other, and then Streible has them look at it together, to "process themselves," as he says, and see what they can do better next time. "They all have to realize they have to speak up," he adds. "I can say that, but the reality doesn't hit them until they see it themselves." Streible evaluates the performances using a checklist that contains items such as creativity, content, props, costuming, songs, and whether students spent time at home developing their skit.

Later that day, in another history class, the presentations center on the role of the Anglican church in England and the sentiments of Catholics at the time. The presentations are not flawless. "I have got to work with that student on the pronunciation of *Anglican*." To Streible the talks are works in progress. One team, for example, was having a disagreement over its presentation, and one of the students wanted to back out. Streible responded, "Once you decide something, you have to follow through on it." The team stuck it out. The others "put pressure on the student and made him stay with it," he said. As the team began its presentation, the other students, now part of an audience, started whispering to themselves. "They are too disorganized," said one. "Their background music is too loud," said another. "Speak up and face the audience," said another out loud. The students in the audience uttered their remarks not in a chiding, taunting, or mean-spirited tone, but out of a concern that the team did not have it together.

One group had a student who did not do any work. Streible watches them closely. He knows the group had been having problems between two of the girls. Later he notes that one girl was absent the first day of the team meeting and initially felt left out, so she never got involved. Yet when it comes time for the presentation, all of the students participate in the report on the French and Indian War. Streible thinks the group needs more time to gel, but they will make it. "That's something you run into in life, and they have to learn to work through it the best they can. They will learn to work together."

Streible says that his students are learning much better than their predecessors in previous years because they are sparked by their own interest and control over their products. "Teenagers, like all kids, have to be active," he says. "You have to keep things moving for them. But more long-term learning takes place this way. Students get a better feeling for the subject they study. They take more responsibility for what they are learning. That's the idea that I try to get across. That is a tremendous change from a few years ago. I think it changes the kids' whole approach to education."

Students tend to agree with Streible's assessment. "In grade school most of the time teachers just gave an assignment and talked *aaaalll* period," said Shannon Hughes. "When I entered Mr. Streible's class last year, I thought it was going to be another *boring* history class—every day read this chapter, answer this question. But his class is not like that. And in other classes, if you don't understand something, you feel stupid asking a question in front of everybody. But here you can ask somebody in a group. They help you, and you all learn together. We work together in groups, and the teacher is there if we have problems understanding the facts, but normally we don't. I wish all my classes were like this." Jenny Abner, a school cheerleader dressed in a navy-blue shirt and skirt, ready for the football game that will be played late in the evening, recalls her doubts at the beginning. "I was confused at first," she says. "Can this really work? What if we can't learn from each other? But you really can learn if everybody works together and everybody does what he tells you to do. It makes you feel in control. You learn not only the book skills and facts but the social skills. The student-as-worker approach teaches you responsibility. Everybody has to help others in the group. If you don't come up with the work, you could lose your friend! Last year I was really afraid, but Mr. Streible really pushed me, and now this year I am doing really good. He's always on you if you aren't doing what you are supposed to do. And if you ask him a question, he says, 'Why don't you think about that for a while, and if you don't understand it, come back.' I needed that."

Streible places high priority on getting students to feel comfortable talking on their feet. Bonnie Ford is a good example of why. This particular day Bonnie has her shoulder-length hair pulled back, tied with a black ribbon. But Streible, who taught her father in 1962, remembers her last year, when she used her hair to hide her face when she started to talk in front of the class. Today, though, as the bell rang to begin her sixth-period government class, Bonnie walked confidently to the front of the room. With a smile on her face and her two cards on the lectern, she waited for Streible to give her the nod to begin her short presentation on the signing of the American Constitution. The ease that she felt in front of her peers was evident, and her confidence appeared genuine as this seventeen-year-old senior spoke to her class only looking at her note cards twice during the five-minute period that she led the class. She talked slowly, with great emphasis, and changed her intonation often. Her peers listened attentively and asked her a few questions.

"The first time I got up in front of the class, I was scared to death," Bonnie admits. "I didn't even look at my classmates. I just read my material because I was as unsure of my material as I was of myself. I stood so rigidly and held on to my note cards. I was afraid to move, and I spoke very softly so the other kids could barely hear me." She also recalls the doubts she had when Streible explained his approach. "When Mr. Streible told us about how the students would be the teachers, I thought, 'There is no way this is going to work.' I thought it will be the same old scenario. But I've really grown. This year I just get up, and it's nothing. Mr. Streible coaches us, encourages us, cheers us on. He sets up a classroom environment where we learn more, and I mean we learn it, not just memorize it. It's like a dream. Everybody dreams about making a speech like on graduation when you could get up and say what you feel. You think about that deep down inside, but it never happens. But now you can get up in front of class, and you make all your dreams come true. You can talk. You are on the spot. You talk about what you want to, and it makes you feel good. You know, my mom used to think I was a snotty little kid. She would call me nonsocial because I wouldn't go to any family reunions. I'd stay home. Now I do things. I don't know if it's because of Mr. Streible's class, but I think it's a big part. Before, I'd never go to a party. Now I'm holding my own graduation party."

After her presentation Streible complimented her as she went back to a group of three girls sitting around a table. He pointed to her eye contact, her strong voice, and her knowledge of her subject. A few moments later, when he stopped at Bonnie's table, her entire face showed her glee as she read Streible's assessment of her presentation—an A-plus. "She is really proud of her growth," Streible commented. "So am I."

Other teachers at Fairdale have applied techniques similar to Streible's but in different subjects, such as mathematics. Jo Ann Mosier, who has a Christa McAuliffe research grant from the state, argues that "there is no better way to learn mathematics than by working in groups, by arguing about strategies, and by expressing arguments carefully in written form." Pam Hardin uses such an approach to teach linear equations. After explaining the essentials to the class as a whole, she divides the class into teams, each of which has a planner, observer, taskmaster, and manager. Students then work collectively to solve problems.

Another teacher who has sought to get students to take more responsibility for their own learning is Judy Phillips, a forty-six-year-old ninth-grade English teacher. Now at Fairdale, she perfected her coaching style while at Seneca High School, an integrated school located in a blue-collar section of Louisville that is a member of the Coalition. In the early 1960s she herself had attended a traditional Louisville high school, one where her teachers were strict and demanding schoolmarms. She had been an eager student and went into teaching because she loved learning, but she quickly discovered that not all students are that motivated. "No one prepared me for what it is really like in a classroom," she says. "It was so frustrating." She decided that the problem lay in her traditional teaching style. "We wonder why kids are so apathetic and passive in school," she says. "It's because schools have taught them to be that way. We promote and reward that kind of behavior. An assignment such as reading pages one sixty-eight to two hundred and answering the questions at the end of the chapter is not an assignment for which a student must do any creative thinking, questioning, theorizing, or reflecting. The kid who is quiet and doesn't make waves is the one who gets all the positive strokes from the teacher."

Phillips's goal now is to get students active in their own learning. Poetry, she says, is a subject that lends itself readily to student-as-worker. "In the past I taught poetry the way I had been taught. I would read a poem aloud to the class. Then we would analyze it to death. We would learn technical terms, and then I would test for recall. It was tedious. It was boring. And of course I was killing poetry for them—and consequently for myself." Now, after informal discussions about the creative process, Phillips has students deal with their own work. In one class two students recited raps they had previously written and performed downtown at a teen club. Then everyone began writing their own raps—about love, problems, haircuts, snakes, ordinary events. Students typed all the poems, a selection committee picked work from every student, and Phillips assembled photocopies into a class book. Everyone got a copy. "The best thing was turning on those kids who are in school simply because the law says they must be here or they don't have anywhere else to go. They felt the spark." Ninth-grader Jami Shartzer likes writing soap operas. "If we need to make corrections, Mrs. Phillips is there to help us," she said. "She explains why we need a comma here, a period there. She sits with us, talks with us, and gets our perspective on what we are trying to say and do. As a result, I write a lot more than I used to. You want to work more." To Robert McMichen, the transformation of his writing skills in Phillips's class was nothing short of magic. He said that last year in middle school he didn't understand what was expected of him on tests. This year, after writing mysteries, speeches, and poems and "rewriting *Romeo and Juliet*," he finds his grammar and punctuation have improved. A district-wide exam on basic skills turned out to be a breeze. "That's because he has been writing," said Phillips, "not studying grammar. But along the way, he has been learning grammar."

But like Streible, Phillips finds the transition to a new way of teaching difficult. "Kids expect me to tell them what to do," she says. "Turn to this page, fill in these blanks. They keep asking me, 'What do *you* want me to say?' But I want my students to learn how to think. It may be a little chaotic at first, but the trick is not to turn back once you start."

Practice of the new approach is by no means limited to high schools—or even to those formally part of Ted Sizer's Coalition. At the Conway Middle School in Louisville, Susan Reich and Debra Colyer team-teach an eighth-grade language arts class in which students take responsibility for teaching themselves and others descriptive writing. The teachers give some initial instruction on the use of metaphors, strong verbs, and the other elements of effective prose. Then students go to work on their own. Students write every day and keep two folders. One is the "Work Folder," containing worksheets and revisions of works in progress. The other is the "Finished Folder." The students do as many drafts as they wish, getting feedback from the teachers, and it is the student who decides when the work is finished and ready to go into the Finished Folder. The grade is based on the folder as a whole, with credit given not only for the quality of the writing but whether all of the work was completed and how much improvement was made in the course of the semester.

Critical to the teaching in this class is the chance for students to read their work and get feedback from their peers. One day the students had all completed papers dealing with "descriptive scenes." The first student up was Latonya Johnson, who read her work:

The sunbeams glided and landed on the ground like an airplane pulling into its hangar. The old dried out fence leaned limp to one side. The stream ran slowly, whispering to the deer that drank from it. The orange leaves bleeded out red as they swayed like dancing ballerinas. The clouds were oceans where the sunrays plunged in and out like divers of the deep blue. The grass was thick and plentiful, like an 8-inch ten-layer wedding cake. Patches of lime-colored grass stretched like elastic as far as the eye could see. The wind sang love songs as it carried the sweet scents of homemade apple pie. But, the smells of autumn dew overpowered it, like gravity holds mankind on the ground.

With Latonya still standing at the front of the room, Susan Reich turned to the class and asked for their thoughts. "It gives you a good picture in your head," said one girl, "and she used nice verbs, like *danced* and *glided*." "She used similes, like *like a ballerina*," said another. Debra Colyer then asked the class what Latonya might still work on, but she had to answer her own question. "Some better transition words would improve it." She takes the paper, circles a misspelled word, and writes, "Awesome!!" across the top.

Next up is Jerry Cardine, who slinks reluctantly toward the

blackboard. "Come on, Jerry," says Debra Colyer. "It's not like this is the first time." "This is dumb," mumbles Jerry. "We don't think so," says the teacher. "Will you humor us?" Jerry stands up against the blackboard, as far away from his audience as possible, and reads as fast as he can his description of a roller-coaster ride:

Magic Mountain called out to a fun seeking soul, for excitement and action. As little children called for their mothers with a scream or two, the car kept on going up and down, up and down. Suddenly a loop on the way seemed to be saying to the children, "No, you're mine." Voices yelled, stomachs were left behind as the twelve story drop full-filled the thrill seekers. One gulp, two gulps and around the turns. The cars continue to go. With diminishing speed the tracks began to moan. Faster and faster the cars went. Whimpers and moans filled the air that looked upon the children. Music like roars from a dragon seemed to affect the speed. As the car stopped, children complained. But they said, "I want to go again!" The cars seemed to look at the children. "Do you want to go again?"

When Jerry was finished, Debra Colyer turned to the class and asked, "What process skills did he do well?" Latonya volunteered, "He repeated what he said. He gave a feeling of going up and down, up and down." Another student commented, "He used good verbs. He said the car moaned." "That's right," said the teacher. "He didn't say the car 'went.' He said it 'moaned.' He made Magic Mountain come alive for us. What other skills did he use?" "He used person-ification," chimed in a boy in the back row. "Right," said Colyer. "Manufactured things don't talk."

Teachers say that the transition to such teaching is not always appreciated by students and parents. "Last year the honor students came in after Christmas with a petition saying they wanted to quit doing writing this way and go back to filling in blanks in the book," said Susan Reich. "These were kids who get A's with a breeze, and they were threatened by the new approach. They could find all the similes and metaphors we threw at them, but they were not sure that they could write good sentences themselves. We had to hold the line. We had to say, 'Mrs. Smith, are you saying that you want your son to apply for a scholarship only to find out that he can't write a sentence?' "

Another expression of teacher-as-coach and student-as-worker is the movement called cooperative learning. Like Ted Sizer, its proponents take aim at the individualism and sense of competition inherent in the factory-model school. Not only do students learn to think and to express themselves orally and in writing, they learn to cooperate with one another. They see cooperative learning as preparing students for the teamwork that is such an important part of the emerging workplace. They also view it as an attempt to overcome the sense of isolation felt by many students today because of the breakdown of family and community structures. In a cooperative classroom the teacher organizes the curriculum, or major parts of it, around tasks and projects that students carry out in small groups. Students function as part of a team. The idea is to create assignments and use grading procedures that give students a stake in one another's progress. The philosophy of cooperative learning holds that it is important for every member of the group to master the lesson. Ideas and materials are shared, labor is sometimes divided, and everyone in the group is rewarded for successful completion of the task.

The major proponents of cooperative learning are David and Roger Johnson, two brothers who are professors of education at the University of Minnesota, and Robert E. Slavin, who directs the Elementary School Program in the Center for Research on Elementary and Middle Schools at the Johns Hopkins University. Researchers have documented social, personal, and academic gains for learners of all ages. "There is now substantial evidence that students working in small cooperative groups can master material better than can students working on their own," says Slavin. Likewise, in more than eighty original studies the Johnsons have shown that children who learn cooperatively—compared with those who learn competitively or independently—learn better, feel better about themselves, and get along better with each other. Not only does cooperative learning increase academic mastery, it also helps students to become more accepting of others who are different. Another strand of research, including the work of Spencer Kagan of the University of California at Riverside, shows that black and Hispanic students learn particularly well in cooperative groups. Moreover, when students of different ethnic backgrounds learn cooperatively, prejudice declines and ridicule practically disappears. Kids who are different from one another start to enjoy being around each other, and they continue to socialize during their free time.

Common sense suggests why. No single student is as smart as a group of students. Moreover, competition works against the concept that there is any intrinsic value to learning. The point of competition is to beat the other person, and the skills required to win that contest have little to do with education per se. "How many times have students waved their hands in class to get the teacher's attention and then forgotten the question?" asks Roger Johnson. Competition says that the minute you lose, your value ends. "That's a terrible thing to tell a kid," he says. "Or an adult."

"Cooperation is the basic phenomenon that distinguishes our species," says David Johnson. "It's the underpinning for everything. It shouldn't be a big surprise that achievement goes up. Cooperation means students share their talents and skills in a way that benefits everyone. The very act of orally reviewing the lesson reinforces knowledge; explaining a concept to someone else is at least as useful to the tutor as to the tutored. And students appear to have so much more fun learning together that they may be more receptive to the material and thus quicker to pick it up."

While all of this may sound fine in theory, the fact is that applying the principles of cooperative learning in the classroom is tricky business. It's not just a question of the teacher giving an assignment to a group of students and then standing back and watching them go at it. It requires carefully worked-out techniques. Teachers must give careful thought to the makeup of each group. They must constantly move about the classroom monitoring group progress and offering advice. Students must be instructed in "helping behaviors," such as giving each other explanations, not just answers. Students must be given specific roles, such as checker, summarizer, note taker. The big talker may be cast as the observer, for example, and thus put in a position to realize how much better the group functions when no one dominates.

Both Slavin and the Johnsons emphasize the need for "positive interdependence"—that is, structuring interactions so that each student depends on and is accountable to the others. Students must realize that they sink or swim together. The Johnsons have a technique whereby the teacher divides the class into groups of four and then into pairs. Members of a pair are assigned to do research on a topic and argue opposing points of view. Midway through they switch roles, and each has to argue the other side. Then the whole group has to distill the controversy into a collectively written report.

Ironically, the brothers who collaborate so closely on their research competed intensely as children, growing up on an Indiana farm in a family of seven children. Roger, now fifty-two, moved to California to teach in the suburbs, while David, now fifty-one, lived in New York City to work with delinquents and poor adolescents. David, a professor of educational psychology, came to the University of Minnesota in 1966. His brother, a professor of curriculum and instruction, joined him three years later. The Cooperative Learning Center has run for more than a decade on grants and other external funds, including a current $541,000 five-year grant from the National Science Foundation.

The Johnsons have traveled the world, from Australia to Saudi Arabia, talking about cooperative learning. A decade ago, Roger Johnson said, he'd have been flattered to have a dozen people show up for training at the university. Now the brothers limit themselves to working with about forty school systems that commit time for intense teacher training and must refer dozens of other requests to people they've already trained and trust. There's a place for competition in the classroom, the brothers say, but they believe that far more time should be spent on cooperation. With teamwork, they say, underachievers learn more and bright kids gain deeper understanding. Students mix more easily regardless of race, economic background, or academic level. And students learn empathy, responsibility, self-confidence, how to work hard, and how to think critically, the kind of skills people need to get along in the world. Roger Johnson likes to tell how once, in a meeting on cooperative learning, a mother interrupted. "I know what this is. I know what you're trying to do. It's what we're doing at work. It's management training, isn't it?" "The big issue is how skillful you are at linking up with people and maintaining relationships," said Roger. "The world requires more communication."

Among the schools the Johnsons work with is the Cornelia Elementary School in Edina, Minnesota, where teachers are in their fifth year of using the program. In Deb Monchamp's third-grade classroom desks are grouped in threes or fours, with students facing each other. Many of their lessons are done in groups that change every six weeks. In a spelling lesson recently students were randomly assigned spelling words and work groups. They gathered in groups of three at their desks or on the floor and decided who would perform each of the tasks: writer, spell checker, or reader. Then, together, they made up a story that included their spelling words. One student wrote the story down; another checked the spelling. Then the class gathered to hear the stories as Monchamp checked the spelling. Each group stood in front of the class as it presented its story. Monchamp asked each group how well they worked together and encouraged them to say something good about each other. "Everybody contributed," one student said. "We all thought of a different story and made it into one story," said another. One girl said, "It went pretty good, but Jeremy was goofing off a little." And Jeremy grinned and rolled his eyes. Monchamp asked, "Were you able to help him settle in?" "Yeah," the student answered.

Monchamp estimates that up to 60 percent of the school day is spent in cooperative activity, especially in reading, math, spelling, science, and social studies. "The kids will definitely tell you it's fun," she said. "They gain self-confidence working with peers, they're less inhibited about making mistakes, and they're able to express wonderful ideas. The gifted children learn to expand their knowledge because they will get someone in their group who doesn't understand something, so they have to explain. And even the slowest child has a spark somewhere, be it in math, or making up stories, or an off-the-wall idea."

Louisa Kennedy, age nine, is new to cooperative learning. It's sometimes frustrating that kids lag behind in groups, she said, but "you learn a lot more because everyone has different ideas." Monchamp's classroom illustrates some of what the Johnsons say are necessary parts of cooperative learning. Students take individual tests, but group activities are usually not competitive. In the math drill, for example, students were practicing for a later drill in which they would share a combined score. That results in what the

Johnsons call a "sink or swim together" attitude, but it also makes it clear that no one in the group gets a free ride.

Cooperative learning is controversial. The most obvious question potential critics ask is, Does it slow down the brighter kids? The research suggests that it does not. "High achievers working in heterogeneous cooperative groups have never done worse than their counterparts working competitively or individualistically, and often they do better," the Johnsons write. "The behavior that correlates most highly with achievements in groups is giving explanations, not getting them." Other critics suggest that since the spirit of competition is so fundamental to our capitalistic culture, the emphasis on social skills may deprive students of the aggressiveness they need to succeed. Indeed, Barbara Foorman, professor of educational psychology at the University of Houston, told *The New York Times* that cooperative learning is "doomed to failure" because it conflicts with the American economic and social system. "It goes against the American grain, the individualism that creates the entrepreneurship we as a people have historically espoused," she said. "In a utopia it would be wonderful. But education should prepare kids for life in a particular culture. In reality the name of the game 'is dog eat dog.' Kids have to learn that you get something through your own smarts."

In response David Johnson replies that cooperation is also an important part of the American heritage. He points to the tradition of barn raising and the pulling together that was necessary to successfully fight two world wars. "Pulling together to get the job done, strong individuality, creativity, and entrepreneurship—that's the heart of capitalism," he says. Moreover teamwork is increasingly the paradigm of the emerging workplace. "A person who cannot cooperate is unemployable," he says. "In real life most people work as part of a team."

Jeff Schneider, who studies educational trends as a program development specialist for the National Education Association, believes that educators are so entrenched in dividing students by ability or performance that cooperative learning flies in the face of practices that many educators now take for granted. If change occurs, he says, it may result from pressure by businesses, which are increasingly using cooperation as a way to improve productivity and foster innovation. David Johnson agrees: "Companies like IBM tell you if you can't work as part of a team, you can't work for us. The days of the lone ranger in companies are over essentially."

No one argues that cooperative learning is appropriate for every student in every learning situation. The point is not to replace competitive and individualistic modes of learning but to put cooperative strategies at least on an equal footing. Even Jaime Escalante, the mathematics teacher at Garfield High School in Los Angeles who became the hero of the movie *Stand and Deliver*, uses the team approach in his advanced calculus classes. "Sometimes I take the weakest student and make him the leader of the team. It does amazing things for students' self-confidence," he said.

But such changes pose tricky problems. Finding alternatives to the factory-model classroom is, in its own way, just as difficult as abandoning the old centralized approach to the management of schools. As with shared decision making, getting students more involved in their own learning bumps up against well-entrenched forces and traditions. Some of the problems are political. It's fine to set up a well-functioning classroom in which students take charge of their learning. But classrooms do not exist in a vacuum. They are part of schools, which are part of school systems, and the outside environment is not always friendly to people who set out to do things differently. Education is a fragile enterprise. Good starts can easily be wiped out by a change in principal or superintendent, by a mistrustful union, or by fellow teachers who resent the attention or resources flowing to an innovative group of teachers and students. Changes at the margin are easily erased.

In fact, Ted Sizer has learned some bitter lessons on this score. At Brighton High School near Rochester, New York, teachers voted to leave his Coalition of Essential Schools after a home-economics teacher was dismissed by the school district. Teachers in "nonacademic" fields, such as physical education and business skills, saw themselves threatened by the Coalition's emphasis on core academic courses and interdisciplinary teaching. Dissident faculty members also thought that the experiment had been thrust on them by Tom Jones, the principal, and they found support among parents who believed that the school, described by one student as "a BMW and Benetton kind of place," was already sending enough graduates on to college. At Finn Hill Junior High

School in Washington State, tensions developed between teachers working in Coalition classrooms and their colleagues in regular classrooms, and principals in other schools resented the attention that the experiment was getting. The district cut a staff position and, with it, the common planning time for core teachers. What has saved it thus far is the help it has gotten from the University of Washington School of Education, which legitimized its existence. If the program is to survive, though, it will have to do so by finding its own resources.

Despite support from the principal, McCullough High School in Texas decided not to support the idea after the switchboard lit up with a barrage of angry phone calls protesting the fact that, with a restructured school day, football players would have found it difficult to make all their drills. At Hope High School in Providence, Rhode Island, near the Coalition headquarters, Sizer found himself up against the deep-seated cynicism of teachers who had endured racial violence, twelve principals in thirteen years, and deep staff cuts. Only the most senior faculty members survived the cuts, and many of them mistrusted Sizer. They even organized themselves into an informal group that called itself the Naysayers. Only after a year did Hope's suspicious faculty permit the creation of a "school within a school"—with five teachers and one hundred students, about 10 percent of the student body. When the program did get established, more than two dozen students transferred out of Hope Essential into less demanding schools in 1988–89.

Jim Streible and other teachers at Fairdale, seeking to redefine their role as "coach," have survived in large part because both the school principal and the district superintendent were committed to fundamental changes and have provided them with political protection. Marilyn Hohmann, the principal, arrived five years ago when Fairdale was, as she puts it, "in the pits." "Fairdale had a high dropout rate, the lowest achievement rate in the district, and low attendance among both students and teachers," she recalls. "Jim Streible was burned out, and he wasn't alone." Hohmann was brought in by the superintendent and told to change the place. No other directions were given. "As a staff we began to talk and ask, What do we want? We talked about what it was like to be a kid here. We did our own research. We talked to other teachers; we started the professional development work. We created pockets of teacher interest. They helped each other." Recalling the time she asked ten teachers to follow a kid's schedule for a day, she said, "They came back saying, 'Nobody spoke to me' and 'Nobody asked me a question.' They said that school was not a very humane place. You never got to make a decision. You never got to think. Nothing was connected with anything else. People began to believe that they could do things differently."

Even before anyone at Fairdale knew who Ted Sizer was, the school had moved toward shared decision making. Teachers elected a governance committee consisting of seventeen elected teachers, six administrators, and three parents. Most of the real work of the school is now overseen by task forces made up of teacher volunteers. Faculty members work in teams, and the concept of teacher-as-coach enhances the concept—central to shared decision making—that the teacher is a responsible professional. Streible functions as part of a team of teachers representing the traditional boundaries in the curriculum: English, humanities, reading, and history. Even the school librarian is part of the team. Likewise, at Conway Middle School, which is not formally part of the Coalition, the faculty has divided itself into six interdisciplinary teams, two per grade. Each team is responsible for 140 students, who give themselves names like Super Sixers and Pacers.

By early October 1990 Fairdale had reached what Hohmann saw as a real turning point. A few years earlier only fifteen parents showed up for a parents' night at the school, and those parents were hostile. On October 4, 1990, there was a standing-room-only crowd, with parents asking about what was happening in school. Parents told the Fairdale staff about their children, who for the first time were interested in school. One parent whose son had never liked school told the principal that the child now loved to come home and talk about what he was doing. Another father told Streible that his daughter would not have run for sophomore-class treasurer if she hadn't had Streible. She gained that much confidence in his class. To Hohmann these reports from parents mean more than any test score. "We know achievement scores are improving," she said. "Our students—62 percent of them—come into our school two or more grades below grade level. It's not a place where you would expect kids to do well. But our kids are doing far more demanding things than people would have expected. They are working far more seriously and harder than they ever have before. We're changing culture here.

"Kids have learned in different kinds of settings. Learning has become something they see from both sides of the desk. In the past American schools turned out a large pool of workers who did not have to think a great deal, but now we're in a different situation and asking for a very difficult thing. We can't afford to lose anyone. Upper-class kids always got jobs, and middle-class kids managed to survive in the old system. But kids today just don't get that much by sitting and listening. But neither can adults. I'd hate to be bored to death. That's why we are trying to build a culture that is far different from the factory-floor model. And students have come to appreciate this new attitude. They have learned that there are no more *fait accompli* diplomas. This in a place where no one ever thought about sending a student teacher, and no one ever wanted to come to teach. We now have more requests to transfer in."

For all of the political and other problems involved in restructuring the classroom along the lines described above, there are—happily—some problems that restructuring *avoids*. The most obvious one is *tracking*, the practice of grouping students on the basis of academic ability rather than assigning them on a random basis to programs, classes, or reading groups. Tracking, known in professional parlance as "homogeneous grouping," is the norm in American public schools. From kindergarten on, every student knows that the names of their reading groups—*robins, bluebirds,* and *cardinals*—are euphemisms for *smart, not so smart,* and *dumb.*

Tracking was the nineteenth century's answer to the built-in conflict of public education in a democratic society: How do you promote academic distinction while trying to teach everyone? The solution hit upon was to segregate students on the basis of academic ability. Common sense suggests that any student will do better when the teaching is geared to his or her particular needs. Likewise, tracking means that teachers no longer face the problem of "teaching to the middle" at the risk of boring the bright students and hopelessly confusing the slower ones.

In practice, though, tracking does not work according to the theories. Study after study has shown that the major consequence of tracking is to lower the expectations that teachers have for the students in the lower tracks—which is to say, most students—and thus to lower these students' aspirations and self-image. Moreover, in practice schools assign the best teachers to the highest tracks. Tracking works to the advantage of the most talented students, but it works to the disadvantage of the system as a whole.

The case for tracking presumes the existence of a factory-model school. It presumes that schools must be organized on the basis of how well students receive information delivered by teachers. But if the emphasis shifts from the teacher delivering information to the students taking responsibility for their own learning, then the reason to engage in tracking disappears. Albert Shanker suggests that, in order to get around tracking, schools should reclaim the vision that existed prior to the emergence of the factory-model school: that of the one-room school. "Teachers in one-room schoolhouses almost never lectured," he said. "These teachers knew that there wasn't much they could say simultaneously to a roomful of kids of different ages and stages of learning. So teachers moved from one group of two or three students to another. Because they couldn't spend much time with any group, they usually assigned some work to each, making sure that the group had a pretty good idea of how to proceed. Periodically the teacher would return to each group to make sure the work was being done correctly and to offer more help where it was needed. And teachers frequently asked students who'd mastered a particular task to help those who were still struggling to learn it. What one-room teachers did out of necessity—avoid teacher talk and get kids to learn on their own or in small groups—is actually a superior way of getting them to learn."

When Ted Sizer created his Coalition of Essential Schools in 1984, the original purpose was to have schools redesign their educational programs using nine principles, which include teacher-as-coach and student-as-worker, and to promote this new approach to running classrooms. But it became clear that just as individual programs needed political support within their school buildings and districts, so schools working with the Coalition principles needed to be supported at the state level. "As Coalition schools tried to do new things," Sizer recalls, "they ran head-on into state and district regulations. While most schools were able to argue for waivers successfully, it was clear that if a large number of schools were going to change, ad hoc waivers weren't going to work." At the same time Sizer's financial backers were urging the Coalition to expand. "Their view was that we were too small," he says. "No one pays any attention to a handful of schools."

The solution was a project known as Re:Learning: From Schoolhouse to Statehouse, which was born in the summer of 1988. Under the program, run jointly by the Coalition and the Education Commission of the States (ECS), seven states—Arkansas, Colorado, Delaware, Illinois, New Mexico, Pennsylvania, and Rhode Island—have agreed to promote Sizer's ideas in at least ten schools apiece over a five-year period. On May 21, 1991, Colorado joined the roster, according to the ECS, and five more states are expected to join the program by next year. Equally important, they have promised to change the regulatory and policy climate in which schools operate to make it easier for reforms to thrive. Some of the waivers granted to schools thus far enabled teachers to teach outside their area of certification, provided for additional days of in-service training during the school year, provided alternative graduation requirements, and allowed schools to experiment with changes in scheduling. New Mexico, for example, has passed two laws that encourage schools to seek waivers from requirements on class size, instructional time, assessment practices, and graduation standards, as long as they can explain how such changes would benefit students.

The primary motivation of governors for accepting Re:Learning was a recognition that current reform efforts are not working. "What we found out," says former governor Garrey E. Carruthers of New Mexico, "is that by sending mandates to school systems, nothing much happened." The 108 schools in the 7 member states range from an Indian reservation school in New Mexico to an inner-city school in Chicago to a state school for the deaf in Rhode Island. New Mexico has put up $750,000, Illinois close to $700,000 for the project. In some states, such as Delaware, corporations and foundations have provided additional contributions.

Overall, the Coalition's annual budget is $4 million, of which approximately $1 million will be spent out of the Denver-based offices of the Education Commission of the States. The money, from private donations and grants, provides for research-and-development efforts as well as direct support of school districts and states that have embraced the Sizer program. An additional $10 million in public and private money has been raised for teachers, schools, and states going through the redesign process. "If a group of teachers in a school decide they want to explore going in a certain direction," said Sizer, "there's money for them to get on a plane and go visit a school that has taken a similar direction. Teachers also have a chance to talk with each other, something for which there's very little time in the regular school day." Teams of teachers from many of the schools attend summer institutes and regional workshops. A small committee of outside experts will be appointed to review and interpret research about Re:Learning, including one project that will track a group of fourteen-year-olds entering original Coalition schools over a nine-year period to monitor their success or failure.

Not everyone, though, has been enthusiastic about Re:Learning. After holding five public meetings, the Rosewell, New Mexico, school board voted not to participate in the initiative. The board cited a lack of evidence that Re:Learning would help elementary school children learn. "We're just downplaying the whole thing," said Pedro Atencio, coordinator of Re:Learning for the state. "I think what happened is that parents were just not aware of the terminology. It's going to take a long time for people to understand what Re:Learning is about."

Sizer has no fixed model for a redesigned classroom. "There is no such thing as a distinct, detailed blueprint for a fine school any more than there is such for a successful family," he says. "We do not have a single model that can be duplicated. What we believe in is a set of ideas. There is no 'it' to this program. The 'it' is what you fashion in your own setting on the basis of some commonly held ideas, including the one that the primary purpose of education is intellectual, that it is to help students learn to use their minds well. Everything else gives way to that. There are no children for whom the habits of serious thought should be denied."

Part of the "it" is a new concept of the relationship between time and learning that is crucial to the functioning of smart schools. To find out more about this, let's board a stern-wheeler for Hannibal, Missouri.

4.

RESETTING
THE CLOCK

SAMANTHA HARDY, a third-grader at the Eugene Field Elementary School in Hannibal, Missouri, was a classic candidate for a "remedial" program. She had entered school a year to a year and a half behind the norm in her language development, and by the end of her first year she was reading well below grade level. Teachers suspected that she was guessing at many of the answers that she put down on her worksheets in class.

Traditional wisdom says that the best way to help a child such as Samantha is to pull her out of her regular classes each day and repeat at a slower pace what she had not grasped the first time around. Instead teachers at the Field School did the exact opposite. They *intensified* the amount of information and stimulation they threw at her. They paired her with another student to read to each other, peppered her with lessons in phonics and literature, and sent her on field trips to museums and historical sites to expand her range of experiences. They suggested that she participate in an extended day program after school, where she received intensive tutoring in reading. As a result, Samantha is now reading at grade level. "We refused to accept the idea that there was something wrong with Samantha," said Barbara Johnson, her second-grade teacher. "We built on the strengths that we knew were there."

The Field School is a pioneer in a new approach to education called accelerated learning. Developed by Henry Levin, a professor of education at Stanford University, accelerated learning is one of numerous efforts now under way across the country to reset the academic clock and rethink the relationship between time and learning.

Nowhere is the industrial model of schooling more obvious than in the way schools use time. Under the industrial scheme of things time is fixed, and production varies. Shifts run for eight hours, and workers are paid in six-minute increments. Union and management negotiate the speed at which products will move along the assembly line, with management pushing to speed things up and workers arguing for a more relaxed pace. Strict control of time is critical to carrying out the "one best way" to solve production problems. Such an arrangement grew up naturally in turn-of-the-century America. It was, after all, "the Age of Efficiency." Americans everywhere were pledging to rid their lives of waste with the principles of science, and the "efficiency craze," as it is known today, permeated every aspect of life, even the home. Housewives were bombarded with books and articles on topics such as "The New Housekeeping: Efficiency Studies in Home Management," and "Scientific Management in the Family." Books appeared entitled *How to Apply Efficiency Tests to a Church.* Emblematic of the time was a 1913 cartoon depicting two lovers shadowed by an efficiency crank with a stopwatch in hand: "Young man," he was saying, "are you aware that you employed fifteen unnecessary motions in delivering that kiss?"

Educators followed the lead of their industrial counterparts and organized schools around rigid schedules, fixed from above. The length of the school year, school day, and even class periods are set by state law, with every student getting exactly the same amount of time. Some states, including Kentucky and Texas, even mandated the number of minutes that every student must spend on each subject each day. Students, schools decided, should start school somewhere around their sixth birthday, go to a new grade and new teacher every year, and graduate after twelve years. The school day was chopped up into arbitrary fifty-minute periods, even in elementary school. Reading at 9:05 A.M., spelling at 9:55 A.M., and so forth all through the day. In case anyone forgets, bells ring to remind everyone that it is time to move on to a new activity.

Accountability in American public education is built around seat time. Just about any student who logs enough time at a school desk will get his diploma. Standardized tests put a premium on speed, not depth. What counts is not so much what you know as how fast you can deliver it. Adults also are minions of time. Teacher pay raises are based on seniority, or time spent getting advanced degrees, and administrators' budgets are based on average daily attendance, that is, on how many students they have for how long.

American educators are paid for logging time, not for getting results. New York City took the industrial comparison to the ultimate limit. Until recently its 61,000 teachers punched time clocks!

There is an important side effect to this concept of time: the concept of "coverage." American teachers feel enormous pressure to "get through the textbook." Not all countries share this compulsion. In a forthcoming book, Harold W. Stevenson, professor of psychology at the University of Michigan, and James W. Stigler, associate professor of psychology at the University of Chicago, argue that Japanese and Chinese schools use time quite differently and that this contributes to their superior academic performance. It is not uncommon, they say, for a Japanese teacher to devote an entire mathematics lesson to discussing a single problem.

In short, learning in American schools is a function of time. The teacher lectures for forty-five minutes and assumes that the bright kids will take in most of what she says, the not-so-swift ones very little. Most students will be somewhere in the middle. In organizing time the overriding value is not student learning but the efficiency of the system. Learning must adapt to formal schedules, not the other way around. Never mind that some students are ready to begin formal learning at four, others not until seven. Never mind that some students learn quickly, others slowly. Never mind that the most exciting part of the story is about to unfold as the bell rings. Never mind that no one is home to greet them when schools disgorge their charges at 3:00 P.M. Never mind that a minute of math instruction is quite different from a minute of social studies or art. There is no organic rhythm to the way American schools are organized. Students are forced to learn not by the natural tick of their internal development and psychological watch—or even the nature of the subject at hand—but by the minute-by-minute tock of preset clocks that move them along at production-line speed from drill to drill, test to test, period to period, subject to subject, grade to grade. And if the student doesn't get it the first time around, the whole process is repeated. The invisible bonds of industrial time are out of sync with contemporary learning needs.

As was the case with centralized management, the very industry that gave birth to this philosophy is now rethinking its priorities. Through innovations such as quality circles and flex time, companies are flipping the old priorities and making time a function of production, not the other way around. In other words, the focus is on getting the job done. Scheduling is no longer an end in itself, but a means to this greater end.

Schools are doing likewise. Virtually every way in which schools made use of time is now up for grabs, from the length of the school year and school day to the amount of time students have to learn their assignments. Schools are looking for ways to let the schedule grow out of learning needs. They are seeking to make time a function of learning. The changes take at least three forms: altering school calendars and schedules, changing the pace at which students progress through the system, and rethinking the way time is used within the classroom.

The most obvious way in which schools are altering their schedules relates to the most anachronistic of all practices: the long summer vacation. This custom precedes even the factory-model school, having its roots in the days when the United States was primarily an agricultural country and children were needed on the farm. The summer months were work months in which boys and girls grew to maturity through hard labor at the plow or in the kitchen. Students in the nation's earliest schools attended class for only three months during the winter while the soil lay dormant below ice and snow. Gradually the school calendar lengthened to accommodate changing economic conditions and the desire to keep children, who were now in the cities, busy while their fathers or mothers worked at the plant. The length of the school year now varies from 170 days a year in Minnesota to 182 in Ohio, with most states—thirty-four of them—settling on 180. That still leaves three long summer months to toil in the fields. But few students ever get very close to a plow.

Critics have frequently pointed to the inherent inefficiency of this system. A task force of the National Governors' Association noted that the country has a tidy quarter of a *trillion* dollars tied up in school buildings. "The overwhelming majority of America's schools are used only five days a week, nine months of the year, and are restricted to the formal education of people between the ages of five and eighteen," it concluded. "This makes no sense." In addition, three-month vacations can be disastrous for educational reasons. Teachers say that it takes them two or three weeks just to get students back to where they were in June, a task that must be accomplished while they are getting to know a whole new group of students. The Japanese have a much better system. School in Japan starts April 1, so the two-month—not three-month—summer vacation comes during the school year. This means that students return to the same teacher, minimizing the negative effects of the down time. Teachers also give reading and other assignments over the vacation to enhance continuity.

A surprisingly large number of American schools have now begun operating on a year-round basis. The National Association for Year-Round Education estimates that 736,000 students in 859 public and 13 private schools were attending year-round schools during the 1990–91 school year. This was a 40 percent jump in students over the previous school year. According to Charles Ballinger, the association's director, dozens of school systems in the nation are looking more seriously at the length of the school calendar. In San Diego alone, 113 elementary and middle schools have gone to a year-round schedule for 89,000 students—20,000 more than in the previous year.

In most cases the twelve-month year was viewed as a way of making more efficient use of space and other resources. The longest-running multitrack year-round school is the Fairmount Elementary School in St. Charles, Missouri, just west of St. Louis, which adopted such a schedule in 1969 as a means of reducing overcrowding. Students at Fairmount are split into four cycles and attend class for nine weeks, followed by three weeks off. The start of each cycle is staggered, so that at any given time three cycles are in session and one is off. Classrooms are always filled. The largest district to move to year-round schooling, Los Angeles, did so to conserve space. After a four-year, on-again, off-again debate, the school board decided in February 1990 to put six hundred schools on a year-round schedule that in most cases alternates ninety days of schooling with thirty days of vacation. By staggering schedules among four separate "tracks," schools could keep a fourth of the pupils on vacation at any one time and thereby increase capacity. As is usually the case, opposition to year-round schooling came primarily from resort and camp operators and from employers who count on students for summer help.

In some cases, however, schools have moved to year-round

schedules for educational as well as economic reasons. Buena Vista, Virginia, embraced it as a way to improve curriculum offerings, cut spending on remedial work, attract better teachers, and keep its young people occupied. A rural industrial town of 7,000, located in the southern Shenandoah Valley in a narrow river canyon at the base of the Blue Ridge Mountains, Buena Vista has been economically depressed since the early 1970s. The downtown area, which was submerged under five feet of water during floods in 1969 and 1985, is still partially abandoned. In the early 1970s, with unemployment so very high among adults, high school students rarely found work, and there was not much for them to do during the summer. Moreover, with increasing numbers of wives working to help make ends meet, supervision in the home declined. A group of parents approached school officials with the idea of opening the school in the summer. In 1973 the Parry McCluer High School began offering voluntary year-round attendance. Instead of a conventional calendar of two ninety-day semesters broken up into three six-week periods, it now operates on what it calls the Four Seasons Calendar. The portion of the calendar that corresponds to the regular high school year is divided into three sixty-day units, while the summer quarter offers an optional forty-day unit, tuition-free, for students who need more time to learn and for college-bound students who seek more challenging courses. Within three years the summer quarter attracted over 50 percent of the students.

Leslie Fitzgerald, a senior at McCluer, attended summer school so that she could get some required courses out of the way and take more advanced courses during the regular school year. So for two years she took her physical education requirements and, as part of the summer program, went swimming, canoeing, biking—"Fun things you can only do in the summer," she said. With those credits out of the way, "That left room for other subjects that would help me excel," she added. She took three college-level courses— psychology, political science, and an advanced computer course. "It was nice," she said. "You do not get burned out this way. You still have some summer vacation, and it leaves room open during the regular year to take extra courses."

Sybil Floyd, also a senior, has been going to school in the summer since eighth grade. During the first two summers she, too, took physical education, but the summer after her tenth grade she took chemistry and, after taking Algebra II during her junior year, she took algebra again during the summer. "I didn't fail, but I wanted to do better," she explained. "It's much easier to learn a subject in the summer. The classes are smaller. During the first two hours the teacher explains things and teaches a new assignment. Then you have time to go over your homework and ask questions. Since there are not as many students in a class, teachers can work with you individually and give you extra attention. It has really helped."

Once the leap to year-round schooling was made, Buena Vista discovered that it was getting applications from top-notch teachers who wanted the extra summer pay, and it was able to increase hiring standards for new teachers. Despite the fact that they are in school 220 days a year, no more than 1 or 2 percent of Buena Vista students graduate early. One reason is that the school system hiked the minimum graduation requirements to 23 credits for college-bound students, well above the 16 to 18 required by the state. The state subsequently followed suit. But today Buena Vista students are still well above the new state requirements. As measured by the usual objective criteria, the plan seems to have paid off in better academics. In 1969 Buena Vista eleventh-graders scored in the 40th percentile on state-mandated achievement tests. By 1986 they were up to the 55th percentile. The dropout rate has also fallen from 5.8 percent in 1969 to 3.9 percent in 1988. One reason for the increase in student achievement, teachers say, is that year-round schooling gives them an alternative to failing students. Instead students can use the summer to make up the work. School officials estimate that in 1987 they saved $120,000 by eliminating the need for remedial work during the regular school year. The school system also saves money during the school year by offering more and different courses during the summer. "We'd have to hire three additional teachers in our high school if we did not have an extended school year," says James Bradford, Jr., the superintendent.

Year-round operation provides the opportunity to run more activities without adding staff members. In addition to regular courses, summer provides excellent opportunity for enrichment activities, such as lifetime sports—canoeing or hiking—that are popular ways to fulfill physical education requirements. The high school sponsors a four-to-six-week trip to Germany every summer for students who elect a course in conversational German. Tim

Deyo, a former student-body president at the high school, says that summer courses are better because of the self-selection factor. "It makes all the difference being in a class when everybody wants to be there," he says.

Year-round operation offers special possibilities for disabled students. Susan Leviton, associate professor at the University of Maryland Law School in Baltimore, notes that students with emotional and behavioral disorders need consistent attention in order to make and sustain steady progress and that for them long summer vacations can be educationally devastating. "How can you have that for nine months and not have it for a longer time?"

If the length of the school year is an anachronism, so is the length of the school day. In the past, schools could shut down for the day at 3:00 P.M. with full confidence that mothers were waiting at home to greet their offspring with milk and cookies. Such, of course, is no longer the norm. Eighty percent of school-age children now have mothers who work outside the home. As a result thousands of schools are now opening their doors at 6:00 A.M. and starting after-school day care. In New York City some even serve dinner to homeless students and family members. In most cases the extra time is used not for heavy academics but for sports, artistic activities, or other forms of enrichment.

Last fall San Francisco schools began extending the school day for 4,000 of their lowest-performing students, those in grades six to nine who ranked in the bottom quarter on state standardized reading tests. The students are required to give up to four hours a week of their free time to stay after school and work on reading and writing. This approach extends a program San Francisco started two years ago called the Saturday School, which provides a literature program to students scoring below the 40th percentile nationally on standardized tests. Each Saturday at ten sites throughout the city, between 150 and 250 students gather at any given site for a program in which teachers seek to build enthusiasm for reading by "applauding" their efforts and building their self-esteem. According to Anthony Anderson, director of the Saturday School, parents have backed the program wholeheartedly, and test scores of participants have increased in both reading and math. The program is voluntary, but 1,500 youngsters have participated thus far.

Parents participate in workshops and pledge that their children will attend school regularly and that they will encourage them to read.

Educators are also rethinking the rate at which students make their way through the school system, starting with the date on which they start formal education.

In keeping with the spirit of standardization that marked the factory-model school, most states use arbitrary dates. Students usually march off to kindergarten or first grade in the September after their fifth or sixth birthdays. Such an approach may make for bureaucratic convenience but it bears little relationship to the way children learn. Developmentally speaking, a year in the life of a preschooler is a long time—20 percent of his or her life! Children who are barely five are often expected to be on par with those who are almost six. It's easy for the former to conclude that they are dumb or, if the teacher pitches instruction to the lowest level, for the latter to become bored and impatient with school. Both scenarios are formulas for disaster. So, too, is the practice of many school districts that, with all good intentions, flunk kindergartners who are not deemed ready for first grade. Imagine what it must be like to have your first experience with school to be one of total failure!

The well-to-do, of course, have never followed these rules. They start their kids in playgroups, nursery schools, and kindergartens. Their kids hit formal schooling running. Common sense—not to mention justice—suggests that we do likewise for all children, and considerable evidence now exists that early-childhood programs are even more effective with disadvantaged youngsters.

One study of nineteen-year-old Head Start graduates found that two-thirds of them went on to earn high school diplomas compared with only half of those in a control group. Nearly 60 percent of the Head Start graduates had jobs versus less than a third of those in a control group. Researchers calculate that for each dollar spent on high-quality preschool programs, society gains $7 down the road in higher tax contributions and lower expenditures on remedial education, welfare, and the criminal justice system.

Because this evidence is so clear, early childhood education has become one of those issues on which liberals and conservatives find themselves joining hands, albeit for different reasons. Liberals see it as a matter of social justice—giving the poor access to what the rich already enjoy. Conservatives argue for it in cost-benefit terms—as prudent social planning. As a result, the country has recently been treated to the fascinating spectacle of hard-headed businessmen arguing that the country must increase its "investment" in preschoolers. The Council on Economic Development, a leading corporate group, has recommended that for purely economic reasons "we should put $5,000 on every single three- and four-year-old head to insure their proper development." Largely because of such pressure, six states and the District of Columbia have recently passed laws requiring all-day kindergarten, and others are considering such measures. The Bush administration has been increasing the budget for Head Start, but even with a 1991 allocation of nearly $2 billion, up by $400 million over the previous year, fewer than half of all eligible students are being served.

There are other ways in which the starting date for schooling can be modified. New Zealand has flexible starting times. In that country children enter school on their fifth birthday, whenever that is. No one expects a child who has just turned five to perform at the same level as a five-and-a-half-year-old or one who is almost six. In England young children are placed in groups of three-year, rather than one-year, spans as a way of dulling the edge of age differences. Then there is the question: Why should everyone spend twelve years in school? Minnesota allows high school students to take college courses at public expense (see Chapter 7). Joseph Fernandez, the schools chancellor in New York City, suggests that schools should come to terms with the fact that thousands of students need *more* than twelve years. As a matter of fact only one-third of high school students in New York City graduate with conventional diplomas in four years, but three years later 57 percent have gotten a diploma.

Still another variation on the traditional use of time is "multiage grouping," which rejects the factory-model notion that each student must be promoted one grade each year. Under this approach students of more than one age level—two to four years is the normal range—work together in the same classroom. The idea is to let pupils develop at their own pace, allowing movement between levels for those pupils ready to advance or needing more help in a subject. Educators sometimes call it continuous progress. Many schools experimented with upgraded classes in the 1960s, often unsuccessfully, but the practice is making a comeback today as a way of avoiding two practices that are seen as a precursor to failure for young children: tracking and flunking. People often criticized open and ungraded classrooms for lacking structure and letting students "do their own thing." Now they have a better chance because we know more about how children learn. "We're missing a bet by trying to educate children in litters," says Lilian G. Katz, director of the ERIC Clearinghouse on Elementary and Early-Childhood Education at the University of Illinois. The longest-running example of the multiage approach is the Lake George Elementary School in Lake George, New York, where the principal is Robert J. Ross. A kindergarten-through-sixth-grade school with six hundred students, it was designed for multiage grouping, with expansive rooms containing several teaching stations surrounding a common area. Students in the various grades are divided into three "clusters." Within the clusters are teams of two or three teachers. About 6 percent of pupils join older or younger students.

When it comes to rethinking the pace at which students move through their schooling, perhaps the most influential school of all is not even located in this country. It is the Köln-Holweide Comprehensive School in Cologne, West Germany, which runs from grade five through eleven and uses what is known in West Germany as the team/small-group model. More than twenty West German schools have incorporated features of it, but Holweide, where it originated more than twenty years ago, is the showcase. The student body of 2,200 has a diversity that is rare in Europe, including the children of Turks, Moroccans, and other foreign "guest workers" as well as many Germans from poor or single-parent families.

The formula it uses to handle such a diverse student body is simple: Teachers are divided into small, relatively autonomous teams, with each team responsible for one group of students. The teams, usually six to eight teachers, stay with their students from the fifth grade until precollegiate education ends in the tenth grade. Adjustments can be made, but first teachers and students must try to resolve whatever problem has come up. Time is set aside during the school week for members of each team to meet with one another to plan teaching. Each team decides how to group students, how to organize the school day, which teachers will teach which subjects, how much time will be devoted to each subject, what materials will be used, and so forth. No one is locked into a schedule for the whole year, because the system allows for readjustments according to the needs of students and teachers. Most of the classwork takes place in small "table groups" made up of four to six students of varying academic abilities and social backgrounds. Students typically stay with their table groups throughout the six grades.

Holweide's approach makes for a more efficient use of time. Since students stay with teachers for six years, there is, as with the Japanese system, no "down time" at the beginning of the year when teachers are getting to know a new group of students. Nor is there pressure at the end of the year to rush through material to prepare the student for another teacher the following fall. Another major benefit of Holweide's innovative approach has to do with accountability. Since teaching teams have responsibility for their 120 or so students for a full six years, no one can blame a student's deficiencies in reading or math on last year's teacher or simply try to tread water until the student can be passed on to a teacher in the next grade. At the same time, since they function as a team, teachers need not face such challenges alone. Holweide, says Albert Shanker of the American Federation of Teachers, who has become an evangelist on the subject, "turns the usual bureaucratic, assembly-line processing of children into a teaching and learning enterprise, a moral community." Studies show that only 1 percent of students at the school drop out, compared with 14 percent in West Germany as a whole.

One American school that has borrowed from Holweide is the David Wark Griffith Junior High School, which is wedged into a neighborhood of modest bungalows and auto-parts shops in a primarily Hispanic section of east Los Angeles. Virtually all of the students come from families poor enough to qualify for reduced-price lunches. Many must be tutored in English. In 1987 Day Higuchi, a science teacher at Griffith, heard about the Köln-Holweide School and spoke to his principal, George Hatem, about replicating the model. After reviewing literature from Germany, they decided to create what they called a Model Core Program under which a team of four teachers would be assigned to the same group of 125 students for the entire three years of junior high school and assume responsibility for their total academic performance during that time. Higuchi recruited three other teachers—Dallas Russell, Leslie Watkins, and Laurie St. Gean—and the quartet spent the next year meeting during lunch periods and over the summer to plan the experiment. The goal was to come up with a structure that would coincide with the special emotional and social needs of adolescents. "We cast them into a sea of thousands of peers who lead lives largely unknown to a constantly changing parade of adults more remote by quantum leap than ever before," they said.

Students were selected on a random basis to participate in the Model Core, and a meeting was held to explain the program to parents. "Parents could veto participation at that time," explained Russell, "but once the students began in the program, it was difficult to drop out." Teachers teach a four-period day, and the students are assigned to study tables with peers of varying academic ability. Instead of receiving grades, seventh- and eighth-graders are given "achievement ladders" listing what they have mastered, skill by skill and performance by performance. Letter grades are then resumed in grade 9. Key to the project was the scheduling of a conference period for planning purposes. "It is imperative to have the time in the school day to create something different," said Russell, the mathematics teacher. "We're changing the way school is structured for these students, and that takes careful planning and preparation. All subjects connect in school, just as in life. It is a team effort to educate a child. We have to talk about a student and compare notes, just as is done in the business world."

Under the plan any disciplinary problem in one class is reported to each of the teachers and then to the home. Students soon learn that it does not pay to break the rules. "Students learn that there are hard consequences for inappropriate actions," said Russell. "Life doesn't give them any breaks—we are obliged to teach them that reality."

At first the rest of the school's hundred-member faculty was suspicious. The Core team enjoyed the luxury of an additional conference period scheduled into its school day, and while the team continually asked for a full contingent of thirty-six students per class, in practice the front office gave them fewer students. "The first year we didn't interact much with the rest of the faculty because we were building our own program, and the need wasn't there," said Watkins. "All four of us had the same students, and we communicated daily within the program." They also had some difficulty with the front office, which followed traditional procedures in disciplining Core students rather than allowing the Core teachers to handle the problem. "We just wanted the front office to let us know when our students were out of line," said Watkins.

Some students rebel at the close scrutiny given them by their four teachers, but 90 percent of students in the original Core program were still there at the beginning of the third year. Those that did leave did not, for the most part, succeed in the regular program. "We have four or five students who are still really struggling, but they came in with few or no skills to begin with," said Watkins. One afternoon, when Higuchi had kept some students after school, he drove them home in a driving rainstorm to speak with their parents. One student lied about where his home was and bolted when Higuchi stopped his car. Not to be outdone, Higuchi took the chance that it was the child's neighborhood and went from door to door until he found the student's home and had a long talk with his relatives. That child was taught a real lesson that day.

Student reactions have for the most part been positive. "It's like family," said Linda, who likened her teachers to parents. "Everyone knows each other." Robert attended another school in the second year of the program and is glad that he's now back in the Core. "The better students and teachers know each other, the more teachers can help us," he remarked. Only two of the original four teachers, Watkins and Russell, are still working full-time in the program. Higuchi left teaching to take a full-time job as vice president of the teachers union, but he continues to keep his hand in the program and is doing an assessment of its results. St. Gean, the social studies teacher, decided to continue teaching in the seventh grade. The remaining two, however, said that they would commit to it all over again. "In a second," said Russell. "Despite the excruciatingly tough first year, when we all had to change our way of teaching and learning, the program works for kids. This year the rewards are rolling in with our students as real citizens. We're a real family. Students don't care what you know until they know that you care." Watkins agrees. "I'd like to have my students even longer than three years," she said. "We work so well together now." Both said that they liked the idea of counseling their own students and working on life skills as well as academic subjects.

Academically, students in the Core program did well. They

also outnumber others on the pep squad and in other clubs and after-school activities. "Our students have manners," said Watkins. "They respect themselves, other students, and us. We've worked relentlessly on interpersonal skills and peer problem solving." Russell was asked by a new teacher how he stopped students from stealing things from his desk. Russell was startled. "Students' stealing is never an issue in the Core program," he said. "We have too much respect for one another. I know the students so well."

Critics of American education frequently point out that students in many other countries spend more time in school than do their American counterparts. According to a survey for *The Atlantic Monthly,* Japan educates its students 243 days a year, West Germany from 226 to 240 days, and the Soviet Union 211. Among industrial countries, only France and the Flemish part of Belgium have fewer school days in their calendars. Some districts in this country have decided that adding to the school schedule might not be such a bad idea, either by lengthening the school day or by having students come in on Saturdays.

But while it's fine to increase the amount of time students spend studying, there's an even more important aspect to the rethinking of time in American public schools: making better use of the time you have. As noted in chapter 1, one of the basic fallacies of the school reform movement of the 1980s was that schools can be improved simply by giving students more of the same. But more of the wrong medicine never made anyone better; more of the same old teacher talk will simply increase the boredom level in the classroom. The trick is to enrich the educational mix and organize the teaching and learning process so that time is a function of learning, not the other way around.

One way to do this is through the widespread practice of block scheduling, or combining several class periods back to back. This gets away from the tyranny of the bell and allows the introduction of a hierarchy of values—some subjects are more important than others. One approach to block scheduling is the Copernican Plan, which is being piloted in Topsfield, Massachusetts. The brainchild of Joseph M. Carroll, superintendent of the Masconomet Regional School District, the plan takes its name from Nicolaus Copernicus, the sixteenth-century astronomer who revolutionized our conception of the universe. Carroll points out that Copernicus did not come up with any revolutionary new findings about the universe. What he did was bring a new perspective to the problem of explaining what seemed to be erratic planetary movements. "If one assumed that the sun, rather than the earth, was the center of the planetary system, the movements of the planets could be explained rationally," says Carroll. "That simple change was a revolutionary idea."

Carroll's "Copernican change" involves the school schedule. "Instead of having students change locations, subjects, and activities seven to nine times each day, we ask them to concentrate on one or two subjects at a time, each taught in an extended 'macroclass,' " he explains. Eighty students—about half of the ninth-grade class—take two hundred-minute classes each day for sixty days, then switch to two new classes. "The other structure is so fragmented, so crazy," said David Donavel, an English teacher. "It's very, very hard to teach that way." Donald Doliber, a social studies teacher, told *Education Week* that the change permits more coherent teaching and learning. "In a hundred-minute span, I can talk about Martin Luther, about the Counter-Reformation, and about the Thirty Years' War, as well as the themes running through all three events," he says. By contrast, he would spend a day on each topic in the traditional program and be unable to discuss the common themes because the lessons were too disjointed. "Some students can't remember what they had for lunch the day before, much less the Thirty Years' War," he comments. He also argues that the "macroclasses" have strengthened the bond between teachers and students and led students to "accept responsibility for their education." He also states that his plan reduces class size, increases the number of courses a school can offer, and cuts down the student-teacher ratio. Carroll's plan has other components, such as differentiated diplomas, awarding credit based on mastery, and the use of small seminars. But he thinks that an institution can only handle so much change at once, and "I'm stretching the limits right now."

The most radical rethinking of the relationship between time and learning, though, involves the Accelerated School, which we mentioned earlier in this chapter. Henry Levin of Stanford University became interested in the way public schools deal with "educationally disadvantaged" students. He estimates that about one-third of the nation's children fall into this category by virtue of poverty and cultural forces that make it difficult for them to succeed in school. Once such students start falling behind, the usual approach is to put them in "remedial" programs, in which they are pulled out of regular classes and taught the same material they have already failed to get, only at a slower pace. The answer to educational failure is not better—or even different—teaching but more time.

The problem with this approach is that remedial teaching tends to be even more boring for the students than the teaching was the first time around, and the major effect—even when students can muster the enthusiasm to take the repetition seriously—is that they fall farther and farther behind their peers in the regular classes. "We start off with the assumption that these students are damaged merchandise and that we have to repair them," says Levin. "When you do that, you have lost the battle. You tell them, their parents, and their teachers that they are incapable of learning at a normal rate, and that becomes a self-fulfilling prophecy."

Levin decided to reverse this logic. Why not treat slow learners the same way as fast ones—by providing as much stimulation as possible? Gifted students are taken on field trips to museums, given "hands-on" curriculums, presented with challenges that require them to work harder and faster, Levin reasoned. Why should slow learners be treated any differently? Levin called this approach accelerated learning and started testing it out in two California schools, one in San Francisco and another in Redwood City. The basic strategy was to identify each student's educational strengths, work with parents to set goals that would assure that students would be functioning at grade level by the time they moved on to the next school, and then provide the time and stimulation necessary to reach these goals.

One school that opted for accelerated learning is the Eugene Field Elementary School in Hannibal, Missouri. Hannibal rests above the bluffs that rise out of the Mississippi River as it winds its way past Missouri. Samuel Clemens, who was born there and wrote about it, made the town famous, and a riverboat parked in front of the town's twin grain silos reminds visitors of the era of Tom Sawyer and Huckleberry Finn. But barges moving along the river reflect the changing times, as does the traffic flowing across the bridge taking people to jobs in Quincy, Illinois. Hannibal is a town with poor rural people who have migrated from the countryside to find jobs or, as many do, survive on public assistance. The principal of the Field School is Larry Degitz, a tall, thin former chemistry and physics teacher in his forties who has two teenage children of his own and speaks with passion about his job. "Given the birthrates of children born to families at risk, the dropout rate is going to double," he says. "I've had teachers tell me that you can't change this. I think we can, but we have to come up with new solutions—now."

Field, one of six elementary schools in Hannibal, is located on Market Street, not far from the center of town. The school site dates back to 1893 and the current building to 1924, and Field has the feel of another time. It has had only four principals in its entire history, and their pictures hang in the school's office. Field's exterior has been modernized with new storm windows to help conserve energy, but inside it looks much as it has for the last sixty years— dark wood, polished oak floors, and even glass-enclosed cases filled with stuffed birds, a vestige from a day gone by. Kathleen Turner, the remedial math teacher, went to Field as a girl half a century ago, as did her four children and her husband. Now many of the rural poor that move into Hannibal send their children to Field, and 70 percent of the families qualify for free lunch. Not surprisingly the students tend to do poorly on standardized achievement tests, and about a dozen first-graders out of fifty were usually held back. Four years ago, just to see where they stood, teachers at Field took a hard look at their students' performance. They were horrified to realize that most were two years below grade level when they left the school and that 43 percent of their former students had dropped out of school. Obviously the old approach to remedial education was not working. "We tried to close the gap by repeating things," said Degitz. "But the gap only widened. If students don't get something the first time, what makes you think that, given the same thing, they'll get it again? Kids only get demoralized, frustrated, saddened about going to school."

Enter Hank Levin, who had been looking for schools willing to try out his theories of accelerated learning and had spoken to a meeting of Missouri superintendents. Degitz heard the word and passed it on to his teachers, who dug deeper into the idea and decided to give it a try. In the meantime—"the funny part" is what Degitz calls it—Field got the word that it had received a $130,000 federal grant for a dropout-prevention program. "It was as if somebody gave us a Cadillac," said the principal. The money meant that Field could go about implementing the principles of accelerated learning the way it was supposed to be done.

Field hired substitute teachers to enable regular teachers to devote more time to thinking and planning; teachers were encouraged to stimulate children in as many ways as they could. "At-risk children need a multisensory approach," Degitz explains. "They need to manipulate items while they are hearing about them. They need to hear it, see it, and do it, instead of sitting at desks in straight little rows. In math they need to work with Cuisenaire rods and use fingers as calculators." To further enrich their experiences, Field chartered buses to take underachieving students to the zoo in St. Louis and the Abraham Lincoln monument in Springfield, Illinois. The school also began offering an after-school program with offerings such as swimming, racquetball, photography, pottery, art, printing, and crafts. But significantly, the greatest number of students actually signed up for tutoring. "They like working with someone one-on-one," said Laura Cunningham, coordinator of the extended day program. "They like the attention." Unfortunately not everyone could afford the fifty cents a day the after-school program cost. "When you are living on minimum wage, that can be a potful of money," says Degitz.

Not all teachers liked all aspects of the new approach. Of the five who've left since 1988, Degitz suspects the new project probably had some effect on the decision of a couple of them. "It wouldn't surprise me if one or more still won't leave or transfer to another assignment, due, in part, to the stress of the change," he said. "It is difficult, once you have established a teaching system that is comfortable for you, to accept wholesale changes. It makes some people question their own competence. But, like I try to tell them, no one is expected to have all the answers. Those who left were all good people, good teachers. Some things just don't fit with some people."

Early results on accelerated learning have been encouraging. The Daniel Webster Elementary School in San Francisco showed the biggest gains in language achievement and the second-biggest gains in math of all seventy-two elementary schools in the city in

1990. The Illinois State Board of Education was so taken by such reports that it has offered to help schools adopt it in place of their regular remedial programs. Twenty-four took up the offer, and the Chevron Corporation recently gave Levin $1.5 million to establish Accelerated Schools in Texas, California, and other states where Chevron has plants.

Accelerated Learning was the key to the academic turnaround of the Hollibrook Elementary School in Houston, described in the opening chapter of this book. Hollibrook opted for this approach after Suzanne Still, the principal, came across an article written by Levin in a professional journal. Principal Still is a rebel. As a young teacher in the 1960s, she was once sent home by the principal to change her clothes because her skirt was too short. Part of her rebellion takes the form of having faith in "at-risk" thirteen-year-olds—like thirteen-year-old Lauro Gonzales.

A dark-skinned Hispanic with penetrating brown eyes and an infectious smile, Lauro lives in a two-bedroom apartment with his mother, stepfather, and four siblings in the public housing project adjacent to the school. When he was six, his mother marched him across the street to Hollibrook, where he failed miserably. He found it difficult to sit and listen and, when asked a question, would bury his head on his desk. Teachers began pulling him out of his classes for remedial work, but he found this embarrassing and frustrating and began getting into fights. The second semester of third grade he spent twenty-five days in the so-called Campus Discipline Center, a windowless room where "behavior problems" like Lauro served time sitting in tiny cubicles filling out workbooks under the watchful eye of a school secretary. When Still became principal, the first child brought to her for discipline was Lauro, who had been caught ripping a star-filled chart documenting student accomplishments—*other* students' accomplishments—off the school bulletin board. Later, at the end of his fourth-grade year, he was suspended for breaking into the school over a weekend to steal ice cream.

Just before school opened the following fall, Still called Lauro in for an hour-and-a-half chat in which she laid out an ambitious expectation: He would not leave Hollibrook until he could read and write. Lauro's teachers, Jennifer Higby and Kippie Curcio, began looking for strengths on which they could build and discovered one in math. They put him in contact with a job-training program where he got to work with computers. They started giving him jobs around the classroom and sending him to the principal's office not to be disciplined but to read his stories to her. Still herself began looking for ways to enrich his experiences. She took him on his first trip to the nearby mall and bought him his first meal in a cafeteria, where he was overwhelmed by the choices of desserts before him. "Miss Still," he said, "I'm in paradise." Still recalls that she did not know whether to be more pleased by his enthusiasm or "by the fact that he knew the word *paradise*." By the end of the year Lauro's standardized-test scores had jumped dramatically. While he still needs lots of attention when it comes to tough subjects like science, Hollibrook's decision to intensify his pace of learning, not slow it down, clearly paid off for Lauro. It also paid off for Hollibrook students as a whole. In 1988, fifth-graders in the school had an average composite score on their standardized achievement tests of 3.7, meaning that they were performing at the level of third-graders during the seventh month of school. By 1991, the average was up to 5.2—a gain of more than a year and a half. The language arts score jumped from 3.7 to 5.6, while the math score soared from 5.3 to 6.6. These gains seem even more impressive given the fact that they occurred during a period when the percentage of students from minority and low-income homes increased. "These kids are *more* at risk than before," said Levin.

By rethinking the relationship between time and learning, smart schools can avoid at least another of those problems that loom as intractable under the lockstep approach of the factory-model school: the debate over flunking versus social promotion. The practice of making students repeat a grade seems logical enough. Students who have failed to grasp the material presented at a particular grade level should, the argument goes, be given another opportunity to succeed. Moreover the threat of failure serves to motivate students to learn, and retention makes life easier for teachers by narrowing the range of abilities among the students they face. The alternative—social promotion—means that they will be forced to confront tasks for which they are not ready. Opponents of flunking, on the other hand, argue that success is a better motivator than failure and cite evidence that mastery of basic skills is not necessarily a prerequisite for learning higher ones. They also argue that, given the wide range of abilities in most American classrooms anyway, it is arbitrary to hold back a few students. Whatever the justification, there is no doubt that retention is costly. The National Association of School Psychologists estimates that the United States spends $10 billion a year to reteach students who have been held back.

The heated debate over social promotion versus retention presents a curious paradox. Few educational causes get more popular applause than refusing to promote a student just because he or she is a year older. Yet few practices have been shown to be less effective. Summarizing the results of more than sixty studies over seven decades, the *Harvard Education Letter* concluded that "most low-achieving students do progress, whether they are retained or promoted," and that "retained students score somewhat lower on achievement tests than similar children who have moved along to the next grade." Roy P. Doyle, a professor of education at Arizona State University, took his own look at the research and concluded, "There is probably no widespread practice in education today that has been as thoroughly discredited by research."

In smart schools the issue of retention versus social promotion becomes moot. Creative use of time, combined with techniques such as cooperative learning, makes it possible for slow learners to move along with their peers. The factory-model concept of fixed time is on its way out. Virtually every aspect of the way schools use time— from school calendars and the pace of learning to the way time is used in the classroom—is up for grabs. Smart schools are making time dependent on learning, not the other way around.

But making effective use of time in the service of better learning presumes that we understand the goals of this learning and that we know when we have achieved them. That's an assumption we must now examine carefully. Next stop: Indianapolis.

5.

Beyond Testing

I T'S THE DAY of reckoning for Josh Roof, a sixth-grader at the Key School in Indianapolis, Indiana. He's about to be tested on what he knows about solar energy, and he's been preparing for weeks. But instead of nervously chewing on his number-2 lead pencil while he fills in blanks on a piece of paper, Josh is standing, even smiling, in front of a video camera and talking to a live audience—his teacher and fellow students—about his topic. He shows them his final product, a model of a solar-powered skyscraper that he designed to illustrate what he had learned during the Key School's nine-week schoolwide study of the theme "Harmony."

"A solar-powered building is much more in harmony with society and nature," he tells his audience. Josh describes the research he did on solar energy and how he converted metric numbers to scale from his architectural drawing. He describes the angles he has designed on the building's exterior to support solar cells and tells how an architect looked over his plans and made suggestions. A fifth-grade teacher, Hazel Tribble, who guided Josh's work on several projects, asks him whether the seventy-story building would generate enough energy to heat itself during Indiana's cold January nights. He stops and thinks, then replies, "Of course." His classmates join in the questioning. "Is such a building really possible?" "How tall would it be?" "Would the solar panels fall off in a storm?" "How long did it take you to draw the plans?" As the dialogue continues, Tribble notes that Josh speaks with much greater confidence than he did on his last video appearance. She also notices that he explains details in clear and informed sentences.

At the Key School individual student video portfolios have replaced paper-and-pencil standardized tests as the primary means of evaluating student performance and development. The results of

Josh's study and building efforts, along with the explanations of the processes he went through to create the final project, are now recorded on video in living color for anyone to see. In fact, an entire history of what Josh has learned is formally captured as a part of his official "video portfolio." His teachers discuss and analyze each section of his video portfolio looking for a wide variety of abilities and skills, as well as areas for improvement. "The most important thing to me about the video portfolio," said Tribble, "is that it gives me a chance to see how the child thinks. It gives me a document of the thinking processes that result in the final product. No written test can do that."

The Key School in Indianapolis is pioneering in an enterprise that might be best described as the "keystone" of redesigned schools: finding new ways to measure what students learn *and* designing a new system of accountability.

At the present time there is, for all practical purposes, *no* accountability in American education. That's because the factory-model school puts its faith in process, not in results. State education departments make policy decisions that then flow down the chain of command to superintendents, principals, teachers, and students. The assumption is that if everyone follows the rules—maintaining the correct class size, using the approved textbooks and curriculums, accumulating the right number of course credits—everything will come out just fine. The one thing that never enters the equation is student learning. "No teacher ever lost her job just because students were not learning," observed Richard P. Mills, the commissioner of education in Vermont. "What counts is following the rules." Nor, we might add, did any school district ever lose state aid because it failed to educate some child. To the contrary, the longer the student is kept in school, the more money the district gets.

But, you say, "American students cannot get the Civil War in the right half-century." And they come in dead last in all those international competitions. Whose fault is it? The answer is: no one's. The fault lies not with any identifiable individuals but with the system as a whole—the complex set of conventions, rules, policies, customs, and chains of command. Any single player in the system can beg off responsibility. You say, Hector isn't learning? Sorry, but I followed the curriculum. You say, Most of our kids are reading below grade level? Sorry, but we pull them out of class for remedial work, just like we're supposed to do. In practice, of course, in the absence of anywhere else to point the finger, educators take the only way out they can: They blame the kid. "We taught him, but he didn't learn." In other words, the operation was a success, but the patient died. Education, says David Kearns, is "the only business I know of where, if you do something good, nothing good happens to you and if you do something bad, nothing bad happens to you."

There is, to be sure, one important exception to accountability based on following the rules: standardized reading and math tests. These tests measure outcomes, and they are very powerful. They are the principal means by which citizens evaluate the performance of their local schools. Newspapers print each school's test scores, and readers scan them with magnifying glasses. School boards use them to judge the performance of superintendents and principals, who put pressure on teachers to deliver higher scores. Standardized tests even drive curriculums. Several years ago the New York City school system announced that it was switching to a new brand of reading tests. As soon as the word went out, teachers bolted to the libraries to find out what kind of questions were on the new test. Much to their horror they discovered that, unlike the old test, the new one did not ask students any questions about *antonyms*. So teachers who for their entire careers had been drilling students on antonyms abruptly ceased doing so. Helping teachers keep their eye on what test makers want has even become a professional field in itself. State boards of education now routinely hire consultants to "align" their curriculums, that is, to make sure that the curriculum coincides with what the test makers want. Whether this is good educational policy is not an issue.

The problems associated with standardized multiple-choice tests are legion, and it is tempting to dwell on them at length. Suffice it to say that they grew out of the efficiency movement of the early twentieth century and perpetuate the values of the factory-model school—authoritarianism, standardization, passivity, and the like—rather than the ideals of the smart schools necessary for tomorrow's world. They measure the wrong things in the wrong way for the wrong reasons.

Standardized multiple-choice tests operate under the dubious assumption that there is a single right answer to any question worth asking. They do not ask students to generate answers on their own; rather the trick is to figure out which answer the test maker has determined is the correct one. Several times in earlier chapters we have made the point that in most real-life situations the major challenge is not to answer a question but to figure out the right question to ask. In standardized tests the important challenge is already done for you. They represent the triumph of passive learning. "It is testing for the TV generation," charged Linda Darling-Hammond, a professor at the Teachers College of Columbia University. "We don't ask if students can synthesize information, solve problems, or think independently. We measure what they can recognize."

The *reductio ad absurdum* of standardized testing is multiple-choice tests of writing. Instead of having students write a passage to be graded as a whole, these tests require students to perform tasks such as selecting the best phrase to insert at a particular point in a given paragraph. Psychometricians, a.k.a. test makers, claim that most students will get roughly the same score no matter which form of test they take—either writing an essay or filling in blanks. For the purposes of argument, let's take their word on that. But consider the message that it sends to teachers and students: writing consists of manipulating the meaning of short, isolated passages by recognizing phrases drafted by other people. Even the old-fashioned tests in which students actually write an original passage are inherently misdirected because they are administered under timed conditions. They measure ability to write a quick, coherent first draft. Any experienced writer will tell you that writing is what you do to refine the rough draft. Moreover, whether you do this quickly or slowly is a matter of individual style and has little to do with the quality of the final product. Timed writing tests measure journalistic writing, a worthy genre to be sure, but, alas, a highly specialized form of writing that most people will never have to do.

Another weakness of standardized tests is that they provide little, if any, feedback that teachers can use in making educational decisions. The reason is simple: They are designed to rank students, not to identify strengths and weaknesses of individual students. Since the scoring system, based on percentiles, is intended to exaggerate minor differences among students, failure is built into the formula. When students are graded on a curve, half are doomed from the beginning to come out looking bad, while the other half get a largely illusory feeling of success. As Grant Wiggins, a nationally known consultant on student assessment, puts it, "The standardized test is disrespectful by design. Mass testing as we know it treats students as objects—as if their education and thought processes were similar and as if the reasons for their answers were irrelevant."

Moreover the discriminatory nature of standardized testing is becoming more and more evident. New York State recently decided that standardized tests could not be used as a criterion for awarding merit scholarships because the tests unfairly discriminate against young women. After a three-year study funded by the Ford Foundation, the National Commission on Testing and Public Policy charged that the American testing system has become a "hostile gatekeeper" limiting opportunities for many young people, especially women and minorities. "Twenty years ago, when testing initially became controversial, there were far more individuals pursuing opportunities than there were opportunities," said Bernard R. Gifford, a former educator and now vice president for education of Apple Computer, Inc., and chairman of the commission. "Testing was used as a major measure of weeding out qualified candidates. Today, in the middle of a growing labor shortage that will grow more acute in the future, it is very clear the emphasis placed on testing in the past of weeding out candidates has to shift."

The results of standardized tests are easily manipulated. George Madeus of Boston College points out that when standardized tests are used for purposes such as rating schools, they generate a *political* rather than an educational response. If superintendents, principals, and others are under pressure to have students do well on standardized tests, you can be sure that they will do whatever is necessary to get the scores up. Any relationship between the raising of test scores and students actually learning is purely coincidental.

Test makers who want to sell their products understand this and do their best to cooperate. Not long ago John J. Cannell, a family physician in Beaver, West Virginia, noticed widespread discrepancies between the academic performance of some of his teenage patients and "the grade level to which they were assigned." As a physician, he found himself handling problems of low self-esteem and depression in many of his teenage patients. Then one day he heard from the state education department that schoolchildren in West Virginia, which has some of the nation's highest illiteracy levels, were performing *above* the national average. Since no one in full command of his or her senses seriously believes that the financially strapped schools of West Virginia are turning out students who perform above the national average, Cannell undertook a survey of thirty-two other state education departments. He found that *every state* was making the same claim. "We could not find any state that was below the national average," says Cannell. The doctor, by now enraged, formed an organization called Friends of Education, Inc., to publicize the problem. His findings came to the attention of Chester L. Finn, Jr., then assistant secretary of education in charge of research, who invited test makers to his office to discuss the situation. The test makers argued that the definition of "average" on most tests had been established in the early 1980s by a national sample. Schools, they said, had improved. So it was to be expected that most students these days test "above" average by what is now an outdated standard. The phenomenon has now come to be known as the "Lake Wobegon Effect" after the mythical town created by folk humorist Garrison Keillor, where all the women are strong, all the men good-looking, and "all the children are above average."

Even the way test scores of individual schools are reported is misleading. Test makers report reading and math scores in terms of the percentage of students who are reading at or above "grade level." Common sense suggests that most eighth-graders in a typical school would be found to be reading at the eighth-grade level. That's what you're supposed to think. Likewise, if an eighth-grader comes home with a piece of paper saying that he is reading at the eleventh-grade level, his parents would be overjoyed because they would assume, reasonably enough, that he is reading as well as the typical eleventh-grader. That may be right, but that's not what the test makers are saying. They cannot make any such claim because no eleventh-grader ever took the eighth-grade test. Nor has any eighth-grader ever taken an eleventh-grade test. In the language of test makers "grade level" is a statistical abstraction. It is the median score—the point at which half the students perform above and half below. The test makers are really talking in terms of percentiles, but instead of saying the student ranks at the 90th percentile, they call it "reading at the eleventh-grade level," because that has meaning—however misleading—for parents. No wonder that parents become confused, like the angry mother of a college-bound senior who told a high school guidance counselor, "I knew Clarence was not in the top half of his class, but no one told me he was in the *bottom* half."

Perhaps the most damaging aspect of standardized tests, though, is their impact on the curriculum. Since states test reading and math, this is what schools emphasize. But in doing so they focus on the basic skills and factual knowledge that such tests measure and direct schools' attention from the new agenda of teaching students to think. "One of the reasons kids don't learn to write in our schools is that they're not asked to write," said Albert Shanker of the American Federation of Teachers. "Why aren't they asked to write? Two reasons. One, it takes a long time to mark papers, and two, there are no standardized tests in writing, so that you don't have these annual things each year which say our district is above average in writing. There are no standardized tests in science, so teachers are sort of told—'Look, it's reading and math that's going to count.' Nobody gives a test in science, so nobody's going to know that until they get these ten-year international comparisons, and that's not done school by school, district by district." Current tests, say Lauren and Daniel Resnick, a husband-and-wife research team at the University of Pittsburgh, "are tuned to a curriculum of the past, one that is not suited to today's social and economic conditions." Testing, they say, "remains in essential respects unchanged from the era in which it was considered enough for schools to teach mastery of routine skills—simple computation, reading predictable texts, reciting civic or religious codes. Goals such as interpreting unfamiliar texts, constructing convincing arguments, understanding complex systems, developing approaches to problems, or negotiating problem resolutions in a group were reserved for an elite."

The situation is becoming worse, not better, for the United States is going test crazy. Nearly every large educational-reform effort of the last few years has either mandated a new form of testing or expanded the use of standardized tests. In a misguided attempt to assure increased accountability, state legislatures have turned standardized tests into political weapons, and a new term has entered our vocabulary: "high-stakes testing." The National Commission on Testing and Public Policy estimated that in any given year elementary and secondary students take *127 million* separate tests as part of test batteries mandated by states and districts. At some grade levels, it said, a student may take seven to twelve tests a year. These consume 20 million school days and $1 billion of public funds—and this does not count the "opportunity costs" of time used to drill students in the narrow skills measured by standardized tests. Scores from standardized, machine-graded sheets are being increasingly used to categorize students, flunk kindergartners, admit students to well-funded gifted or magnet programs, hire and fire teachers, award diplomas, evaluate curriculums, and dole out money. "The amount of testing of American schoolchildren is greater than at any time in our history," said Archie E. LaPointe, executive director of the National Assessment of Educational Progress. LaPointe should know, because his organization is expanding its operations to provide more state-by-state comparisons of student achievement. It is a "high stakes" game in itself. "Whoever controls those powerful tests will control a large measure of what is taught and learned in American schools," said George Madeus of Boston College.

Reversing this reinforcement of the factory-model values of assessment—standardization, passivity, and so forth—will be difficult. But the direction and basic principles that must be followed are clear as crystal. The goal is to describe what today's youngsters need to know and be able to do in the twenty-first century and then to develop tests that measure this knowledge and these skills— tests that respect the values of smart schools. Schools must abandon the traditional preoccupation with process and inputs and focus instead on results. But the results must be genuine educational goals, not the contrived skills that make for success on standardized tests. The new assessment devices must respect diversity and reward the ability of students to generate answers on their own, not merely repeat information they have soaked up like sponges.

The operative word here is *authentic*. Grant Wiggins, who has done as much thinking about this as anyone else, points out that most tests that students take are "proxies." Instead of having students do what they are supposed to be learning to do—write clearly, think, problem-solve, put events in historical perspective, and so forth—teachers come up with shortcuts that supposedly reveal whether, if asked to do these things, they could in fact deliver. With authentic testing there are no shortcuts or proxies. Students are actually asked to do the writing, problem solving, and so forth and are then evaluated on how well they do so. Wiggins suggests that we take the concept of performing in the arts and apply it to every classroom subject. "If we wish to design an authentic test," he says, "we must first decide what are the actual performances that we want students to be good at. We must design those performances first and worry about a fair and thorough method of grading them later. Do we judge our students to be deficient in writing, speaking, listening, artistic creation, finding and citing evidence, and problem solving? Then let the tests ask them to write, speak, listen, create, do original research, and solve problems."

Wiggins lays out several principles for the development of "authentic" tests. First, he says, they should require the performance of exemplary tasks. That is, they should "replicate the challenges and standards of performance that typically face writers, business people, scientists, community leaders, designers, or historians. These include writing essays and reports, conducting individual and group research, designing proposals and mockups, assembling portfolios, and so on." He points out that the root word of *assessment* means to "sit with." Thus, authentic tests should be administered in settings that enable the evaluator to ask the student to explain or clarify answers. There should be no arbitrary time restraints or secret agendas. They should be designed to let students "show off" in whatever way comes most naturally to them. "There is room for the quiet techie and the show-off prima donna in plays; there is room for the slow, heavy lineman and for the small, fleet pass receiver in football. In professional work, too, there is room for choice and style in tasks, topics, and methodologies. Why must all students be tested in the same way and at the same time? Why should speed of recall be so well rewarded and slow answering be so heavily penalized in conventional testing?"

There is another all-important quality of authentic tests. They should *encourage* teaching to the test. No one complains when a basketball coach drills youngsters on foul shooting or setting a pick.

Everyone knows that this is what they will have to do when the game starts. He is teaching them what they will need to know, and the game is, in effect, an authentic test of what they learn in practice. Likewise, classroom instruction should be aimed at preparing students to demonstrate their knowledge of writing, mathematics, English, history, Spanish, or whatever, and the tests should be set up in such a way that when the instructor "teaches to the test," he or she is doing exactly what you want to happen. If the tests are well conceived, teaching to the test becomes a virtue.

All of this sounds obvious, even banal, but the situation in which American schools find themselves is such that even common sense can sound quite revolutionary. The reason is that "proxies" are cheap and easy to administer, while "authentic" tests are difficult to develop and more costly. Nevertheless, the movement is on to refine the art of developing authentic tests and, thereby, to develop an accountability system suitable to the values of smart schools.

The Key School in Indianapolis has been a trailblazer in authentic testing—not only because of ingenious assessment techniques, such as Josh Roof's video portfolio, but because of the educational goals against which it measures itself. Key is the nation's first school to be organized around a theory of multiple intelligences that Harvard University cognitive psychologist Howard Gardner advocated in his 1983 book, *Frames of Mind* (Basic Books). Gardner argues that people possess a range of abilities, most of which are undernourished in the typical school. "Most schools focus their attention on language arts and math," said Patricia J. Bolanos, principal of the public elementary school. "We want to develop the full range of their talents and discover where they are particularly strong." Gardner argues that people have at least seven distinct intelligences, among which are *spatial* (the ability to perceive and manipulate the visual world), *bodily-kinesthetic* (skill in using one's body), *musical* (the ability to think in sound), *interpersonal,* and *intrapersonal.* Interpersonal skills are social, such as understanding another person's motivations or feelings or being able to arbitrate a problem, while intrapersonal skills have to do with the vast realm of self-understanding, a topic that few American schools even approach.

Key owes its existence to eight bold elementary teachers who used their collective creativity and intelligence to invent a new kind of public school. The eight teachers were team-teaching at P.S. 113, an Indianapolis elementary school. Over coffee one day in the teachers lounge and later in each other's living rooms, they began working collaboratively to define and communicate their ideas about what a school should be like. "We had an optimistic view of human nature," recalled Bolanos, one of the founders. "We believed that people have certain innate abilities, and that if these are given the right nurture, they will develop, and everyone in society will benefit. But when we limit the areas that the culture thinks are important, such as schools do with linguistic and math skills, then we limit the entire culture." Together they developed a curriculum that they thought could make education more creative. They applied for grants, investigated the work of researchers, lobbied, and finally decided that the only way to put it into practice was to start their own school. One day the Gang of Eight, as they came to be known, piled into a car and drove fourteen hours to a conference in eastern Pennsylvania to corner Gardner and get his opinion on their plans. He in turn was surprised and excited to see how the teachers had developed practical applications for some of his ideas. The idea of a video portfolio was one Key-teacher innovation that particularly intrigued him. This idea was sparked by Gardner's comments to the teachers about "process portfolio work," something his group at Harvard was starting in Pittsburgh with art and music in a project in the schools called Arts PROPEL. He agreed to work as a consultant to the school.

In 1987 the Key School opened as a K–6 program. It was located in a blond brick 1938 art deco building with rounded corners and sweeping curves, near a revitalized downtown Indianapolis. Bolanos was designated by the school system as principal. Its 20 staff members, including 14 teachers, served over 150 kids. The Key founders were convinced that a creative and flexible school could benefit all children, not just "the gifted or talented." They were convinced that "gifted" and "special education" were false categories based on the mistaken notion that kids require special and separate learning environments and that the separation does them good. So the Key teachers insisted on selecting ordinary kids by lottery, and thus representative of the city's cultural diversity, so that their ideas could not be dismissed as applying solely to exceptional or prosperous children. In 1989 minority students accounted for 42 percent of the students. Forty-one percent came from single-parent homes. A third were officially poor.

Key's curriculum is designed to give equal emphasis to all seven abilities and to allow children to intensively develop particular areas in which they have the greatest interest and ability. "There are jobs out there that require these different intelligences, and we want our students to be ready," said Key teacher Sharon Smith. Key fits its education to the child. "The thrust of Key School is to get the child exposed to all these areas at an early age," explained Bolanos. "It is a matter of equity for all children to learn where they have strengths and provide extra time in those areas."

One way Key teachers learn about a child's particular strengths is through another form of alternative testing, which takes place in the "Flow Activity Center." Key kids will tell you these "tests" are a lot of fun. They should be. The flow center is a game room, a special kind of game room. Kids simply play with a variety of board games, puzzles, audiotapes, and other devices while their teachers and a specialist, Gwendolyn M. Staten, observe which choices they make. A record is kept to create an intelligence portrait of each student.

In designing more sophisticated ways of interpreting the play data, Key teachers worked with another team of researchers from the University of Chicago, headed by Mihaly Csikszentmihalyi, professor of human development and education. The team was interested in motivation and creativity. Csikszentmihalyi coined the term "flow activity" to describe the feeling people get when they are successful at an activity they enjoy. Rooted in the Key School vision of testing students is a fundamental belief that children learn in many different ways, that they have multiple intelligences that traditional tests are not able to capture. Key School teachers look at the development of the whole child and give each kid the chance to discover and build his or her strengths in the context of a general education. The video portfolio then allows for qualitative evaluations.

"We are not interested in competition, exterior rewards, or grades," said Bolanos. "We don't have evaluative grades. Instead, we want kids to develop an intrinsic motivation and link it with a student's area of strength. Instead of remediating weaknesses during the regular school day, we want to motivate through success."

At the beginning of each school year, students choose a special-interest pod that includes kids from all grades. The pods represent all seven areas of intelligence. Key kids spend one class period of forty minutes a day working in pods that include math pentathlon games, problem solving, communications, art, choir, Spanish, physical sciences, mind and movement, acting, or becoming young astronauts, young entrepreneurs, young naturalists, and so forth. The pods enable kids of different ages to work together.

"One of the beauties of the pods," explained Bolanos, "is that teachers get an hour a day to work in their areas of high interest. I have a background as an art educator, so I conduct a ceramics pod for ten children. For the child it is almost like an apprenticeship. And the experience is wonderful for all of us."

Key's general curriculum is organized around twelve-week schoolwide themes, such as "Connections," "Animal Patterns," and "Changes in Time and Space." The idea for the thematic approach was stimulated by Ernest L. Boyer of the Carnegie Foundation for the Advancement of Teaching and his notion of the Basic School. The themes are designed to get students to think across traditional subject divisions. "This is what you do in later life," pointed out Beverly J. Hoeltke, a second-grade teacher and another member of the Gang of Eight. Standard subjects such as reading, writing, math, and social studies are woven into and developed organically with these themes and explore different aspects of interrelated ideas. But all students also spend time each day on art, physical education, Spanish, computers, and music.

But it's the video that captures the kids at their peak learning moments. The portfolio provides an intellectual profile upon which teachers and the students themselves can build.

While working on his model, for example, Josh further developed his passion for drawing and building. Both Josh and his friend Mark have special strengths in spatial thinking, which were detected early on in school by Key teachers. Thus they are given a full class period each day to mature in the school's architectural group, or pod. "With Josh, for example, I look to see if he used thinking and problem-solving skills in his project and how he answered questions," Hazel Tribble, Josh's teacher, said. "I look to find a crystallizing experience that got him interested in this project in the first place. I see if he has evolved through the learning experience. I look to see if he used the available resources and how he collaborated with others."

"We also look to see if there is evidence that the children present ideas that are grounded in their life," Bolanos noted, "rather than regurgitating information. We want them to link projects with their experiences and their goals."

Josh's video portfolio is filled with performances that show a variety of his interests and abilities. Personal interviews at the beginning and end of each year informed his teachers that he liked music and drawing best, that the class period a day spent with his architecture pod had advanced his ambition to become a professional architect someday. It also showed his social and personal growth at Key. "I am learning about myself," he said. "I think that is important. I learned a lot this year."

What does the Key School do with video portfolios like the one Josh made? His teachers look at his video closely to see whether he is more self-confident about his work than on the last video he made, to see what kind of thinking went into his final project, to see how well he defends his work in the face of peer questioning. A group of teachers can watch the video of the child or involve parents in a conference. "It is authentic," said Bolanos, "because what they do on the test and what they do in class are the same." To Josh Roof, solar energy was "a hard subject to do. It was complicated," he said. "And it took guts to stand up in front of a camera." But Josh says he got used to it. And what he liked best was doing the actual research for his presentation and preparing the visuals that he would need for the video. "A lot of thinking went into that project," he said. The videos ultimately go home with students and Josh will be able to look back at himself in the years ahead. Meanwhile, the video becomes a part of his permanent record that travels on to another school.

"The tape also tells teachers how well their instructional program is influencing student thinking processes," said the soft-spoken Bolanos. Video portfolios also document a teacher's professional judgment about the children they teach and their strengths and weaknesses. It represents more than just the teacher's word on how a student performs. Her judgment is confirmed when others watch what she sees in class.

On another segment of his video portfolio, Josh showed the class a large chart and time line tracing the twenty-eight houses that his father occupied since childhood. The project was part of a nine-week schoolwide unit on "connections."

"I picked this project because I wanted to know about my dad," Josh told one girl, who asked about his motivation. "I wanted to be connected to his history. And I am interested in houses." To complete the job, Josh designed interview questions and created charts and graphs to show results. The videotape showed that his handwriting had improved a little and that he could use mathematics to organize statistics.

"Will you do it for your mom?" a boy asked.

"Maybe . . . probably . . . yes," answered Josh.

In another segment Josh led a tour of historic cottage homes in the neighborhood of the school and demonstrated his knowledge of architectural terminology in describing an 1890s Victorian structure. His architecture pod adopted other neighborhood houses, and Josh interviewed several owners about the histories of the buildings. The result? He became an expert, and the historic landmarks association even requested that Josh and his classmates conduct tours.

The video portfolio captured Josh as he described the history of two extinct species—the dodo and the carrier pigeon. In another episode, he assembled a photo history of interstate highways. On still another piece of tape he demonstrated knowledge of mass-production techniques he witnessed on a field trip to a local factory by mass-producing peanut butter and jelly sandwiches for the entire class. Each tape showed Josh interested in—and enthusiastic about—his project and learning new skills and ideas along the way.

Following his presentation on the solar-energy design, Josh watched the tape to see if he was less nervous on this "test" than in earlier sessions and to see how well he answered questions. "Students get insight into how they appear to others," said Tribble. "The tape is a mirror to show them who they are to the rest of the world. It strengthens their interpersonal and intrapersonal skills and helps them to find the acceptable symbol to present themselves to the rest of the world. Through the video portfolios kids can become an expert on themselves. They see who they are, what they like to learn, how they learn. The taped performance helps make the invisible visible."

Key School may let parents see their son or daughter in action as well. It is a view they would not find if they simply visited the classroom. Students act differently when their parents are attentively watching in person. Key teachers are working on ways to help the parents interpret and use what they see. With the Key "test" they can bring their son or daughter's educational highlights into their living room with a cassette copy of the portfolio.

"Parents need to see what Key School considers a good project so that they can reinforce what we are doing," explained Hoeltke. "We can use the tape to model for them."

Key School has developed its new assessments based on new academic objectives and values. Fortunately, its students also do well on old-style tests based on old values. "We don't like to talk about the test results because they don't relate to what we are doing," insisted Bolanos. "But our scores were good. Key tested much better than the Indianapolis public school system as a whole. And in 1989 three-quarters of our graduates applied for the highly competitive junior high magnet programs, and all but one were accepted."

Authentic testing is important to Ted Sizer's concept of the student as "worker." He calls them "exhibitions." For example, when Jim Streible asked his students to synthesize what they had learned about the war in Vietnam and present it to their classmates, he was engaged in authentic testing. Another teacher who has perfected the art is Kay Scheidler, an English teacher at Hope High School in Providence, Rhode Island. Scheidler works closely with the social studies and science teachers and has stayed with the same group of students for four years.

One of her exercises in the tenth grade pulls together information from literature, history, and science relating to the use of nuclear energy. Students read John Hersey's *Hiroshima* and study the history of the dropping of the atomic bomb on Japan. In science, students also study about nuclear energy. At test time, recently, the assignment was to write a letter of at least two pages that would be sent to an important person to persuade him or her of the student's viewpoint in relation to nuclear energy. The letter must show that the student understands the scientific aspects of nuclear energy, such as how nuclear reactions change the nucleus of atoms, and can handle mathematical components, such as calculating the half-life of a radioactive isotope. It must also demonstrate a sense of historical perspective about how issues of nuclear energy relate to foreign-policy issues, and the writing style must offer a persuasive argument that clearly points to one main viewpoint.

Shelley Weeden, a senior at Hope, was surprised to be able to put so many different subjects together. "When nuclear energy is getting explained to you, usually it's science," she said. "It's not usually referred back to a historical point. It's usually about nuclear fission and what happens and how it reacts. But you don't get the personal side to it, how people felt, how they lived years after the bomb was dropped or when it was dropped or what caused the atomic bomb. You just mainly get what the nuclear bomb can do. It's not just working out a problem on the board, or knowing that Einstein knew how to create an atomic bomb, but knowing the history behind it, which was why we needed the atomic bomb. You couldn't cram things into your brain and then forget it. You remember it longer. You know more. You really think in more than black and white. You can take the work home. You can't just copy from someone. You can't study for it."

Scheidler has asked her classes to translate *Romeo and Juliet* into black dialect and then perform their version for another class. Once she handed out a sheet with examples of Edgar Allan Poe's flowery Gothic style and asked them to rewrite a Poe passage in the humorous style of Mark Twain. Shelley Weeden picked a section of Poe's "The Black Cat" that read: "From my infancy I was noted for the docility and humanity of my disposition. . . . I was especially fond of animals, and was indulged by my parents with a great variety of pets." Her rendition of how Twain would have written it was as follows: "I was always a bit of a loving tyke. 'Specially wit' animals. Ma and pa was always givin' me some. All time was spent talking to dem creatures."

In another of Kay Scheidler's classes students write a "medieval romance" as a way of getting fourteen-year-olds in the 1980s to understand and appreciate literature of the 1300s. After studying the Middle Ages in history, students write stories using a school word processor, taking a month to complete a story that is bound into a class book with a color photo of a bold knight attacking a fierce monster on the cover. The titles, in Gothic lettering, are: "Medieval Romances," "Chivalrous Deeds," and "Courtly Manners."

According to Scheidler and fellow teacher Noreen Drexel, writing a medieval romance of their own helps students internalize the genre. "As an evaluation in medieval romances, normally an English test would be questioning them on Percival, or King Arthur, or Sir Lancelot," said Scheidler. "To have them create their own medieval romance is really a whole different level of understanding." Students, some with reading levels as low as fourth grade, first read the story of Sir Gawain and the Green Knight and the stories of Percival and Tristan and Isolt. Then, to test their knowledge of the period and understanding of the main elements of these tales, the assignment is to write their own medieval romance. Like many a tale from legends of the Knights of the Round Table, the ninth-graders' stories expressed obstacles and frustrations of both love and ambition, the need to prove oneself, family reconciliations. One student imagined a Golden Key of Tintagel, which must be found to save the kingdom. Another had a beautiful and evil sorceress sent to seduce a young knight and deter him from his quest. Students put their heroes to tests of strength, loyalty, and humor. The stories are, in a word, *authentic,* re-creations of a time far removed from them. "The initial reactions to our readings ranged from apathy to a certain disgust: 'You mean they really believed in all that stupid stuff back then?'" Scheidler said. "Through the process of doing the writing themselves in imitation of the genre, the students proved not only to understand, but to be able to skillfully manipulate the conventions of the genre. They also managed to project their own interests and problems into the stories with a surprising intensity. When I think back to high school, I got A's on tests, but I forgot all that stuff. These kids are not going to forget the medieval romances they wrote. It really stays with them in a more thorough way. I've been teaching for twenty-two years, and I've never seen them enjoy writing so much."

Authentic testing is also now moving to the state level. State education departments have begun redefining the knowledge and skills that students will need to function as effective citizens and workers in the twenty-first century and then devising new techniques to measure how well students are learning them.

The first state to make such an effort on a statewide basis was Vermont, where Richard P. Mills, the commissioner of education, became concerned that traditional standardized tests were sending the wrong messages about what students should be taught. Three years ago, with solid backing from teachers and the business community, he persuaded the legislature to come up with $450,000 for pilot tests of new approaches to assessment in English and mathematics. Forty-seven schools were selected for the first year of the program, but ninety-one others joined in on their own.

Vermont's strategy is to supplement—and eventually replace—standardized testing in the two subjects by collecting and rating portfolios of students' actual classroom work. Instead of the usual "snapshot" approach—capturing what a student does or does not know at a particular moment—the new approach judges student performance over a period of time. These portfolios are then judged on the basis of common standards for the subject and grade level in much the same way that a critic or employer might evaluate the portfolio of an artist or photographer. State officials expect to validate and refine such standards during the first year of the project and then require their use in grades four and eight in the state's 340 elementary and middle schools beginning in the fall of 1991. "We'll be able to say, Here is the standard, and here is actual student work that meets the highest standard, and here's student work that is not acceptable," said Mills.

In mathematics, state officials, working with teachers and outside consultants, drew up a list of teaching goals reflecting new standards of the National Council of Teachers of Mathematics. The basic goal was to get away from the traditional emphasis on the rote learning of mathematical procedures and to teach students to value mathematics, to communicate using mathematical symbols, and to become "mathematical problem solvers." Vermont teachers are encouraged to give students "real problems that take days or weeks to solve," including those that are "truly open-ended, with no single correct answer." The state education department also laid out a set of general principles for creating mathematics portfolios. A portfolio, they said, is "a showcase for student work, a place where many types of assignments, projects, reports, and writings can be collected." Portfolios should document students' progress throughout the school year. They should contain a wide variety of materials, including drawings, models, journals, and essays describing how students approached a particular problem. They should cover a wide range of categories of problems, from the direct application of functions like long division to the solution of "nonroutine" problems with "multiple possible approaches and solutions." Portfolios should also contain work from another subject area that relates to mathematics, such as a graph of data collected for social studies.

Ann Rainey, who teaches eighth-grade mathematics at the Shelburne Middle School in Shelburne, helped develop Vermont's new approach. Students in her class keep all of their work in folders and periodically designate five to seven examples of what they consider their "best pieces." She also asks students to write a "math autobiography," to do a short essay on "the color of math," and to write a research paper about a mathematician. Rainey said that her goal is to "empower students" to think mathematically. "For too many years mathematics has been taught as a separate entity, as a bunch of isolated symbols," she said. "You'd say, 'Division is the opposite of multiplication, so you turn the second number upside down and multiply.' The kids would look at you and go, 'Huh? OK.' But it was rote learning that went out the window as soon as they went out of the class. Today, all students need to acquire math power, not just the select few. These kids may forget a formula, but they can still solve the problems because they understand the how and why of mathematics."

To make sure that her students understand the concepts they are dealing with, Rainey frequently asks them to explain their mathematical reasoning with words. For example, she gave her class the following question: "You and a friend read in the newspaper that 7 percent of all Americans eat at McDonald's each day. Your friend says that that is impossible. You know that there are approximately 250,000,000 Americans and approximately 9,000 McDonald's restaurants in the U.S. Convince your friend (in writing) that the statistic is possible." The obvious starting point is to calculate that 7 percent of Americans is 17.5 million persons, divide this figure by 9,000, and arrive at the conclusion that, on the average, each McDonald's store serves 1,944.44 persons a day. Every student in the class was able to do these calculations, and several stopped at this point. "But what does the number 1,944 tell you?" asked Rainey. "Is that a reasonable figure or not?" Indeed, a few left the answer at 1,944.44. "They didn't use common sense," said the teacher. "They took whatever the calculator told them and forgot they were dealing with people."

Hilary Milens did the necessary calculations and then went on to reason that McDonald's stores "are open eighteen hours a day and on the turnpikes they are open twenty-four hours a day" and that their "production lines are set up to make food very quickly." She pointed out that many students are located in large cities and wrote that when "you think about how many people are in big cities, it sounds pretty convincing." To bolster her argument she then wrote out some estimates of how many people might come by for each of the three meals. For example, at breakfast, served between 6:00 and 9:00 A.M., she estimated that a restaurant would serve 180 people per hour at seats and 24 per hour at the drive-through window. Her daily total came to 2,182, which she said was "very close" to the 1,944 figure. Jill Trongo, another student, began her justification of the 1,944 figure by noting that "some places are busier than others." She reasoned that most restaurants have eight cash registers, five at the counter and three for drive-through, and then estimated how many persons could be handled at each meal, noting that "lunch takes longer." Her answer was seven pages long and received a "nice job" comment from the teacher. "You convinced me," said Rainey. Another student got a similar rating by doing a one-page chart showing the number of people eating at ten-minute intervals during meal hours, the number of people per hour, the total number of people between specific hours, and the number of drive-through customers.

The trick, of course, is to figure out how to grade portfolios in such a way that they can be used to determine whether students are performing at an adequate level and to compare the performance of students in different schools, districts, and, eventually, entire states. This sounds complicated, given the fact that portfolios are far more subjective than a list of answers on a standardized test. But proponents point out that standards have been devised for measuring other "subjective" activities, such as Olympic figure skating or diving.

In Vermont, portfolios are graded on a scale of one to four. At the bottom is Level 1, the Not So Good Portfolio, showing "almost no creative work" or "evidence of student thinking." It typically consists of little more than duplicated sheets or pages copied from a textbook. At the top, Level 4, is the Outstanding Portfolio, one that is "exciting to look through," replete with projects, diagrams, reports, or letters explaining why a particular piece of work was chosen, audio- or videotapes, or other evidence that the students have been led to "think for themselves." In between are Level 3, the Good Portfolio, which indicates a "solid mathematics program" that nevertheless lacks evidence of "student enthusiasm, self-assessment, extensive investigations, and student analysis of information," and Level 2, the All Right Portfolio, which indicates an "adequate" mathematics program, "somewhat bound by textbook requirements" and showing "little evidence of student original thinking." Evaluators then grade each piece of work in a student's portfolio according to seven criteria: understanding of the problem; quality of the procedures used to solve it; quality of the decisions made along the way; the answer; use of mathematical language; use of graphs, equations, and other mathematical symbols; and clarity of presentation. Jill Trongo's McDonald's question got 3's and 4's from the committee working to define the new standards. "She understood the problem, and she explained every detail," said Rainey. "Every 'why' was in there."

Rainey encourages students to discuss their work among themselves, and thus to come to understand that there are a variety of approaches to most problems. One day recently Ryan Galt, who is thirteen, explained to the class how he had solved a problem on the blackboard. From the back of the room Rainey, trying to keep up, declared, "Whoa, Ryan, your mind is just zipping along there." Suddenly, out of the darkened classroom came a cry of admiration. "Jeez, that's sweet," said Casey Recupero. He had the same correct answer, but he was delighted by the other student's elegant methodology. As the class ended, clusters of students noisily compared their approaches to the problem. "I had an interesting way of doing it, but I messed up," one student said. "That's because you did this here," his classmate said, pointing out an error. Rainey's reaction was one of pleasure mixed with trepidation. "Oh, the math teachers in high school are going to wonder what I'm doing—teaching all these unorthodox things."

Having students write, and then periodically update, their "math autobiographies" gives Rainey insights into how to teach them most effectively. Lindsey Stillman said that she has "always hated time tests" but that "one thing I really like are word problems." Another student let it be known that he felt much more comfortable working in groups than on his own.

In addition to using the portfolios to assess the quality of individual students' work, state officials will use them to rate the quality of the mathematics program for entire schools and districts. Evaluators will look for variety, growth in student performance over a period of time, evidence that students have discussed their work with the teacher and with peers, and "evidence of the students' ability to revise."

The use of portfolios in the teaching of writing involves a different set of problems. "Even those who do write well have never been held to any consistent set of criteria," said Rick Mills, the state superintendent. "Most students think that writing consists of doing a first draft and handing it in. Portfolios send the message that writing takes work and that first drafts don't do it."

Joan Simmons, who teaches eighth-grade English at the Craftsbury Academy public school, requires her students to assemble portfolios with a variety of forms of writing, including a poem, a short story, a play, and a personal response to a cultural, media, or sports event or to a book, current issue, math problem, or scientific phenomenon. In order to document their progress, Simmons asks for drafts as well as finished pieces. Every quarter the students, in consultation with fellow students, reevaluate their portfolios and pick out a "best piece." They must explain their decision in writing.

As with mathematics, Vermont's English teachers have worked out a four-level scale for judging portfolios. The criteria are clarity of purpose, organizational coherence, the use of detail to support the main theme, the establishment of voice and tone, and, finally, mechanics such as spelling and punctuation. Simmons said that laying out such specific criteria for students is a big help in teaching. "When most eighth-graders think of writing, they think of the mechanics," she said. "When they realize that other factors are equally important, they look at what they are doing with a very different eye." For example, Patty Waterhouse, a thirteen-year-old, showed her portfolio to a visitor and explained, "I've changed my mind about which is my best piece because my work is different now than at the beginning. It didn't have details, and it didn't have my voice." Simmons said that having specific criteria also makes writing seem more "scientific" and gives students a more sophisticated basis for determining their best work. "Most students are inclined to pick something long, like a research paper, because they have a lot invested in it," she said. "They also tend to value expository writing that reports on what other people say. They have not been taught to value their own ideas."

To enhance the personal value of students' work, Simmons has students read everything they write, except for research papers, to one another. One day recently, for example, Tammy Flint read aloud a moving poem about the confusion brought on by a father's sudden death. When she finished, the class was silent, and many eyes were moist. Then Simmons asked the students to assess the work. Hands shot up. "I'm still trying to recover," said Jody Houston, swiping at his eyes. "After that experience Tammy knew that she had something wonderful," said Simmons afterwards. To Tammy's mother, Peggy Marckres, such new approaches have helped her daughter enormously. "I was thinking about keeping Tammy back because of her spelling and reading," she said. "But this year she got an A in language arts and reading. If she writes a story and she wants to rewrite it, she can rework that piece. She has learned that she can really do it."

Mills said that the goal of the portfolio pilots is to "provoke an explosion of writing and mathematics in this state." The point, he said, is not to rank teachers or schools but to find out how well students write and understand mathematics and writing. "We'll be able to point to schools that have been able to deliver and say they're using these kinds of strategies," he said. "Schools that aren't delivering can learn from the ones that are." Forty percent of the funds are going into the training of teachers, and groups of teachers and others are already at work on the next round: the use of portfolios in social studies, science, and the arts.

Another state that has been moving toward new ways of measuring student achievement is Connecticut. The process started with the drafting of a new Common Core of Learning that spells out what the state expects of students when they graduate from high school. The Core stipulates that students must be competent in reading, writing, speaking, and listening, and be able to solve problems in math. They need to understand the arts, cultures and languages, history, literature, and science and technology. It also specifies that students should understand the world of work, develop a positive self-concept, be motivated and persistent, and develop effective interpersonal relations. With the Core in place, Connecticut has now turned to the task of developing assessment devices designed not only to measure these outcomes but to prod teachers into emphasizing them in the classroom. "Testing often is a catalyst for change," said Joan Boykoff Baron, a researcher with the Connecticut Department of Education. "They tend to send a message more loudly than curriculum."

A glimpse of Connecticut's future can be seen in the classroom of Peter Kavall, a forty-eight-year-old chemistry instructor at Norwalk High School in Norwalk. Kavall's classroom has the usual clutter of balance beams, beakers, and test tubes scattered on black slate tabletops illuminated by rows of fluorescent lights. But he uses these traditional tools in ways that reinforce the view, spelled out in the Core, that his role is not to fill students with scientific facts but to teach them to think and to solve problems in a scientific manner.

Last spring Kavall was teaching his students, most of them juniors, about chemical reactions. They learned, among other things, that when magnesium is placed into a solution of water and hydrochloric acid, a reaction occurs that produces hydrogen gas. He set out to test their understanding of the concept of the rates at which such actions take place. Kavall handed each student a sheet of paper that pointed out that chemists are frequently interested in controlling how fast reactions take place—slowing down the rusting of a car, say, or increasing the speed at which an antacid works in someone's stomach. The assignment told the students to pretend that each of them was a "research chemist who is interested in controlling the rate of the reaction of magnesium and hydrochloric acid." The goal was to "investigate the factors that affect the rate of this reaction."

First, each student was given fifteen minutes to write down the theory of how to determine the rate of a chemical reaction. Then the class was divided into four-person teams that were given twenty minutes to brainstorm about factors—the temperature or concentration of the acid, the surface area of the magnesium, and so forth—that might affect reaction rates, and they selected one of them to measure. Each team was given a bottle of hydrochloric acid and a long test tube with a cork at the top and told to devise an experiment using this equipment to determine the effect of the factor they selected on the reaction rate. "This is different from other science classes I've had," said Michelle Warszawski, a petite girl with long thin hair who was wearing a green sweater and an Indian-bead necklace. "It's not like following instructions in a cookbook. We have to think it up." Before proceeding, each team had to get a go-ahead from Kavall. "That's for safety reasons," he explained. "I make no judgments about whether I think they are on the right track or not." As a matter of fact, one team started off on the erroneous assumption that the reaction could be speeded up by increasing the amount—but not the concentration—of acid in the test tube. "I'll have a talk with them at the end about what they learned," said Kavall.

One team consisted of David Long, Kyra Salancy, Colleen Taylor, and Taurus Wright. During the brainstorming period they decided to study the effect of temperature on the reaction by doing the experiment three times: first at room temperature, then by respectively chilling and heating the test tube containing the acid solution. They disagreed, though, over what they would measure. Taurus wanted to see how much hydrogen would be created in, say, five minutes, while Kyra wanted to see how long it would take at the various temperatures to create a fixed volume, twenty-one milliliters. The team decided to record data on both, but in the end Taurus's method triumphed because they ran out of time before the last reaction was completed.

As the students worked, Kavall moved about the laboratory. Sometimes a student would ask him how to do something, but he would deflect the question by suggesting a way that the students could discover the answer for themselves. He made mental notes about how the teams were working together and which students were contributing what to the process. When the hands-on laboratory work was completed, each student was given another written question to complete on his or her own. The question recalled that each team had brainstormed about "factors that might affect the rate of a chemical reaction" and then tested one of the factors. "Now, devise an experimental plan to test one of the other factors," it said. Kavall then gave each student two grades, one reflecting the performance of the student's team and the other based on the student's written work and contribution to the team effort. "This is something that parents sometimes find difficult to accept—being graded as part of a team," said Kavall. "But that's the way it is in real life. In business, if a group makes a bad decision, everyone pays for it. Kids have to learn to work as a group."

To Kavall, who has been teaching at Norwalk for eighteen years, the whole point of the new assessment techniques is to get away from the cookbook approach and make science itself more realistic. "You'll notice that nothing is said in the exercise about getting an answer," he commented. "The whole focus is on process. Students go to English class and read stories and discuss possible interpretations, but then they expect science to be boom-boom-boom. Actually, real science is trial and revision. There are lots of routes to solutions, some good, some bad. It's important for students to try things and learn from their mistakes. OK, you had an idea, and it didn't work out. Now what do you do?" Students seemed to like the idea of coming up with their own experiment designs. "Science is supposed to help you think," said Taurus, "but if someone tells you exactly what to do, you're not thinking."

Another Connecticut teacher who has become dissatisfied with the "cookbook" approach to science teaching and assessment is Robert Segall, a forty-three-year-old science teacher at Windham High School in Willimantic. Two years ago he signed up to help state officials experiment with new testing methods under a National Science Foundation grant. Segall's students, too, ignore the usual testing rules and work in groups of three and four. They open their books, use their notes, go to the library, or even seek help from experts at nearby colleges. And they take several days to finish their exam. On one occasion he gave them two cans of soda, one diet, the other regular, and asked them to design and carry out an experiment to determine which was which. The only rule was no fair tasting them. Then there was his "nutty" problem. He gave each team of students a collection of nuts—peanuts, almonds, and cashews—and told them to pretend that they were consultants to a

Third World country hired to advise the country on which kind of nut would give residents the greatest amount of energy for their money. The assignment was to devise and carry out an experiment to determine the most suitable nut. The most common approach was to set the nuts on fire, one by one, under a tube of water and measure the temperature change of the water.

To Chad Saba, a junior who plans on being a marine biologist, the science tests are "fun," but more than that. "Instead of responding to a single question on a piece of paper, you test out each procedure," he said. "You make up your own hypothesis, and if it doesn't work out, you try to keep figuring it out. You are more involved. My partner and I have to figure out things for ourselves." Segall has not totally abandoned traditional tests such as multiple-choice exams. But he says that performance tests have given him another tool and have prompted him to look for new problems. "The group work and projects like this add a little more energy and enthusiasm to the class," he said. "The ownership is theirs. They have to be creative and take responsibility for their work."

California has taken a different approach—instead of starting with a list of goals, it revised curriculums and then set out to develop testing mechanisms that assure that the curriculum guidelines are being followed. The new curriculum in English–language arts, for example, includes the integration of listening, speaking, reading, and writing. It insists that students actually read literature rather than wade through textbooks—an unusual approach, as textbooks have come under fire for providing either watered-down passages of literary classics or badly written new "literature" for students.

Assessments are based on individual consultations between students and teachers, audio- or videotape recordings of students' oral reading, students' writing of original endings to stories, and other criteria. At the Torrey Pines High School in La Jolla, California, for example, Winfield Cooper, an English teacher, has her students develop portfolios that include writing in the style of James Joyce as well as writing a piece of original fiction. The students write an introduction to the portfolio that explains what they have learned about themselves as writers. "We were amazed at what we saw," said Cooper. "These weren't just honor students." Authentic testing is being applied to other academic areas. Thus, in California, a student may be instructed to look at three geometric diagrams, decide if anything is wrong with them, and write an explanation in his or her own words. Or a student may take a science test by designing, performing, and reporting the results of an experiment to determine which of two magnets is stronger, using a variety of magnetic and nonmagnetic objects provided in the classroom.

State Superintendent of Public Instruction Bill Honig says that assessments will "drive the curriculum" in the right way. "Teaching to these tests is what we want, because the tests and the curriculum are aligned. These tests are one hundred percent connected with real-world, on-the-job performance. We're finished with tests that measure only isolated low-level 'basic' skills." There is evidence that this is happening. The Center for the Study of Writing at the University of California at Berkeley found that teachers in California claim they assign more writing and a greater variety of tasks than before the writing assessment was introduced. Students report an increase in the number of reports and papers they have written. Schools are changing their programs, and teachers in a wide variety of content areas—from history to science—are assigning more writing within their disciplines.

One thing is clear, though, and that is that performance measures are likely to produce more, not less, controversy. Parents of poor and minority students claim that most standardized tests are culturally biased and discriminate against their children. In an effort to deal with this criticism in its 1988 writing test, the National Assessment of Educational Progress gave students more time to complete their essays, but it found that this *widened* the disparity between whites and blacks. No one knows what will happen when portfolios and other forms of authentic tests replace current national tests. Perhaps the reported gaps between whites and other students will narrow; perhaps they will widen. If the latter occurs, though, it will become much more difficult to blame the tests. Instead, such data will expose just how unjust the entire school system is. Authentic tests will emphasize the deep trouble our factory-model schools are in and how poorly they serve the students who most need them.

There is another way in which authentic tests will be unsettling: by exposing the weaknesses of the country's "most successful" schools. The residents of well-to-do areas like Scarsdale, New Trier, and Beverly Hills tend to be satisfied with the quality of their schools—and why not? Their students routinely rack up the best standardized test scores in their respective states, and graduates successfully compete for places in the best colleges and universities. Given the fact that they are competing against students from far less favored backgrounds, they certainly should. But performance testing changes the reference point. Instead of comparing students with each other, authentic assessment measures *everyone* against absolute standards for reading, calculating, writing, and thinking. The satisfaction that parents in Wilmette enjoy from knowing that their children do far better than those on the south side of Chicago is likely to be quickly dissipated by documentation that some still cannot string together a series of coherent paragraphs. It will further dissipate as international comparisons of student achievement become more sophisticated. It's nice to make the Final Four of the Pygmy basketball championship, but that laurel will not carry you very far in the Barcelona Olympics.

Three years ago executives of the New York Life Insurance Company decided on a bold plan to handle the medical claims that pour in each day. Every evening they put them in bags and load the bags on an Aer Lingus plane bound for Dublin. Upon arrival, they are trucked to the nearby rural market village of Castleisland in a region where there is a large pool of well-educated young people who need jobs. They process the claims and send instructions back by a transatlantic line to the company's data processing center in Clinton, New Jersey. It's interesting to speculate on how that decision might have been made. Some executive at a meeting probably raised the question of how to handle all those claims. Someone else suggested sending them to Dublin. OK. Why not? If you think about it, what this means is that American schools—Hillcrest High School in Queens, for example—are competing for jobs for their graduates with schools in Dublin.

It's a staggering thought.

6.

NEW TECHNOLOGIES

BY THE TIME Emma Camille Schwartz was five years old, she knew high-tech. At the age of two she had mastered the buttons on the VCR at home in Chicago. By three she could manipulate the mouse that operated her mother's Macintosh computer. Soon she was calling her friends and her grandmother on her father's car phone and contacting her father on his pencil-size pager. Emma knows how to operate the family's CD stereo (though she's not allowed to). She records her own songs on a Radio Shack tape recorder and uses a play calculator to experiment with numbers. At play group she can easily converse with the other preschoolers about the video worlds of *The Little Mermaid* and *Bambi*.

In the fall, when Emma starts school, she is in for culture shock. When she walks through the schoolhouse doors, she will leave the plugged-in, wired-up world she has known thus far and enter one that still considers television an innovation. "Schools today reflect their nineteenth-century technological roots more than do most other institutions," admits James Mecklenburger, the technology expert for the National School Boards Association. "Lectures, standardized tests, letter grades, tracking, textbooks, field trips, chalkboards, courses, credits, busing, and the like remain the technologies of choice."

Educators have always been supercautious about new technologies. When printing was invented, professors held out against the development of textbooks, which loomed as a threat to their authority. Socrates even opposed the most basic of technologies—writing. "If men learn this, it will implant forgetfulness in their souls," he says in the dialogue *Phaedrus*. "They will cease to exercise memory because they rely on that which is written, calling on words that can't speak in their own defense or present the truth adequately."

The Congressional Office of Technology Assessment, in a 1989 report, "Technology and the American Economic Transition," concluded that education invests a smaller portion of its resources in technology than any other major industry. Lewis Perelman of the Hudson Institute calculated that the average job in the American economy requires $50,000 of investment in plant and equipment for every employee. For schools the figure is a mere $1,000. If you go along with the notion that the real "worker" in the teaching and learning process is the student, that figure drops to $100. While the rest of society goes through a technological revolution, schools are lingering in the Stone Age—not only in the way they deliver information but in virtually every other activity in which they engage.

Educators are quick to reply that their occupation is a "labor-intensive" industry, one in which 80 percent of the budget goes for salaries. Thus their craft differs in a fundamental way from manufacturing, where greater efficiency can be gained by replacing people with machines. This argument, though, is fatuous. For one thing, education *can* be automated. Perelman points out that as a percentage of their total budgets, corporate education departments are spending at least 300 times as much on computer-based instruction as public schools. "Companies like Unisys and IBM are restructuring employee education programs to replace the great bulk of classroom teaching with instruction delivered by computers and telecommunications—to achieve better results at less cost," he said. "Two decades of research show that computer-based instruction produces at least thirty percent more learning in forty percent less time at thirty percent less cost compared with traditional classroom teaching. A technological revolution now is totally transforming the role of learning and teaching in the modern economy. The 'Yak in the Box' model of instructional technology—the thousand-year-old lecturing classroom professor—will have as much place in the twenty-first century's learning enterprise as the blacksmith shop has in today's transportation system."

Actually, the "education is labor-intensive" argument should be flipped. When it comes to the use of technology, the problem with American schools is not that they differ from manufacturing enterprises but that they are too much *like* them. As with the other structures we have been discussing, the current technology of public education is grounded in the values of the factory model. Chalkboards and textbooks are extensions of teacher talk. They contain the implicit assumption that the purpose of education is to transfer knowledge from the teacher to the student and that students learn at similar rates and in similar ways. The absence from classrooms of that most basic of modern technologies—the telephone—is revealing. The telephone is a means of communicating horizontally with parents, with professional colleagues, and with external data bases (assuming, of course, that you have a computer). The nineteenth-century factory model, though, says that teachers need not communicate with each other. Teacher communication should be vertical—with their superiors. For this you do not need a telephone.

When new technologies do find their way into the classroom, they tend to be co-opted by the system. Television, to the extent that it is used at all, is plugged-in teacher talk. That's why the heated debate about whether to allow commercially sponsored newscasts into the classroom is, in the long run, beside the point. The most compelling argument against allowing these newscasts into the classroom is that, for those eight to ten minutes, they are replacing the teacher. Teaching time that would ordinarily be filled by a school employee has in effect been transferred to a private enterprise, and students are forced to sit through a commercial message. But if you get away from a classroom organized around teacher talk, whether it be human or electronic, the authority issue evaporates. Few people would object to having such broadcasts available as an option for those students—students-as-workers—who found them worthwhile.

According to Jay Becker of Johns Hopkins University, 96 percent of the nation's schools have computers in at least some classrooms. There are now 2.25 million such machines, but this is still only about one for every twenty students. Computers first entered American classrooms in the early 1980s, not because of some farsighted educational vision but for political reasons. The key event, oddly enough, came in December 1983, when *Time* selected the personal computer as its "Man of the Year." That drove home to the American public the fact that computers were changing the world and that, unless their children were familiar with them, they would not be prepared to function in the twenty-first century. The pressure from parents on schools was immediate and striking. As one suburban elementary school principal said at the time, "I no longer had to go to the school board to beg money for computers. They came to me and asked if I shouldn't be spending more!"

Since more teachers and principals at that point did not have the foggiest idea what to do with the new machines, they took the obvious and rational approach: They taught students *about* the machines. They set up courses in "computer literacy" and marched students through computer laboratories once or twice a week to learn how computers worked and to do some simple programming—a skill that most would never need again. One wonders if educators in the mid-sixteenth century responded to the invention of the pencil by offering courses in "pencil literacy."

Then, once the political task of assuring parents that their offspring were becoming proficient on the new machines was accomplished, teachers began to realize that computers might have some genuine educational applications. For one thing, they found, computers are very good at delivering information to students, especially factual information that can be learned in rote fashion. Computers present such information in entertaining ways—certainly more entertaining than some teachers. They are a welcome break from the usual routine of chalk and talk. Computers are infinitely patient, so slower students can take the time they need without feeling embarrassed. Moreover students *like* them! In short, computers were welcomed into American classrooms as a new, improved form of factory-model instruction. Lessons were programmed into them, and students were plunked down at keyboards to extract them. The most ambitious "integrated learning systems" used large mainframe computers that sent information out to "dumb" terminals, meaning that the information all went in one direction, and the concept of "computer-assisted instruction" entered our vocabularies. It is a revealing term. Like everything else in the factory-model school, the computer is obedient and uncomplaining, carrying out the teacher's orders just as he or she is supposed to do for the principal and superintendent.

At its best, electronic teacher talk has the same payoffs in schools as it does in industry, especially when dealing with basic subjects like arithmetic and grammar. At the Zenos Colman Elementary School in Chicago, in a low-income housing complex, students spend forty minutes a day in a computer laboratory working on lessons drawn up by WICAT Education Systems. Harry Donahoo, the principal at the time, credited the computers with dramatic increases in reading-test scores. "Last year, for the first time, the whole school gained the equivalent of a whole year," he said. John Gottsman, then the vice president of WICAT, predicted that eventually students should be able to master twelve years of basic skills by the end of the fifth grade, and can spend the rest of the time on great books or whatever they want. Other manufacturers make similar claims.

There is nothing particularly surprising about the fact that educators at first viewed computers as a tool for doing what they have always done—only better and faster, with more bells and whistles. That's the basic rule that applies to the introduction of any new technology anywhere. "When Edison invented motion pictures, the early filmmakers set their cameras up in front of theater stages," said Bill Atkinson, the guru of Apple Computer, Inc. "Then they went to another theater, set up a screen, and showed the film. It wasn't until D. W. Griffith came along that filmmaking became a medium in its own right." John Naisbitt, in *Megatrends* (Warner, 1982), talks about three stages of technological development. First, he says, new technologies, following the line of least resistance, are applied in ways that do not threaten anyone. The first widespread applications of microprocessors, after all, were in toys. Then technology is used in ways that improve on previous technologies, a stage that can last a long time. And finally, he says, "new directions or uses are discovered that grow out of the technology itself." When it comes to the use of technology, educators are still in phase two. They are still sticking cameras up in front of stages.

Computers are very good at delivering information, and conveying information is an important part of education. But the emergence of smart schools requires far more imaginative use of technology. Previous chapters have described how educators are decentralizing school governance, rethinking the relationship between student and teacher, resetting the academic clock, and finding new ways to assess student learning. Now it is time to see how computers and other new technologies fit into this picture. Technology is pedagogically neutral. Put into the hands of an authoritarian district superintendent, it can make an efficient, top-down system even more efficient and top-down. Alternatively, it can be used by principals and management teams to help manage a school budget under shared decision making. Teachers can employ computers to download what's in their heads, or they can view them as "tools" to empower students to take charge of their own learning. If we are talking about empowering an entire school community—parents, teachers, administrators, even students—then they all need access to the newest technology. Otherwise, we are trying to prepare students for the twenty-first century world using Stone Age tools.

One of the first districts to frame the issue this way was the Central Kitsap School District in Silverdale, Washington, across Puget Sound from Seattle. Central Kitsap's voyage into the world of high-tech dates to 1983, when the school board, inspired by the spate of national reports on the condition of American schools, appointed a Task Force on Excellence to suggest ways of improving its schools. After trying some quick fixes, the board decided that fundamental changes were in order. "We had reached a teaching limit," says Warren E. Olson, administrative assistant to the superintendent. "We were working our staff to the maximum, yet changes in family structures, the nature of the student body, and other forces were making our job more difficult every day. Clearly we needed some whole new concept." The school board also decided that the use of new technologies would be central to any new concept of schools. "We wanted to go from teacher power to collectively stored intelligence," said Olson. "We set out to use computers to bring about a cultural transformation of the school."

To do so, school officials hit on an ingenious approach. First, they appointed a committee of parents, teachers, and others, bought them each a copy of John Naisbitt's *Megatrends* and told them collectively to curl up with the volume and ask themselves, How should a school be designed to meet the needs of students in the year 2020? Then they named a Technology Task Force to make suggestions on how technology could be used to create such schools. All this brainstorming eventually led to "Strategy 2020," a planning effort that involved an additional 150 teachers, administrators, parents, and other volunteers, who laid out the educational principles for the two new schools. The vision laid out in Strategy 2020 took the form of what the committee, succumbing to educators' chronic penchant for jargon, even before the Bush administration made the term famous, called paradigm shifts. Translated into street English, this means new ways of doing and thinking about things. The key shifts included the following:

- Administrative and educational decisions should be made at the lowest level, preferably by the teachers and students directly affected.
- Teachers should be "managers of instruction, not presenters of information." They should function as teams of professionals, sharing ideas and communicating frequently.
- Students should learn both on their own and in flexible groups and should play an active role in their own learning.
- Technology should be employed to "manage learning as well as diagnose, present and evaluate" it.

Central Kitsap's first big investment in its high-tech future was a conventional system of computer-assisted instruction for teaching basic skills. Units were installed in the one elementary school and one junior high school, and teachers such as Deborah Blickhan used it to drill her twenty-eight fifth-graders on skills such as grammar and reading comprehension. Her students spend about three hours a week at the keyboards in the school's computer laboratory, proceeding as fast as they can through the curriculum. At the end of each day Blickhan gets a printout documenting each student's activities, including how long a youngster spent on various items and how many tries it took to get the right answers. She then uses these data to choose the student's next lesson—and passes that choice on to the aide who runs the computer laboratory. The district estimates that it would take an aide a whole workday to compile the data that the computer provides instantly. "No more correcting worksheets," said the teacher. More important, the computer enables her to individualize the instruction she offers. Instead of handing out uniform spelling lists, she has each student develop personalized lists from his or her own reading. "I teach fifth grade, but the reading range of my students goes from second to sixth," she said. "I no longer have to teach to the middle." By using the computer to handle relatively straightforward teaching chores

such as grammar, she is freed to devote more time to other purposes, such as having students read books, offering personalized
math instruction, and counseling students. "I've become more of a
manager of instruction." In short, the computerized instruction did
not replace the teacher but became a vehicle to change her function
as teacher—from disseminator to coach.

The next big step came in September 1989, when Central Kitsap, aided by a $300,000 grant from Tandy Corporation, opened the
first of its two new schools, Cougar Valley Elementary School. With
221 computers for 518 students—nearly one for every two
students—Cougar Valley is one of the most computer-intensive
schools in the nation. Physically it resembles many of the "open
classroom" schools of the 1960s, with large open spaces and low,
movable walls rather than rows of self-contained classrooms. Karen
Dyrness and Pat Bonds team-teach a class of first- and second-
graders, occupying half of a large room organized around a half a
dozen "learning centers"—groupings of students and instructors. In
a recent class six students knelt or sat at computers working on reading while four others played a phonetic-alphabet game on the floor.
Benjamin Struble, a volunteer from the nearby Trident submarine
base, sat on an undersized chair helping individual students with
their reading. In the corner Susan Davey, a special-education
teacher, sat on pillows working with some of her charges. A teaching
aide worked with a small group of students at a nearby table. The
two teachers moved around the room, occasionally stopping to help
a child or to give directions to an instructor. Small-group instruction
carried out in a variety of learning centers is hardly a new idea. Earlier attempts at putting it into practice nationwide floundered,
though, not because it was a bad idea but because the average
teacher could not keep track of what each student needed and was
doing. "Now, with computers, we have a managerial tool to do it,"
said Eugene R. Hertzke, the superintendent of schools.

One change that turned out to be much more important than
anyone had anticipated was the "local area network," or the linking
of the computers on each teacher's desk that allowed them to communicate with each other. Teachers and administrators used its
electronic mail feature to take attendance, assemble lunch orders,
schedule meetings, and exchange information on items such as assignments for particular students—details that rob teachers and

students of learning time in the factory-model school. They found they could do this detail work whenever they had a free moment and not interrupt classes. The so-called E-mail thus saved time and freed teachers from lots of busywork. Even more important, it broke down the isolation that has been such a fixture of traditional schools. "Even if they go through a whole day without seeing each other," said Hertzke, "teachers can work together. Education has become a collective enterprise." The power of this device became apparent the morning of October 18, 1989, the day after the California earthquake, when Gerry Erickson, the school librarian, learned that Yolanda Brennan, one of her parent volunteers working in the school that day, had survived several earthquakes in Guatemala. At 10:02 A.M. she typed a message into the electronic mail system that links the computers on the desks of each of the school's eighteen classroom teachers. By 10:08 A.M. the first request had come back for Brennan to visit a classroom to give students a firsthand account of earthquakes.

Such experiences led teachers and administrators to conclude that, if a choice has to be made, it is more important to put computers in the hands of staff members than in the hands of students. Backed by a $3.5 million bond issue, the district is now putting large numbers of computers into all sixteen schools. "Anyone who has to communicate—from principals to custodians and food service managers—gets a computer and printer," said Hertzke.

The Cougar Valley school library has an electronic encyclopedia that students can use to print out articles. Students used the computers to help organize a production of *The Nutcracker,* and they write compositions on the computer. "They're even putting out a newspaper," said Steve Anderson, the principal. "I've never seen that before." Students like the new approach. "Sometimes you get mad at the computer because it's never wrong," said Chris Breese, a fourth-grader. "But it can also be more fun. A piece of paper doesn't ask you questions."

Going electronic has by no means been problem-free, and Cougar Valley learned some lessons during the first year. Teachers discovered that students don't like to use headsets while working at the computer and that they prefer to work with partners rather than alone. Attempts to create a parallel electronic mail system for students had to be scrapped when someone gained access to another student's electronic files and destroyed some work. Becky Feller, a sixth-grader, complained that her parents "don't think I get enough homework." One reason is that parents don't see the telltale paper trail that they remember from their own school days. They don't realize that much of what once went home as homework is now being done—more quickly and efficiently—in school on computers. "We didn't realize how much communicating we were doing by sending home worksheets," said Anderson. Teachers at Cougar Valley have installed a voice-mail system so that parents can call after working hours and get oral reports on their children's progress. Ultimately, Anderson would like to see the entire curriculum tied into the computer, along with records of student performance. Among other things, this would eliminate much of the need for testing, since a teacher, parent, or state education official could determine exactly where each student stands at a given point. "The problem is that all the software programs are freestanding," said Anderson, and the district's software doesn't dovetail with the schools' own curriculums. "We'd have to bring in someone to link all the lessons to our own learning objectives."

Not everyone approves of Central Kitsap's plunge into the world of high-tech. Some children were pulled out of Cougar Valley by parents who were suspicious of all the talk about "thinking skills" and thought that computers were just the latest gimmick. "We had some parents who were successful in their professional life, who learned with paper and pencil," said Anderson. "They felt that what was good enough for them was good enough for their children. People are real comfortable with spelling books and lists of words. We tried to tell them that what was good enough for them wouldn't serve their children well twenty years from now. But for everyone who pulled their child out, we had others from outside our attendance area wanting to get their child in."

Central Kitsap's second high-tech school, Silver Ridge Elementary School, opened in September 1990. Taking note of the problems that Cougar Valley had encountered, planners were careful to bring parents into the planning process from the very beginning. Parents worked together for a year before the school started. One issue for them was how to handle a shorter day caused by the need to schedule planning time for teachers. The parents organized a variety of activities, such as scouting, dance, and athletics. While teachers are planning, students are taking foreign language, drama, or magic classes.

Physically, Silver Ridge has many of the same features as Cougar Valley, with twenty-five open classrooms built around a central library and media center. There are also some significant differences. Planners decided not to have a central computer lab. Instead the classrooms are grouped into four "pods," or clusters, each of which has a bank of thirty computers that rest on movable tables and can be moved in and out of classrooms as needed. "We want to emphasize that computers are an integral part of every aspect of teaching and learning," said B. J. Wise, the principal. "We did not want to treat them like water fountains," said Hertzke. In order to make peer tutoring possible, the pods, named Air, Earth, Fire, and Water, contain students from various classes from kindergarten to sixth grade. Each class has a "teaching wall" that looks like an ordinary modern blackboard. Push it to the side and there is a twenty-seven-inch television, a VCR, and a video camera with a mirror and normal lenses. Each classroom contains a light table. This is a small video camera, mounted on a movable table, that can be used either to project pictures on the wall—a map, for example—or to make videotapes.

Teachers in Silverdale are already finding that technology forces them to rethink the kind of assignments they need to give students. Ron Gillespie, the librarian at Central Kitsap High School, recalls a visit from an eleventh-grade history student seeking demographic and other information on half a dozen different countries. The teacher had assigned the task as a research project and gave the student three days to complete it. Instead of sending the student to the usual reference books to copy the information, though, Gillespie pointed him to an electronic data base. Soon he was on his way back to the class with a neat printout—the three-day assignment completed in ten minutes. Moments later the teacher appeared, demanding to know why the librarian had messed up his lesson planning. "At first he was pretty angry," Gillespie recalled. "Then we started talking about the purpose of the assignment, and it became clear that the traditional concept of research—gathering information—just isn't viable anymore. Information is cheap. It is too easy to get. So we developed some new questions that caused students to make use of the information they obtained. Is there a relationship between a large military budget and the infant mortality rate? What is the relationship between illiteracy and the gross national product in various countries?"

Scottsdale, Arizona, is another district that has approached the new technologies in a comprehensive way. As Mark Share, director of educational technology for the Scottsdale Public Schools, puts it, "We view computers as tools in the hands of students, teachers, and administrators." Aided by $6 million from a bond issue, the twenty-three Scottsdale schools now have 2,600 computers, mostly Apples and Macintoshes, for 20,000 students, one of the richest ratios in the country. At appropriate ages students are taught three basic skills—word processing, using spreadsheets, and building and manipulating data bases. Three-year-olds in the preschool program draw and learn colors by moving their fingers across computer screens; high school students learn how to build computer-controlled robots. Math teachers use them to teach problem solving, and science teachers simulate frog dissections. Computer games incorporate geography lessons. Students can even take portable computers home. It is commonplace to assert that tomorrow's thinking society will put a premium not only on what students know but on how well they can track down and organize large amounts of new information. On this score computers are a natural. "Anyone can take a problem and find an answer," said Share. "The hard thing is to figure out the right question. You might be looking at a lot of data on the American presidents and then ask yourself: Why did so many come from Virginia? Then you can start to find out why."

At Yavapai Elementary School in Scottsdale, students use the Apple Global Education Network to exchange information with students on Martha's Vineyard on their respective environments. They are also collecting water samples for a student in Chicago studying acid rain. "For the first time we can really take the information needs of students seriously," said Judy Voran, head librarian at Chaparral High School. Steve Richardson and his fellow sixth-graders became curious about the political changes in East Germany. So they went to a computer and tapped into a satellite network linking schools in North America, Europe, and the Middle East. Back came a message from students at Luitpold High School in Munich describing the excitement of West Germany's young people. "Imagine, the younger generation in East and West have never had a chance so far to see their neighbors and to get to know their way of life," the German students' message said. To Steve and his friends, checking out the views of students 5,800 miles away comes as naturally as a trip to the school library did to previous generations of students. "You find out what is happening right now," he said. "And besides, we like to hear what kids have to say."

Computers are the most important new technology for writing instruction since the invention of the pencil—maybe even more so. Learning to write is essentially self-editing. The craft requires writing and rewriting. For little children, the biggest obstacle to learning to write is the physical act of moving the pencil across the paper, but computers make this unnecessary. For older students word processing allows endless revisions. Some teachers have students spend the entire semester writing and rewriting one or two papers. At Supai Middle School in Scottsdale all students go through a two-week word-processor course as part of their language arts class. Language arts teachers report that the experience alters their writing style, even when they "go back" to paper and pencil. One reason, according to Jim Reith, the district language arts coordinator, is that when they work on the word processors, students learn that the placement of a word in a sentence makes a difference. They discover this by using the cut-and-paste functions to move words around and see how the meaning or emphasis of a sentence changes. On the word processor this is easy.

Not long ago sixth-graders at Kiva Elementary School in Scottsdale who had been studying Egypt showed the power of the computer by writing, designing, and publishing a four-page newsletter that was a clever roundup of the latest news of that period. The students called it *"King Tut's Chronicle* (Vol. 1, No. 1, 2500 B.C.)" and edited it in the style of the *National Enquirer*. One headline screamed CLEO IN TROUBLE ONCE AGAIN? over an article speculating about why Cleopatra "might not be able to make her annual trip down the Nile." Another dealt with whether the Hyksos had developed new weapons. "Are they thinking of attacking once again? NOTHING FINAL YET! . . . Inquiring Egyptians want to know." The newsletter contained news articles on King Tut's murder and a Nile River boat race, horoscopes, puzzles, and a "Dear

Cleopatra" column of advice to readers. The movie listings ("Currently playing at your local pyramid") included *The After Life* and *The Mummy's Curse*, while upcoming concerts included "Walk Like an Egyptian" by Hatshepsut. The stock market report showed that pyramid blocks were up nine dinars while mummified cloth was down seventy-one dinars. A classified employment advertisement read: "Wanted: Navigator. Help Cleopatra sail across the Nile. Must have a good sense of humor. Call 1-800-PYRAMID." The computer facilitated a project that required students to pull together an enormous amount of information and reformulate it using what Share calls "the higher order thinking skills: application, synthesis, creativity."

Computers are powerful tools for working the curriculums of schools away from rote learning and toward the problem-solving skills that students will need in the workplace of the future. They can serve as brain amplifiers. Researchers at the Apple multimedia research laboratory in an unmarked building in San Francisco have developed an exercise that starts with a videotape of children making a small merry-go-round go faster or slower by leaning in or out. The student can use the computer to plot the speeds on a graph. The potential for teaching complex subjects like calculus is obvious. Students can sit at a blank screen and put together combinations of images or play with "what if" questions that would have been impossible to create. Indeed, education comes from the Latin word *educere,* "to lead out." What makes the merry-go-round so impressive is that it constitutes a concrete representation of abstractions. Intelligence is, in many ways, the ability to make connections and to play with "what if's."

Computers promote the value of respect for diversity. Whereas teacher talk appeals to the minority of students who learn best by hearing abstract ideas, computers offer a dazzling array of visual images. For a generation that has grown up on television and music videos, the significance of this is considerable. Moreover, since computers are inherently social devices—a document on a computer screen is public property—they enhance cooperative learning. Students work together naturally on computers. The emergence of videodisks will make computers an even more powerful tool.

In November 1990 Texas became the first state to approve a

videodisk-based curriculum program as an approved "textbook." The program, *Windows on Science,* developed by Optical Data Corporation of Warren, New Jersey, will now compete with two publishers of standard textbooks for a piece of Texas's $40 million elementary-school science book market. In San Fernando, California, a third-grade teacher, Alfreda Soriano, uses the program. As she teaches her eight-year-olds about the formation of plants, she visually shows her students the beautiful slow-motion opening of a petal. In fact she can quickly retrieve any moving picture of any topic she is trying to describe—in seconds. Videodisks combine the power of computers with the graphic and auditory capabilities of video, giving teachers and students the ability to quickly summon materials ranging from statistics and documents to news footage of a presidential speech. A teacher may freeze images on a television screen to further explain them or stimulate pupil reaction. In Scottsdale, Donna Schell, the media center specialist at Yavapai Elementary School, uses a laser disk to explore how slaves viewed the Civil War by moving back and forth between a journal kept by a slave at the time and photographs. The Scottsdale school system is also developing a laser-disk program for middle school humanities instruction that will make it possible for teachers to integrate themes of literature, art, and music. "Teachers have always been able to teach about art with slides," said Share, "but if a student asked a question that referred to a slide that was in another tray, it was almost impossible for the teacher to find it fast enough to retain the teachable moment. The ability to call up any item—a slide, a document, a few seconds from a videotape—at the push of a few buttons encourages students and teachers to deviate from the lesson and respond to ideas, questions, and situations that come about. This will greatly enhance the teacher's role as a facilitator of learning."

There is no way—nor, for the purpose of this discussion, any reason to try—to forecast all the snazzy new things that technology will generate. Current trends are toward the use of computers not as a means of delivering instruction but as a means of controlling and managing the interaction of all sorts of other technologies: written documents, films, videos, audiotapes, CD-ROMs, information from outside data bases, and the like. The sky's the limit, both literally and figuratively. "Technology is a license to think creatively," said Eugene Hertzke, the superintendent at Silverdale. But, as we have seen, the real power of computers lies in their own power not only to transform what happens in the classroom but in their capacity to transform virtually all aspects of the factory-model school.

Silverdale, for example, has used computers to decentralize its system. School administrators put purchase orders into the computer, and the central purchasing office then fulfills the order and charges that school's account. No more approval slips flowing back and forth. Whereas most school districts have a central depository of information on items such as test scores, Silverdale stores such data in each school. If individual schools are going to make budgetary and other decisions on their own, they need information that under the old system either does not exist or that, under the factory model, is hoarded by the central office. Dade County school officials recognized this, which is why the system developed a computer program that gives principals and cadres up-to-the-minute information on matters such as how much money they have left in their budget for various purposes. Similarly if the regulatory authority of middle managers is to be reduced, then central administrators charged with overseeing the functioning of the system as a whole must be given the electronic tools to monitor student progress, school progress, and so forth.

Central Kitsap schools have used computers to foster the "paradigm" of teacher-as-manager and student-as-worker responsible for his or her own learning. Teachers use E-mail to communicate with colleagues, to minimize the time required for chores such as grading and attendance taking, and to keep track of a complex range of learning exercises that would be impossible if they perceived themselves in the old role of dispensers of knowledge. Computers are tools—assistant coaches—that allow teachers such as Deborah Blickhan to delegate rote exercises or delivery of information to students. In many cases, these programs have "tutorial" components that analyze students' mistakes, point them in new directions, and monitor their progress.

For their part, students use computers as tools to take charge of their own learning—to become "workers." As the students at Yavapai who networked with their German counterparts demonstrated, computers have the capacity to pose problems and suggest lines of inquiry for which neither the student nor the teacher has the answer. Computers make possible the *creation* of knowledge on the part of the student, not simply the dissemination of knowledge by teachers. Bill Atkinson of Apple sees his company as a "tool maker" and views computers as essentially a way to "facilitate creativity and empower people." Technology helps the teacher to create an environment in which kids can build connections, not simply parrot their teachers, and to create knowledge that is new even to the teacher. All thirty pairs of eyes are no longer on the teacher. When the teacher accepts that, things happen. "The teacher as source of all information has died," said Vicki Durbin of Yavapai. "They're becoming project managers." Students today are moving into a world for which there is no right answer to most problems. In industry, foreman and worker confront problems to which neither knows the answer. The teacher can say to the student, "I want to empower you as a learner, and here is this enormously powerful tool that allows you to do things that I could never conceive of."

Computers also permit more flexible use of time. If a student needs more time to master a particular skill, the teacher can often use a computer to provide that extra time. An example of this is Central Kitsap's Extended Education Program, an after-school program in which students can enroll for extra help, especially in English. The teachers use computers to teach grammar and word processing for practice in writing. The teachers then devote their time to working with groups of half a dozen students on editing. Students at Silver Ridge will be grouped by age rather than by grade, and teachers will stay with the same group of students for more than one year. The school will make liberal use of team teaching and students' tutoring one another. Computers, in short, are tools for restructuring virtually every aspect of American education.

James Mecklenburger of the National School Board Association points out that, in the final analysis, we must come to think of schools and classrooms themselves as a technology that is in the process of being restructured. "Like mass schooling, classrooms are a technological invention designed to accomplish an educational task," he declares. They are devices for assembling students and putting them at the feet of teachers and in contact with textbooks and curriculums. "In the era of electronic learning, school is where the learner is," he says. Networks of learners can be organized across town or around the world. "The kinds of experiences that educators today call 'distance learning' and 'on-line telecommunications' may be the forerunners of such arrangements, though they are small-scale and underfunded today."

Actually, much of the learning revolution is already taking place outside of schools. Bill Bowman, vice president of Jostens Learning Corporation, whose children have grown up surrounded by computers, tells the story of his four-year-old daughter coming into his home office and walking over to an old typewriter that he keeps around to type envelopes. After several minutes of frustration at being unable to get the machine to do anything, she turned to him in frustration and said, "How do you boot this thing?" After he showed her how it worked, she became equally frustrated at the fact that the backspace key would not erase her mistakes. Lewis Perelman of the Hudson Institute notes that over the last decade some 60 million people learned how to use personal computers, adding, "We know that almost none of this economically and socially crucial learning took place in schools. It was 'delivered' by vendors, manuals, tutorial software, videos, telephone hot lines, user groups, books, magazines, electronic bulletin boards, built-in 'help' systems, much trial-and-error, and a great deal of schmoozing. And many parents and teachers will testify that kids often led adults in climbing up the PC learning curve. Today students and educators alike can create, receive, collect, and share data, text, images, and sounds on a myriad of topics in ways more stimulating, richer, and more timely than ever before—if they have access to the appropriate technology and the ability to use it. And many do, if not in school, then outside. Calculators, camcorders, audio books, data bases, simulations, drill-and-practice exercises, VCRs, the Discovery channel, music synthesizers, and the wide array of computing devices are all among the educational tools broadly distributed in our nation. Add to these technologies broadcast television and data distribution via cable, satellite, and phone lines. And more and better technologies are on the way."

It has taken us more than two thousand years, but we have

finally begun to address Socrates' concerns. He spurned writing because it was static, unresponsive, and lent itself to one-way communication. The same accusations can be made against the factory-model school. New technologies, though, are transforming not only the relation between students and teachers but the basic structures of the learning enterprise.

So maybe, just maybe, Socrates would have embraced computers for the very same reasons that he opposed writing. As Chris Breese, the Cougar Valley fourth-grader, put it, "A piece of paper doesn't ask you questions."

7.

THE LAST
MONOPOLY

WHEN GEORGE and Prilla Brackett moved to Cambridge, Massachusetts, they enrolled their eldest son, Ethan, in the fourth grade at the Tobin Elementary School. It was a logical choice. The school was located only a block and a half from the Bracketts' three-story brown frame house on Lakeview Avenue in West Cambridge. It had a strong open-classroom program, which seemed to appeal to Ethan. Like the neighborhood itself, Tobin was racially and culturally mixed.

Ethan, a tall, thin boy who did gymnastics and played the piano in his spare time, did well at Tobin. But two years later, when Ethan was in the sixth grade, the school announced that its highly popular seventh-grade science teacher was leaving. Moreover, the upper two grades at Tobin, which runs kindergarten through eighth, were much more structured than the more open environment in which he had so far done so well. "It didn't look good for Ethan," recalled George Brackett, a heavily mustached man who operates a small computer software company out of their home. "So we began looking at other programs."

The Bracketts sat in on classes at the Longfellow School, about a mile and a half from their house, but decided that the Intensive Studies Program there that had intrigued them was "much more regimented" than what they had in mind for Ethan. Then they visited the King School in Cambridgeport, which offers several different programs, including a minischool—King Open—in which seventh-graders study algebra. "That wasn't available anywhere else," said Brackett. That fall Ethan transferred to King Open. Later, when it came time for their younger son, Matthew, to begin school, he, too, started at Tobin, and they subsequently decided to keep him there.

The Bracketts were able to exercise these options with their different children because Cambridge is one of a growing number of communities across the country that has challenged the monopoly that public schools have traditionally exercised in determining where students will go to school. In the past the Bracketts would probably have enrolled all of their children in the same school, and they would have had no options to make changes. In all likelihood the school would have been their local "neighborhood" school, and they would have given little, if any, thought to whether that particular school was educationally appropriate for each child. Even if they had, they could not have done much about it since their children would have been mandatorily assigned to the same school anyway.

Cambridge, though, has now abandoned the concept of the neighborhood school in favor of an enrollment policy known as controlled choice that seeks to accommodate the individual educational needs of different children by giving them access to different schools within the same public school system. Parents can select the schools they think are best for their kids. Schools, in turn, can no longer presume a captive group of customers and must compete for the parents' business.

Choice is a radical departure from the norm in American public education. Americans value choice and competition in most things. They want to be able to choose between McDonald's and Burger King, beaches and lakes, rare and well done, Tom Brokaw and Peter Jennings. Competition is viewed as essential to a vibrant economy. How else do you keep those who are providing goods and services on their toes and in touch with their customers' changing needs? When it comes to public schools, though, Americans have been content to tolerate a monopoly. Students have traditionally been assigned to school on the basis of their street address. Elementary schools feed into specific junior high schools, which feed into a specific high school. With the exception of an occasional magnet school—one organized around a particular theme, such as science or the arts, and available to students throughout the district—public education offers a one-meal menu. It is the Last Great Monopoly.

Such an arrangement, of course, fits nicely with the factory model of schooling, in which the primary concerns are standardization, the efficiency of the system, and the convenience of the professional educators who run it. The factory model of education assumes that each and every school is adequate for each and every student. Thus assignments can be safely and quickly made at the stroke of a pen without reference to the differing needs or learning styles of students. Another plus is that principals and teachers can assume a captive audience and go about their business knowing that even if they fail to please parents and meet students' needs, they will not suffer any negative consequences.

American public schools are now being stripped of their monopoly. Parents are becoming increasingly sophisticated about the differing needs of their children, and as the failures of the factory-model school become more and more apparent, they are becoming increasingly reluctant to surrender the freedom of choice that they presume in virtually every other sphere of their lives. On the other side of the fence, teachers, buoyed by the emerging sense of their own professionalism, are becoming excited about the possibility of introducing diversity to the school system and creating smaller educational units geared to specific programs and learning styles. Perhaps most important, an unlikely combination of outside political forces has arisen to push for change, an odd group of bedfellows united only by a conviction that traditional pupil-assignment policies now constitute a disaster.

Giving parents a voice in deciding which schools their children will attend at public expense is hardly a new idea. As early as 1955 the economist Milton Friedman was pushing the notion that parents should be given chits, or vouchers, that they could cash in as tuition at any school, public, private, or parochial. The basic argument was that if competition were introduced, the system would have to improve. Giving people the freedom to vote with their feet, the argument went, would force schools to shape up or shut down. Although the Office of Economic Opportunity ran a $7 million experiment with vouchers in the early 1970s, liberals were, for the most part, suspicious of the idea, viewing it as a cover for the channeling of public funds into private and, even worse, parochial schools.

In recent years the flag of parental choice has been taken up by a number of prominent corporate leaders interested in the improvement of public schools. The most prominent has been David Kearns, the former chairman of Xerox Corporation, who characterized public education as "a failed monopoly, bureaucratic, rigid and in unsteady control of dissatisfied captive markets." Kearns said, "Competition makes businesses perform. Choice can do the same for public schools." Now political liberals have taken up the cause as a matter of social justice. Parental choice, they argue, is already a fact of life for middle- and upper-class families, who exercise choice by purchasing houses or renting apartments in neighborhoods served by good schools. Justice says that the poor and lower middle class should have the same privileges. As Sy Fliegel, one of the architects of parental choice in Community District 4 in New York City, put it, "What's good enough for the rich is good enough for the poor."

Until recently any joining hands of liberals and conservatives in the cause of school choice was impossible because the Reagan administration, in pushing vouchers and tuition tax credits, made it clear that it wanted such devices to apply to nonpublic as well as public schools. Reagan administration officials expressed open admiration for the plan pushed through by then Prime Minister Margaret Thatcher in Britain under which parents who are dissatisfied with the school their children are attending can "opt out" of it and start up their own schools at public expense. The irony was that, even as the administration was ramming up against brick walls in seeking aid to the nonpublic sector, prominent liberal Democrats such as former governor Rudy Perpich of Minnesota and Governor Bill Clinton of Arkansas had come around philosophically to the wisdom of school choice. They simply wanted to limit it to choice among *public* schools.

On the eve of President Bush's inauguration in January 1989, Republican leaders saw the handwriting on the wall. They convened a White House conference on the topic of school choice, invited participants from across the political spectrum, and made a point of conspicuously avoiding any mention of the V-word—*vouchers*. School choice was, in effect, politically liberated. President Bush has described public-school choice as "a national imperative" and made it the centerpiece of his push to become the "education president." The administration created a new Center for Choice in Education with a toll-free number (1-800-442-PICK) for anyone wanting to learn more about it. Choice has also been formally endorsed by the National Governors' Association, which called it a necessity if the public is to come to terms with "the nation's diversity and its demands for compulsory education." According to the Center for Choice, at least thirteen states now have laws offering some form of choice—Arkansas, Colorado, Idaho, Iowa, Kentucky, Massachusetts, Minnesota, Nebraska, Ohio, Utah, Vermont, Washington, and Wisconsin. Researchers estimate that 5 percent of public school children now live in areas where they have options that extend beyond the neighborhood school, double the percentage only two years ago.

School-choice plans take three basic forms. The oldest and most popular is *intradistrict* choice, in which local districts stop assigning students to schools automatically on the basis of their home address and in effect open up all schools to all students. Researchers estimate that as many as two thousand districts, from Montclair, New Jersey, to Irvine, California, have such plans. Most districts began doing this on their own, but now that the idea has spread, some states are taking steps to encourage it. Massachusetts has an aggressive program to promote intradistrict choice, and Colorado recently became the first state to mandate that all districts allow students to transfer freely within their borders.

Then came plans under which students have the opportunity not only to move around their home district but to attend school in other districts. This approach, known as *open enrollment,* was pioneered by Minnesota in 1988. Since then Arkansas, Idaho, Iowa, Nebraska, Ohio, and Washington have enacted programs that permit interdistrict transfers. The plans vary widely in details, such as who, if anyone, picks up the transportation tab for students who want to study out of their home district and how much of their per-pupil state aid they can take with them to the new district. Some, such as Minnesota's open-enrollment plan, also permit high school students to study at colleges and universities. Tennessee has permitted interdistrict choice since 1925, and the number of students taking advantage of the option jumped to 20,000 in 1991, up by 4,000 over the previous year. The third, and latest, development has been a series of efforts to extend choice beyond the limits of the public schools. Wisconsin adopted a voucher-type plan that, starting in the fall of 1990, allows up to 1,000 Milwaukee public school students to enroll in private nonsectarian schools at state expense. By early 1991, the Bush administration was supporting this type of broader choice plan.

Although the basic motivation for the recent spate of school-choice plans has been to get kids into the schools that will best serve their needs, many of the earliest and most successful ones were initially established for quite a different social purpose: desegregation. That was the case in Cambridge, Massachusetts.

Though known primarily as the home of Harvard and the Massachusetts Institute of Technology, Cambridge, a 6.2-square-mile city on the shores of the Charles River, is actually a diverse, bustling urban area, one of the ten most densely populated cities in the country. The population of 95,000 persons ranges from prosperous occupants of stately homes along Brattle Street, many from families that have lived there since colonial days, to immigrants from Haiti or Cambodia freshly arrived in the Cambridgeport area. Cambridge citizens come from sixty-four different countries and have forty-six mother tongues. Eighty-five percent of their children are enrolled in the public school system, which consists of thirteen elementary schools running up to the eighth grade and a single comprehensive high school. Half of the 7,500 students in the system are white. The other half breaks down into 30 percent black, 13 percent Hispanic, and 7 percent Asian. Half of the Cambridge students come from families poor enough to qualify for free and reduced-price lunches. Eleven percent are in bilingual programs, from Portuguese and Haitian to Korean and Vietnamese.

Cambridge had always run its schools in traditional fashion. The wealthy bought homes in the Peabody or Agassiz school districts, and if they were politically savvy and aggressive and knew the right kind of people, they could get their children into one of the system's alternative programs for the "academically talented." Residents who were poor, or who lived in one of Cambridge's working-class neighborhoods, had their own neighborhood schools, unless the children qualified as "culturally deprived" and went to Follow Through, a federally funded program, designed with Head Start "graduates" in mind, that emphasizes parental involvement and having students work at their own pace. There was also a thriving nonpublic sector that, during the 1950s and 1960s, attracted more than half of the city's school-age children. Hundreds of Italian and Irish families opted for Roman Catholic parochial schools, while many wealthy residents patronized exclusive private schools such as Belmont Hill or Shady Hill. The city's academicians thought so little of the public schools that Harvard University did not even mention them in the informational literature it gave to married graduate-school students!

In the 1970s Cambridge residents looked with horror across the Charles River at racial strife in Boston, which was struggling to desegregate its schools under a court-ordered busing system. Whites were fleeing the system. Buses carrying blacks into white ethnic neighborhoods were stoned. "It was a nightmare," recalls Mary Lou McGrath, a school administrator who is now superintendent of the Cambridge school system. "We kept asking ourselves, Are we next?"

Cambridge already had its own problems. Despite the closing of several Catholic schools in the late 1960s, the number of white students in the system was declining. The city had several schools that were on the edge of being ruled segregated, so political and educational leaders decided on a preemptive strike. Rather than run the risk of having a judge step in and order forced busing—with all the disruption, hassle, and embarrassment that would have entailed—they decided to try to lure students into integrated settings of their own free choice.

The first stab at this came in 1979, when the School Committee, working with parents and teachers, adopted an open-enrollment option that gave all Cambridge students the option to transfer to schools outside their attendance zones so long as the change did not increase segregation. Not many students made the move, so the following year attendance zones were redrawn to bring about more racial integration. Students already assigned to a neighborhood school were grandfathered into it, but new students were assigned under the new rules. This was still not enough. So finally, in March 1981, neighborhood school zones were completely abolished. Cambridge decided to bring about racial balance by giving *every* student a crack at attending *every* school. The hope was that this would not only head off a court order but bring middle-class whites back into the public schools. For the first time Cambridge schools would be competing not only with the private and parochial sector but with each other!

Cambridge calls its system "controlled choice" because, while parents indicate their preferences, the school district makes the final decision. Here's how the system works: Parents of students in kindergarten through eighth grade gather information about the thirteen schools and then list their first, second, and third choices in order of preference. Actually there are more than thirteen choices, since some of the schools have as many as four separate programs within them that qualify as distinct options. Families can, of course, choose the neighborhood school to which the children would have been automatically assigned before controlled choice went into effect. The preferences are then collected by Peter F. Colleary, the Student Assignment Director, and every month, starting in January, he assigns students to schools. Placements are made with racial balance in mind, with a school being considered desegregated if its racial balance falls within five percentage points, plus or minus, of the racial balance of the district as a whole. In addition to parental preferences, other priorities include availability of space, keeping siblings in the same school, and geographical proximity. In the event that there are still too many applicants for a particular school or program, a lottery is held. Students who are not accommodated with their first choice are automatically put on a waiting list for the next suitable vacancy. If they do not get any of their choices—something that happens to about 15 percent of students— they are put on waiting lists for all three preferences.

To help parents make their selections, each school hires a part-time "parent liaison" to meet with prospective families, give tours of the school, and answer questions. The district also operates a Parent Information Center that disseminates information on all thirteen schools as well as the ins and outs of the overall system and coordinates the work of each school's parent liaisons. No parent can register for elementary school unless they visit the official information center. A major task for Margaret Gallagher, who runs the Parent Information Center, is to educate parents who might not otherwise be aware of their rights, especially poor families and recent immigrants. Every November the district conducts three Kindergarten Information Sessions, where parents can hear presentations on the programs and the philosophy of each school. Gallagher canvasses local day-care centers and writes at least two hundred personal letters to parents of Head Start children. The center holds dozens of community meetings and advertises them on the radio and in foreign-language newspapers. Staff members follow up by calling parents who are known to have school-age children but fail to register. Flyers are distributed in laundromats and supermarkets in several languages, and a twenty-four-hour telephone recording carries information on how to enroll. "Giving parents the information they need to make intelligent choices is the name of the game," says Gallagher. "You never think you have done enough."

Clearly, controlled choice makes no sense unless students and parents have legitimate options from which to make their selections. If every school is the same, then the right to choose is a hollow privilege. On this score Cambridge has done well. For demographic reasons, two elementary schools have closed over the last decade, reducing the number of options to thirteen, but the remaining schools have staked out their own particular character. Agassiz and Peabody, which in the old days were the elite schools populated by the Harvard Square crowd (Agassiz was dubbed the "Yuppie Puppy Palace"), continue to emphasize traditional basic academics, but they are no longer isolated enclaves of the white upper middle class. Robert F. Kennedy makes heavy use of the arts in teaching all subjects, while Morse makes creative use of drama. Haggerty, the smallest school in the system, offers conversational Spanish for all students and staff. Teachers at Fitzgerald have won fame for an emphasis on creative writing that has since spread to other schools, while Fletcher, whose test scores have traditionally been subterranean, has initiated a Coordinate Learning Project that puts a teaching aide in every classroom to focus on language skills, as well as a one-on-one reading program and an Early Morning Math and Computer Program that opens its doors at 6:45 A.M.

As a way of broadening their appeal, many of Cambridge's schools developed "schools within schools." Maynard adopted some ingenious approaches to bilingual education, including a so-called Amigos Program that puts Spanish-speaking and English-speaking students together in a two-way bilingual program. Harrington operates both a traditional curriculum and a Follow Through program. The Graham and Parks Alternative School specializes in open classrooms but also runs a Haitian bilingual program. Martin Luther King, Jr., combines a regular program emphasizing basic skills with an Open School program that promotes individualized learning, multicultural instruction, and parental involvement in running the school. Tobin has three different options: an open-classroom track, offering individualized education and requiring heavy involvement by parents; a Computer School of the Future program, emphasizing basic skills through technology; and a Follow Through program. Cambridge has also extended the principle of diversity to its sole high school, Cambridge Rindge and Latin School. The regular school is divided into seven smaller houses, each with separate administrations, staffs, and special programs and its own academic style. Options include vocational education, a Fundamental School that focuses on discipline and traditional academics, a Pilot School built around a close-knit educational and social community of two hundred students, or the Enterprise Cooperative, a career-oriented program for students who have dropped out or who are unsuccessful in school. Its students operate food-service or woodworking shops, with profits divided among them at the end of the year.

Given Cambridge's abundance of world-class universities, research institutes, and schools of education, it is no surprise that a large number of the community's parents take their children's education very seriously and approach it in a sophisticated way. For such parents, controlled choice has obvious appeal. Take, for instance, Art and Betty Bardige, who live in a large, charcoal-blue, three-story house on Raymond Street, just off Porter Square on Avon Hill, about four blocks from Radcliffe College. The house, built in 1893 by a ship's captain from Martha's Vineyard, is situated near the "top of the hill"—an area mostly populated by professors at Harvard, journalists, and professionals. It has a large front porch that opens into a spacious hardwood entrance hall. The Bardiges use the basement and the first two floors and rent out the top floor to a mother and two children. The Bardiges have three children: Kori, Brenan, and Arran.

Art, born in Chicago, has a master's degree in education from the University of Chicago and taught high school physics in Florida before moving into the field of educational films. He now owns a computer software development firm. Betty, born in Boston, went to high school in Florida, where she and Art met, and has a doctorate in developmental psychology from the Harvard Graduate School of Education. She has spent most of her subsequent career working in curriculum development. When they moved to Cambridge, the Bardiges became involved in school politics, working for liberal groups interested in improving education. "You have a bunch of parents here who do not want to send their kids to private schools," says Art.

Kori, the Bardiges' oldest child, went to an alternative cooperative nursery school in the neighborhood and then enrolled in Peabody, the neighborhood school. Her parents plunged into school activities, with Art becoming head of the Parent-Teachers Organization and Betty, a room mother. Kori, a quiet child with light brown hair, large eyes, and a sweet, shy smile, had a hearing problem caused by ear infections and was struggling with reading and spelling. By the time Kori reached third grade, her parents began to worry about the curriculum and whether Kori was receiving the help she needed. She was making A's, but was having to work harder than her parents thought was advisable. "There was not enough attention to individual differences," said Betty. "There was a lack of educational leadership." They looked ahead and concluded that the two fourth-grade teachers at Peabody would simply be offering more of the same. Now was the time to switch. What Kori needed, they decided, was a more flexible and supportive classroom where she would get added attention. "She's a very bright child," said Betty. "That wasn't the issue." That spring they signed Kori up for the magnet program at the Tobin School. "It was a hard decision," says Art. "We felt like we had put a lot of effort into Peabody, but it was too rigid, too academic, too stiff. They were using a lot of textbooks and a lot of worksheets. We wanted a class where she would not be judged on how many problems she had done."

The Bardiges' second child, Brenan, was born in 1979 and was beginning to read at eighteen months. When it came time to enroll him in elementary school, they opted for the computer program at Tobin. Brenan was young for his class, socially and physically, but since he knew how to read, he was sent to classes with older students. Betty and Art liked the stimulation for their son, but they still wanted him to be in classes with his own peers. So they switched him over to the Follow Through program within the same school. "We feel our kids have gotten an excellent education here," said Art.

But the benefits of choice are by no means limited to professionals. Julio and Domingas Tavares, who live in a pastel-yellow three-bedroom house on Cardinal Medeiros Street, are Cape Verdian by birth and spent most of their lives in Luanda, Angola, where both taught in an elementary school. They tired of the ongoing civil war in Angola, so in 1987 they followed other members of their family to Cambridge. Julio, who is thirty-eight, is a dishwasher at the Westin Hotel. Domingas is a utility aide in Cambridge Hospital, working from 7:00 A.M. to 3:00 P.M. On Tuesday and Thursday nights she goes to the Cambridge Adult Learning Center for English classes.

When it came time to enroll their two eldest daughters, Paula, now eleven, and Claudia, now ten, in school, Domingas had long talks about programs for foreign students with Donna Sousa, the parent liaison at the Harrington School, and decided that they needed the support of a Portuguese bilingual program. She enrolled them both in the program at Harrington. One of the things that she especially liked was the fact that the principal could speak to her in Portuguese. "If there are problems, he can explain it to me," she said.

With their sons, though, the Tavareses took a different approach. Hernani, now eight, an inquisitive child who wears heavy-framed glasses and cocks his head to one side when inspecting something new, started off in the Harrington bilingual program but after a year and a half was moved into the regular English-speaking classes. By the time their youngest child, Ivan, was ready for school, they decided to get him into an English-speaking program from the outset. All of the regular classes at Harrington were full, however, and it looked as if the only English-speaking classes would be at either Fletcher or Maynard, which would mean separating the children, something they did not want. So instead they arranged to keep Ivan at Harrington by enrolling him in its Follow Through program.

Domingas and Julio, who try to check their children's homework each night, concede that keeping up with so many different programs can be difficult. "Last year I really didn't have enough time to find out if the Follow Through program was good for Ivan," said Domingas. "Sometimes I can't get to the parents' meeting, and many times when I do get there, the meetings are finished and I don't have a chance to say anything. But I can't work only part-time and still pay the bills." Still, they are grateful for the choices that they have. Domingas said that, with the help of the parent liaison, she feels as if she got good advice and was able to make wise choices for all of her children. Because of their language limitations her daughters needed to be in the bilingual classes, while the boys, who did not speak Portuguese as well, fit more easily into regular classes. "I like having so many programs," said Domingas. "Before I put my kids in a program, I like to talk to the teachers and to Donna. I try to talk to people whose children are in the program a long time and know what the programs taught. Here the teacher gives me a more important role in deciding what happens with my kids. They call me at work sometimes to let me know what my children are doing."

For some families, though, things do not go all that smoothly. Jim Sanders and his wife, Lin Tucker Sanders, lived in a triple-decker home on Magazine Street in Cambridgeport. When their eldest son, Justin, was about to enter kindergarten they began looking around at their educational options. They wanted a school with a structured classroom atmosphere and one where the principal shared their ideas about education. Unfortunately, they did not get any of their first three choices—Peabody, King Open, or Graham and Parks—and Justin was assigned to Morse. Since Morse was right down the street and Lin knew the teachers, she decided that the assignment was one that they could live with. But she asked to keep Justin's name on the waiting list at Peabody. When his name came up he was transferred to Peabody for his second year.

Peabody turned out to be something of a misfit for Justin. Kindergarten went smoothly, but during first grade Justin began showing signs of stress. After consulting with their family physician the Sanders decided that Peabody might be one of the reasons. When new signs of stress appeared early in the second grade, they knew he needed a change. They decided to try another school—this time an alternative program. But the alternative programs were already fully subscribed, and Justin was not reassigned. So the Sanderses took their only other course of action. They submitted a hardship appeal—one that, under the rules, allows parents to make special requests that their child be assigned to a particular type of school or program for medical or serious personal reasons. "By no means is it good enough to say that your child is not happy," Mrs. Sanders explained. "You basically have to paint your child as a psychological basket case." The committee approved the petition, and Justin was placed at the top of the list for an alternative program. The following fall he entered Graham and Parks.

When it came time for the Sanderses' second son, Robert, to enter kindergarten they once again received none of their first three choices. He, too, ended up at Morse. "We have no luck in the lottery," said Jim. The Sanderses then joined forces with other parents pushing for more alternative schools in Cambridge, and they met with success. This year a new alternative kindergarten was opened at Morse, and Robert is enrolled. "I am basically a pro-choice person," Mrs. Sanders says. "We were ecstatic about the Graham and Parks transfer and the new alternative kindergarten. But just because we finally got our way with Justin doesn't mean the system doesn't need to change. We have persevered, but there are people who would have given up. The system needs to be more responsive to these people as well."

In other cases, frustration leads to changes within the system. Charles Wisner, an architect, and his wife, Kata Hall, moved to Cambridge from neighboring Somerville because they believed in public education and had heard good things about the choice system. They were especially enthusiastic about the chance to enroll their two sons, Benjamin, five, and Samuel, three, in alternative schools. "In Somerville we didn't feel like there was enough energy in the nontraditional classrooms," said Chuck. They settled in a newly renovated white Victorian house on Pleasant Street in the Cambridgeport section that was right across the street from the Graham and Parks School, which, as Kata put it, "was supposed to be one of the best alternative programs."

When it came time to enroll Benjamin in kindergarten, Kata, a graphic designer, visited eight different schools, but they listed Graham and Parks first because of its proximity. The other choices were also alternative schools. "We just figured, hey, something is going to work out," said Chuck. "The word was that, even if you didn't get one of your first three choices, you would get on the waiting list." When assignments were announced in March, though, the Wisners were disappointed. They were one of more than sixty families, out of more than five hundred with children entering kindergarten, who did not get any of their first three choices. The Wisners contacted some of these other families, and several meetings were held with school officials. "People were outraged that they could live a block away from a school and not get their kids in it," recalls Chuck. So they came up with a bold idea: Why not start a new alternative kindergarten? The parents shot off a series of petitions to the School Committee, and, accompanied by engineers, Chuck canvassed abandoned Roman Catholic parochial schools to test for asbestos. They found a suitable site in a former parochial school but ended up opening another kindergarten at Morse. "There is something exciting about opening a new program," said Kata. "Parents really feel they will be able to participate in this." In the end, since they needed only one classroom, school officials decided to go with the Morse site.

Such sensitivity to parental wishes and bureaucratic response is critical to the concept of "controlled choice"—not only for reasons of public relations and politics but because it is the key to building educational quality. "The rank ordering of schools of choice is a referendum on the attractiveness of all schools," says Charles Willie, a professor of education at the Harvard Graduate School of Education. "Those schools that are least preferred are alerted that they must develop plans to make themselves attractive to students. This process encourages the system to be continuously improving least-attractive schools." In short, the district seeks improvement in the overall system by constantly building up the weakest links in the chain. Michael Alves, a consultant who works closely with Willie, describes Cambridge's controlled choice as a "living reform" in which the system is, in effect, "re-created" every year. "Educational improvement becomes an explicit concern, and improvements are self-generated," he says. "The recurring question becomes, What do you do with schools that people do not want, like Kennedy and Fitzgerald?"

What are the results of controlled choice now that Cambridge has been doing it for a decade? Clearly the plan has achieved its original social purpose of creating a stable desegregated school system. Since 1981 the percentage of students opting for nonneighborhood schools has risen to 63 percent, making voluntary desegregation possible. No Cambridge school has drifted toward resegregation. Moreover choice has brought students back to the public schools. Ninety percent of Cambridge children opt for public schools, up from only 70 percent in 1981. Standardized-test scores, flawed though they may be as measures of achievement, have also improved steadily since 1981.

Within the overall rise, some interesting positive trends can be discerned, including a narrowing of the gap between the performances of black students and white students. Cambridge can no longer identify racial minorities by test scores. Indeed, by eighth grade, minority students are actually outperforming white students in math and reading in 60 percent of the public schools. In some schools middle-class minority students outscore their white counterparts. Students from poor families do less well than those from more affluent homes. Social class alone now divides high-achievers from low-achievers. "I think we're a better school system," says McGrath, the Cambridge superintendent. "More children come to school with positive attitudes. Because of the competition, professional staff members have to pay attention to the educational program. The quality of leadership has improved, and there is more respect among the kids. There is greater understanding of cultural diversity. Kids from the projects go to birthday parties on Brattle Street. State basic-skills tests are going up."

One of the things that controlled choice had going for it politically in Cambridge was the fact that the concept of the neighborhood school had already begun to erode. The young middle-class newcomers who moved to Cambridge in the 1970s settled wherever they could find space in the city's tight housing market, and they shared none of their blue-collar neighbors' loyalty to neighborhood schools. Their eyes were quickly drawn to the Cambridge Alternative School and the handful of other magnet programs that got extra state and federal funds, were encouraged to be innovative, had school-based management long before the term became fashionable, and, most important, drew students from throughout the district. Indeed, by 1979 about one-third of the system's white students were enrolled in schools outside of their neighborhood school attendance district. This "unregulated choice" was one of the causes of racial imbalance in the first place.

Buoyed by the success in Cambridge, the state of Massachusetts is doing what it can to spread the concept. Sixteen other Massachusetts cities now operate controlled-choice plans. Since many of the cities are not as small or as compact as Cambridge, they frequently subdivide into manageable attendance zones for assignment purposes. In 1987 Fall River, Massachusetts, began operating a controlled-choice plan with four attendance zones, each one conforming to existing middle-school attendance zones. Parents and students have the choice of six to ten elementary schools and any of the district's middle schools.

Boston joined the choice bandwagon in the fall of 1989, starting off by providing choice for students entering the early grades of elementary and middle school and then extending it to all grades and all 56,000 students the following fall. Boston's choice scheme replaced a fifteen-year-old court-ordered desegregation busing plan that had bitterly divided the city. The new approach sets racial quotas at each school, but parents will be able to choose where they would like to enroll their children. Boston uses the zone concept, with each child eligible to list preferences for about twenty elementary and six middle schools. Blacks in Boston contested the plan on the grounds that the system would work to the disadvantage of many minority students, and there are still complaints that schools in poor communities, which tend to have mostly minority populations, have not been maintained as well as schools in other areas. But the program has been upheld by a federal court. Michael Alves, the consultant, says that in the first year of implementation 78 percent of the 15,000 students eligible to choose got their first choice, with 92 percent getting one of their first three.

This approach has spread nationally. Since 1986 Little Rock, Arkansas, with 26,000 students in fifty-two schools, has divided itself into two enlarged attendance zones containing similar racial and socioeconomic student compositions. Interzone transfers are permitted if they facilitate desegregation. On the other hand, East Baton Rouge Parish in Louisiana, with 59,000 students living in an area that embraces 500 square miles, has opted for completely open enrollment. To do so, it has set up an elaborate busing system with a network of transfer points. Students are picked up at their home in one bus and travel to a collection point, where they are picked up by another bus that completes the route. The system, which constitutes the fourth largest busing system in the country, builds on a concept originally developed to transport students in special-education programs.

Other districts have come at choice in different ways. In Community School District 4 in the East Harlem section of New York City, the issue was not desegregation but educational quality. The superintendent and several groups of teachers were looking for innovative ways to improve the education of inner-city youngsters. Choice was not implemented, as it was in Cambridge, as a full-blown plan to improve schools. Rather it evolved over a period of time, starting with a few elementary schools and then moving up to the junior high level, as a way of giving both freedom and structure to some alternative approaches to education.

District 4 is one of the thirty-two local school districts that make up the New York City public school system. Its boundaries stretch from 96th Street to 125th Street on the east side of upper Manhattan, and virtually all of its students are members of minority groups, two-thirds Hispanic, one-third black. The high poverty level means that almost 80 percent of the district's fourteen thousand students are eligible for free or reduced-price lunches. In the early 1970s the district's test scores reflected the cycle of failure that doomed many of its students. The district regularly came in dead last or near the bottom among the thirty-two districts on reading and math tests, and only 15 percent of its kids were reading at or above grade level. With such overwhelming problems District 4 was, as Sy Fliegel, the associate superintendent at the time, put it, "an unlikely site for ground-breaking educational reform." On the other hand, it had little to lose.

The superintendent at the time was Anthony Alvarado, a maverick educator who believed that the structure of the system was too rigid and that teachers needed to be free to design the most effective programs they could. He invited teachers and administrators to think of innovative ways to improve the learning in their classrooms and then entrusted them with the authority and resources to turn their ideas into little schools. Attendance at the schools they created would be voluntary on the part of parents and students who shared that school's particular vision. To get the ball rolling, the district itself set up two special schools. The first was the Beta (Better Education Through Alternatives) School for troubled youngsters who could not function well in traditional settings and needed more counseling and a less-rigid curriculum. The second was the East Harlem Performing Arts School, which later became the Jose Feliciano School when the Latin singing star adopted the school because of its inspiring work.

Later that same year, 1974, Deborah Meier, a former kindergarten teacher, took up Alvarado's challenge and opened the Central Park East Elementary School, housed on two floors of a dilapidated elementary school on East 103rd Street. The school had only one hundred students, kindergarten through second grade, and just one rule: Children would come only because their parents chose it. Central Park East is student-oriented, with less focus on specific skills and a greater emphasis on content and team teaching. The school tried to teach students to think, experiment, discuss, and do research while emphasizing creative writing and mastery of subject matter. The original Central Park East proved to be so popular that two spin-offs were also opened, Central Park East II and River East School. In 1985 the Central Park East Secondary School opened and became affiliated with Ted Sizer's Coalition of Essential Schools. District 4 has fifty schools in twenty-one buildings: sixteen regular elementary schools, nine bilingual elementary schools, twenty-three alternative schools, and two high schools. The alternative schools were so successful that they led to others, many organized around themes. There are the popular themes that are found in other specialized magnet schools across the country—math and science, performing arts, gifted and talented. There are also some not-so-common ones, such as a biomedical program and a maritime program. All of the schools started small, typically with only a few classes in one grade. The most popular schools were duplicated to prevent them from exceeding the enrollment levels considered ideal by district officials. Eventually, by the mid-1980s, District 4 had twenty-three separate elementary schools operating on an option basis. Then they extended the idea up to the junior high school level. "We didn't set out to create a choice system," said Fliegel. "It was really an organic kind of process—we were never certain what the next step would be."

Students are matched to a school through what is called an open-zoning process, which begins each February, when sixth-grade students receive a booklet describing the curriculum and requirements of each alternative school. Sixth-grade teachers attend workshops on how to help students select the junior high schools that will best meet their needs, and parents attend orientation sessions held by the alternative-school directors. Parents and students are invited to visit schools and sit in on classes during the months of March and April. In May each student submits a junior high application with six choices. Estimates of the number of students placed in one of their two top choices range from 90 to 97 percent.

Jennifer Kratz is an example of how students benefit from District 4's expanded range of choices. The thirteen-year-old youngster has a learning disability and, while bright and inquisitive, does not perform well on standardized tests. After years of frustration in a traditional New York City school that placed a lot of emphasis on such tests, Jennifer began skipping class. By the fifth grade she had grown to 150 pounds and was severely depressed. Jennifer's parents heard about District 4's alternative school programs and took Jennifer to visit the River East Elementary School. Jennifer immediately fell in love with the open atmosphere and what she viewed as the positive attitude of teachers, and she applied for a transfer. "We read books that allowed us to think, and I learned how to work in groups," said Jennifer. "I had a teacher who encouraged me to do my best. And for the first time someone was telling me I did something right." She lost fifty pounds and gained a great deal of self-confidence. Eventually Jennifer transferred to the Central Park East Secondary School. "I think I would have eventually dropped out if I had stayed in a traditional school," she commented. "Most kids in the traditional city schools can't wait to get out. If we had more schools like this one, the percentage of dropouts would be way down."

Not all the new schools were success stories. In a misguided attempt to be relevant to student interests, a group of teachers tried to organize their teaching around athletic themes—reading sports stories, calculating the area of a baseball field, and so forth. It has now been closed and reopened as New York Prep, with a traditional curriculum.

District 4 is no longer at the bottom of the educational system. Over 60 percent of all District 4 students are now reading at or above grade level—"a far cry from the 15 percent when we started," said John Falco, the assistant superintendent. The district is now in the middle of the city's thirty-two districts on math and reading tests. The average daily attendance rate in 1987–88 was 93 percent, up from 82 percent in the early 1970s. In 1973 fewer than 10 junior high school students from District 4 were admitted to New York City's selective high schools, such as the Bronx High School of Science. The figure has now soared to 300. Critics have questioned some of these statistics, arguing that the scores of some 1,500 students who travel from other parts of the city to attend East Harlem schools have inflated the test-score increase. Administrators, though, say that their own analysis has shown that incoming students have little impact on overall figures. But the criticism itself is telling. Why would 1,500 students choose to travel to East Harlem to get an education? In fact, ten of the alternative schools have now been designated as citywide "magnet" schools because they draw a large number of nonminority students from outside the district.

School officials attribute much of this increase to the choice plan. "A choice system treats kids differently," said Fliegel. "Students and their parents become clients instead of a captive audience. It says to kids, 'We care what you think because we try to cater to some of your interests.' The whole purpose is to motivate youngsters to take part in their educational process." Falco believes that free enterprise plays a role. "You now have schools that are competing for students, so it's like industry—if the schools have a quality program, they are going to attract students. You have everyone who is involved seeing to it that students are getting the maximum."

Choice in District 4 has produced some unanticipated but salutary side effects. For one thing schools have become smaller. Instead of the usual 1,400 students and 100 teachers per school, District 4's junior high schools average about 150 students and 12 teachers. Some buildings contain four or five small alternative schools. "Having broken the mind-set of one school per geographic location, we were free to design schools as we felt they should be designed, reflecting our own biases and imagination," said Fliegel. The district's motto is "Less Is Better." Fewer students per school and classroom, less bureaucracy, and less top-down management make up their reform formula. "Small schools are not the answer, but without them none of the proposed answers stands a chance," said Meier. "Hugeness works against lively intellectual intercourse. Apathy develops as a rational response to large, anonymous schools. Young people cannot learn democratic values in a setting that does not value individual achievement, that cannot notice triumphs and defeats, has no time to celebrate or mourn, or respond with indignation or recognition as the situation requires. Small schools offer opportunities to solve every one of these critical issues." Rather than let her Central Park East Elementary School grow larger, Meier has chosen to help start two clones.

Just as the Empire State Building houses many companies, large school buildings can, indeed, house many small schools. One problem, though, is that many of District 4's pint-sized "schools" do not technically exist. The New York City Board of Education recognizes only the twenty school buildings in District 4, not the fifty-two schools that the district recognizes. Moreover the schools are run not by principals but by directors, who are technically teachers. "Officially we've never existed," said Meier. "We're living a fiction."

The state that has taken school choice the farthest is Minnesota, whose embrace of the concept of "open enrollment" has its roots in the personal experience of Rudy Perpich, the state's former Democratic governor. The son of poor Croatian immigrants, Perpich grew up in Hibbing, in the rugged iron-mining region of northeastern Minnesota, and became a dentist. Education, he frequently says, was "my passport out of poverty." When he was first elected to the Minnesota legislature, he and his wife rented a home in St. Paul and sent several of their children to the neighborhood school, which turned out to be an educational disaster. The children quickly became bored because they were covering material they had already had in Hibbing, but school officials, saying they believed in equal education for all students, refused to move them into advanced classes. Two years later, when Perpich was reelected and returned to the Twin Cities, he and his wife made sure that they rented in a suburban district with a first-class school. The experience made a lasting impact on Perpich. His social conscience was offended by the fact that he could purchase a public school education for his children that was not available to the less affluent. He resolved that if he ever got the political opportunity to do so, he would give every parent and child the same freedom of choice that he enjoyed. His views struck home in a state where students in public schools have one of the highest graduation and college-going rates and where public education has widespread public support but where populist traditions are strong.

Minnesota's open-enrollment policies evolved over a period of several years. The first step, by the Democratic-controlled legislature, taken in 1985 in response to Perpich's "Access to Excellence" plan, established a program called "postsecondary options." That fall high school juniors and seniors were allowed to take one or more courses in public colleges or vocational schools at no cost. Instead some or all of the money that the state would have spent on them in their high schools followed them to the new institution. In 1987 the state set up a "second-chance" option designed for students who have problems in a traditional school setting. The High School Graduation Incentives Program allows students who had not graduated to attend any school, learning center, or technical institute to acquire marketable skills. In 1988 the program, which initially had an age limit of twenty-one, was expanded to include dropouts of any age. A December 1990 report by the Minnesota Department of Education and the U.S. Department of Education, based on a study of thirteen thousand students in open choice programs in 1989–90, found that students who had switched schools had dramatically increased their educational aspirations and felt more confident that they were doing better in school.

But the jewel of Perpich's choice initiatives was open enrollment, which permits elementary and secondary school students to elect to attend any school in the state. With each student goes state aid that, in the case of secondary school students, totaled almost $4,000 in 1990–91. Open enrollment began on a voluntary basis in 1987 and three years later became mandatory for all 435 school districts in the state. While districts can choose not to admit students, usually for lack of space, districts cannot prevent students from leaving. The exceptions are in Minneapolis, St. Paul, and Duluth, where transfers in or out of the districts can be stopped if they will upset desegregation guidelines. In practice, white students find it difficult to leave Minneapolis, but St. Paul has adopted a liberal exit policy, thus allowing parents and students to become education shoppers, and forcing school districts to pay attention to the wants of students and parents.

Parents and students take advantage of their rights to cross district lines for reasons ranging from a desire for better academic programs to logistical convenience. For example, Salli Weston of Palisade, a small town in north-central Minnesota, lives at the far end of the Aitkin school district. Her bus ride to Aitkin Secondary School would have been almost two hours each way. Instead she enrolled in the Hill City Secondary School in the neighboring district. Her mother drove her two and a half miles to the nearest bus stop, where she was picked up for the forty-five minute ride to school. "We knew Hill City was a good school because our neighbors had kids who went there," said Katherine Weston, Salli's mother. "She was welcomed there, knew quite a few of the kids, and was very active."

Salli Weston also took advantage of the postsecondary enrollment option allowing her to get a head start on college. By her junior year in high school she had taken precalculus, physics, and chemistry, and the only courses left for her senior year were "what I hadn't taken or didn't want." Salli, who wants to be a chemical engineer, attended Itasca Community College, taking precalculus, psychology, advanced English, and computer programming her first quarter. The state paid her $540 tuition and, because she qualified for a transportation subsidy from the state, paid her mileage costs to and from the college each month. Straddling high school and college is a challenge. Salli still played flute, piccolo, and tenor saxophone for the Hill City band and was a member of the Knowledge Bowl team. But she admitted it felt strange to go to band practice when everyone was talking about homecoming and she, the class valedictorian, had been going to college full-time. But not strange enough to regret the decision. "Some people take it just to get out of high school, but if you're prepared and taking classes, it's great," she said. "It's a really good idea because it gives kids a chance for college who might otherwise not have it. Four years of college is really expensive; it's not easy to do."

As a child Teresa Harlow of north Minneapolis attended the public junior high and high school in Brooklyn Center, then a small blue-collar suburb of Minneapolis. She and her husband lived in an apartment there until affordable home prices lured them into the city. When her marriage ended, Harlow, a clerk in the city of Minneapolis's finance department, remained in the house. She loves the neighborhood, where the plain, neat outsides of the stucco-and-clapboard homes belie the sometimes extravagant woodwork and stained-glass windows inside. The neighborhood is quiet, and even on school nights children play and run in the tree-lined front yards, the night air ringing with their shrieks and laughter. At first her son, Sam, ten, attended Olson Elementary School about a mile from their home, walking to school. Later Hannah, eight, went to kindergarten at Shingle Creek Early Childhood Center. Both children did well in school, and Sam attended a free summer school enrichment program that concentrated on computers. But Harlow, who was active in the PTA, was disturbed by the high turnover of students at Olson, and when city schools hit a budget crisis and cut the summer school courses, Harlow became concerned. She feared that Sam's classes, already at about thirty children, might get bigger.

A friend from Brooklyn Center told her about the state's new open enrollment, and Harlow began calling for information. She decided she'd feel more comfortable with her children attending school in the area where she grew up. Minneapolis schools readily gave her information on open enrollment and released her children to Brooklyn Center. The city district's release of Harlow's children is unusual—Minneapolis schools, with a perennial problem maintaining racial balance, have permitted very few white children to transfer out of the district. Harlow said her transfer sailed right through, possibly because she lives only four houses from the district boundary. "My kids would probably have done fine in Minneapolis schools, but I just like having them there, and I think maybe the schools are better over there," she said. "And my folks and my sister live in Brooklyn Center. It gives a community feeling to have them going there. I know people, and I feel involved. That's important to me." Harlow said that she values the chance to select what she thinks is an appropriate school for her children while staying in the neighborhood they love. "I think I was very lucky to get in when I did," she said. "I have the best of both worlds." For Harlow, at least, being able to send her children to another district did not end her interest in the schools in her resident district. She said she plans to support a tax referendum to raise operating money to cut class sizes at Minneapolis schools because she lives in the city and wants it to stay a good place to live.

In the case of Jennifer Cirkl, who is seventeen, open enrollment led to the reverse migration, from suburb to city. Her parents, Edward and Janell, both grew up in Minneapolis and attended local schools, but with the advent of busing in the 1970s they moved to suburban Bloomington in search of better schools and a bigger house. The Cirkls live in a comfortable, middle-class neighborhood of boxy 1950s-era ramblers. Janell, who once taught physical education, was always active in her children's schools, and their youngest children, Betsy, twelve, and Ben, seven, still attend Bloomington schools. But the Cirkls were unhappy with what Jennifer was doing—or not doing—at John F. Kennedy High School. "Most of the teachers were good, and they tried to keep her mentally stimulated," Janell Cirkl said. "But it just wasn't working." A willowy, outgoing blonde whose fair features contrast with her mother's dark eyes and hair, Jennifer took the most advanced classes she could, got A's, and won awards. But still she felt unchallenged and ill at ease. "I was bored," she said. "I never had any homework in science. And I was a geek because I took the honors program. I only went to one or two parties my whole year at Kennedy. Why go if you're a geek?"

Then Janell Cirkl heard about a program known as the International Baccalaureate (IB), a demanding program with an emphasis on international education and interdisciplinary studies. The program is headquartered in Switzerland, and students in more than fifty countries take IB exams on the same day. These exams are graded by IB-trained teachers and professors around the world, and many colleges offer credit to students who win an IB diploma with high grades. Janell Cirkl was sorely disappointed when a committee at Kennedy rejected a proposal to start the program in Bloomington. At the dinner table with her family she offhandedly remarked that the program would be good for someone like Jenni. To her mother's surprise, her daughter went through the information her mother had collected and announced that she thought that she might like to transfer to Southwest High School in Minneapolis, which had an IB program.

One January day in her sophomore year her parents dropped Jenni off at Southwest to spend the day. The low-slung, neat brick building is in an affluent, stable area of Minneapolis, but its urban aura was still a shock to the teenager from sprawling, modernistic Kennedy with its imitation marble floors, wide hallways, and circular design. "The first thing I saw when I walked in the door was this massive fight," she recalled. "At Kennedy you had maybe two kids in a fight, and then it was over. At Southwest it filled the entire hallway, and security guards with walkie-talkies ran up, and I was looking for directions to the office! I was scared to death. It was like, my God, I just want to go home. I saw guys with ear-rings, kids with things in their nose, all kinds of interesting hair-cuts, graffiti on the building, no doors on the bathroom stalls. I knew it would be different, but I was just totally shocked!" But Jenni liked the IB students she met, was excited by the classes, and decided to transfer. The Minneapolis school system, which had ini-tiated the IB program as a vehicle to retain the middle-class and white students in an increasingly poor and minority student body, was happy to accept her. Dealing with the Bloomington schools, though, was another story. While Jenni's teachers were supportive, asking her to keep in touch and let them know how she was doing, a counselor told her, "I hope you know you're ruining your life. You'll be begging to get back." The transfer request got "lost," and Janell Cirkl went to school headquarters to personally walk the papers through the bureaucracy. "They found Jenni going from Bloomington to Minneapolis, from suburb to city, insulting," she said.

Jenni admitted that while she desperately wanted to be in IB, she was "terrified" about going to Southwest, a fear reinforced by the warnings of friends. But she found her niche rather quickly, immersing herself in her classes and absorbing cultural and class differences she never experienced at Kennedy. The former self-described "geek" has in fact become a cheerleader, something that has her mother shaking her head in wonder. As a little girl Jenni refused even to run with her mother, rebelling against Janell's past as a physical education teacher. Jenni found that when she trans-ferred, she was behind city students in math. Her near-A average is a decline from past years. She's a little behind in French, and that may be a barrier in winning her IB diploma. But Jenni, who wants to be a biological research scientist, is no longer devastated at getting a B. "Some of the kids are just brilliant," she said. "We all feed on each other. It's great." Jenni rarely gets to study with the rest of her friends, who often gather at night to quiz each other. The drive to the area around Southwest is eighteen miles round-trip, and the lost time often isn't worth it. The Cirkls pay Jenni's gas costs, even though she has a one-day-a-week job at a doughnut shop. She's a member of the National Honor Society, works for the school newspaper and yearbook. "I have so many friends. I'm popular," she said with surprise. "I'm always challenged. Open enrollment has changed my life."

When Perpich first proposed open enrollment in 1985, reaction among educators and legislators was overwhelmingly negative. Officials in hundreds of small rural school districts, already hit by declining enrollment and limited local resources, saw open enrollment as a veiled attempt to force school consolidations or closures. Teacher union leaders and others in the state's politically powerful educational establishment warned that students would transfer so that they could play on better athletic teams or be near friends. But strong political support came from the business community, which saw it as a way of improving the quality of education and the efficiency of the school system. Key allies were the Twin Cities Citizens League, a business-supported research group, and the Minnesota Business Partnership, consisting of the chief executive officers of the state's eighty largest corporations. Much of the criticism faded as open enrollment took effect and only small numbers of students participated. In 1990–91, the first year that every district had to participate, 6,134 students used open enrollment, up from 3,200 the previous year. That figure was less than 1 percent of students.

As officials had feared, small school districts were affected the most. As of 1989–90 only 12 of the 343 districts that participated experienced more than a 5 percent change in enrollment. But almost all districts that lost more than 4 percent of their enrollment were districts with fewer than 300 students. Choice, though, became merely the latest blow to Minnesota's small schools. Once, the state had more than 8,000 tiny, scattered districts. That number dropped to fewer than 450 by the 1980s. The smallest districts found themselves fighting shrinking enrollment, decaying buildings, and heightened criticism from state officials, who said small districts were unable to provide the science, math, and language classes students needed for the twenty-first century. The fight to retain small districts was more than a defensive response by school officials. For many Minnesotans, small schools were a proud symbol of the state's agricultural heritage. The school was often the largest employer, a source of community pride, and a center of community activities.

Some small districts seized on open enrollment not as a threat but as an opportunity. Cyrus, a tiny school district in the farmland of west-central Minnesota, is surrounded by larger districts and had already lost its high school when, in 1989, officials decided to turn the elementary school into a math-science-technology school. Using equipment from the defunct high school and money from parent-run bake and rummage sales, the school now has one computer for every three children. Eight young, enthusiastic teachers shaped a curriculum that has grade-schoolers measuring simulated earthquakes on computers and the hallways whirring with computer-controlled Lego cars. "We decided that if we couldn't have a secondary school, we'd have a hell of an elementary school," said Dennis Lokken, the school board chairman. The school marketed itself with brochures in banks and offices in the region and by putting red-shirted students and the school mascot, a plywood robot called Dr. Megabyte, on flatbed floats that traveled to area festivals and parades. The gentle marketing effort was planned carefully. Competition for students is a touchy issue in towns where schools are a source of pride and identity. Margaret Strand, who works in Cyrus schools, transferred her two children to the district from her resident district of Starbuck. "It was a hard, hard decision," she said. "Community pride rides high in rural Minnesota, and when you do something like this, you're highly visible." Whether Cyrus's gamble pays off depends on the school's ability to attract outside students. If enrollment drops to about eighty students, as it has in the past, the school would be near financial collapse. But in 1990–91 about 10 percent of Cyrus's ninety-five elementary school students came from outside the district.

Not surprisingly, open enrollment's harshest critics have been in districts that lost students to other schools or districts. Westonka, a Minneapolis suburb plagued by financial problems after two tax referendums failed, lost 120 students over two years to surrounding districts. Although a subsequent tax increase succeeded and the exodus of students has ebbed, Superintendent James Smith sees little good in open enrollment. "There is nothing that has occurred with open enrollment that would be positive," he commented. In Westonka the program meant that those who were most disappointed with the referendum failures—the schools' supporters—were those who fled the district. That made it harder to pass a tax increase, he added, and meant that some parents were taking advantage of more costly school programs in nearby districts without supporting them with their own taxes. "I'm not going to fight it," Smith said. "It's here, and we're going to deal with it." But he added that he considers open enrollment "a politician's dream," which has resulted in glitz without substance. The only good, he said, is that it has forced school officials to be more responsive to parents and students.

Some think that's a worthwhile change. "Psychologically it's been good for schools," said R. J. Rehwaldt, superintendent in the Rosemount–Apple Valley–Eagan schools, a growing suburban district that is too crowded to accept many new students. "The fact that you could lose some kids, it keeps you on your toes," he said. "You know you've got to do a good job." Open enrollment has also been criticized as favoring wealthy and middle-class students because, until 1990, transporting students was left mostly to parents. In 1989–90 the state's $50,000 fund to assist needy parents with transportation costs was exhausted before the end of the school year. The law has now been changed, however, so that nonresident school districts can pick up transferring students if their resident district agrees. If that district protests, an appeal can be filed with the state. By the fall of 1990, 250 such requests had been granted.

To make sure that Minnesota's poorest citizens know about school choice, the state Department of Human Services mails information on choice to all its clients. A state toll-free phone line dispenses information on the program, which is also marketed through booths at events such as the state fair. A grocery store was persuaded to print information about choice programs on more than a million grocery bags.

One of the arguments against choice is that not all parents have equal access to information about the variety of schools, particularly poor parents and rural parents. The Harlows, you will recall, found out about a school from a friend.

In 1989–90 Minnesota colleges and vocational schools received about $4.2 million in state money for educating high school students, money that otherwise would have gone to local school districts. College reaction has been mixed. Some of the state's most selective private colleges have declined to take part, saying that they are worried about the maturity and ability of high school students. In some of those institutions the amount of state aid that could be funneled to an institution for a full-time high school student would cover less than a third of the cost of tuition and fees. But others have subsidized students' educations, eating the cost as the price of luring bright high-schoolers who will eventually enroll as regular college students.

The true impact of school choice in Minnesota will not be fully clear until the programs have been running for several years. School officials already say they feel that they have greater flexibility to add new programs. Officials say they know that, in an effort to hang on to their brightest students, high schools have greatly increased the number of Advanced Placement programs and other challenging courses. Statistics are hard to come by, but the number of Minnesota public high schools offering advanced-placement courses doubled, from 65 to 130, between 1985 and 1990. More than sixty high schools have signed up for College in the Schools, a cooperative program that brings college-credit courses to high schools. The program gives high school teachers the opportunity to teach a college-approved course under the supervision of a professor, for which students may receive both high school and college credit. Colleges receive $650 for each student who takes the course. Colleges see it as a helpful recruitment tool, while high schools like it because their students stay around.

Schools have started marketing themselves, some producing glossy promotional brochures as slick as a college publication. Some districts in rural areas have even placed newspaper advertisements listing curriculums. Such activity is distasteful to school officials like Westonka's Smith, who nevertheless concedes that it is inevitable and that his own district is investigating magazine advertisements. "We all have to be more marketing conscious," he said.

Joe Nathan, a senior fellow at the University of Minnesota's Hubert Humphrey Institute of Public Affairs and a choice advocate, argues that numbers do not matter so much as the recognition that schools are accountable to parents and students. "You don't have to have large numbers of students crossing district lines for parental choice to be effective," he said. "The important thing is that schools know that they no longer have a captive audience and that kids know they have a choice."

With the exception of studies of some long-standing individual programs, such as at Cambridge, most choice programs, especially the open-enrollment type, are too new to provide conclusive evidence of their effects. But studies are beginning to come in. Mary Anne Raywid, of Adelphi University, looked at 120 districts nationwide and found evidence that indeed choice programs lead to higher academic achievement, graduation rates, more parental satisfaction, and higher teacher morale.

Insofar as school choice has a salutary effect on student learning, the reasons lie in the way in which choice overturns specific aspects of the factory-model school. Choice is yet another step in the decentralization of school systems. It extends to parents the same sort of "ownership" of the educational process that shared decision making gives to teachers and that restructured classes give to students. Since parents are concerned with results, not with rules and regulations, the effect of this empowerment of parents is another shove in the direction of an outcome-based accountability system. Choice also encourages decentralization by making school administrators more dependent on the creativity and dedication of teachers to design programs that will be attractive to parents.

Choice affirms the importance of diversity in education. The goal of choice, says Mary Anne Raywid, is "to create a system that, instead of trying to fit students into some standardized school, has a school to fit *every* student in this district." Choice presumes that since students have different needs, interests, and ways of learning, a school district must offer a variety of educational approaches. The same applies to teachers: There is no single best school for every teacher. Choice puts pressure on districts to develop these differing programs. It also frees up teachers to facilitate this process. "Human beings are so extraordinarily diverse, and in District 4 we have made a virtue of that quality," said New York's Deborah Meier. "Teachers are empowered to try new things, meet new needs, etcetera. For students with divergent learning styles or special needs, it builds diversity into the system and allows a school system to be responsive to different needs, on the part of both teachers and students."

The experience of districts that have implemented parental choice suggests that there are several prerequisites for making it successful. First, parents must have a *range of high-quality alternative schools from which to choose.* Choice is a hollow privilege if there are no choices worth making. "Having parents choose from inadequate programs is a hoax," said Alice K. Wolf, the mayor of Cambridge.

Second, the choices must be legitimate ones. *Every child must have a crack at every school.* There must be no hidden agendas that allow parents with inside knowledge or influence to work the system to their advantage. A strong centralized selection process must be established so that schools themselves cannot stack the deck in favor of students with high test scores or good behavior records or against those who are weak in English or have learning problems. As the National Committee for Citizens in Education put it, "Student assignment should not depend on past behavior, test scores, or academic achievement. Neither should families need to camp out in line in order to be assured their first choice. These methods favor the most informed, assertive parents and students who are already succeeding in school. Lotteries and expansion of popular programs provide more equity in the assignment process."

Third, *parents must be educated about their options—all parents.* An effective parent information system is the key to avoiding the creaming effect. Information must be readily available to parents who do not speak English or fill out complicated forms or who cannot take a day off from work. Steps must be taken to overcome the difficulties such parents face, such as less time, the lack of a car, or the absence of a sophisticated understanding of how to assess accurately what makes one school better than the next.

Fourth, *transportation must be made available* to those who cannot afford it. Otherwise, there is no equity.

Fifth, all parties must acknowledge that *choice will cost more.* Cambridge watched its busing budget rise from $54,000 in 1981 to $1,225,000 in 1988. Other costs are incurred by the need for an effective parent-information system. Parents are hired as liaisons between the school and the community. "But you can't have the finances driving the system," says Cambridge's Mary Lou McGrath. "If you do, you'll always have a reason not to do something—not to open an alternative program at Fitzgerald, not to help the parent liaisons, or whatever. You have to decide what kind of educational system you want to operate."

Sixth, *districts must be ready with training.* Some teachers and administrators are nervous about innovations such as parent liaisons. "It can be intimidating to have someone in the school for twenty hours a week with a telephone," says McGrath.

At the beginning of the chapter, we noted that the current popularity of choice resulted from the convergence of two distinct social traditions. On the basis of the choice plans described here, it is clear that the tension between the two groups of adherents not only persists but has considerable practical consequences for the future direction of choice in public schools.

The first tradition, rooted in an alliance of conservative and populist political forces, favors choice because proponents see it as a way of empowering citizens, increasing options, enhancing competition, shaking up the bureaucracy, and in effect setting up a free market of public education. This position is reflected most fully in Minnesota's open enrollment plan. The assumption is that by giving parents and children control over where they will attend school, teachers and principals will be forced to improve the quality of their offerings. To back this up, the plan provides for state money to follow the students wherever they happen to go. If a school fails to attract enough students, then so be it. The laws of supply and demand must take their toll. *Caveat vendor!*

The second, which can be described as the liberal position, views choice as a way of rectifying social inequities through a careful balancing of various social values, of which freedom of choice is only one. It is best reflected in the concept of "controlled choice" as seen in Cambridge. It asserts that the empowering of parents to choose the school their child will attend is a useful, though by no means absolute, value. It must be balanced by other values, such as racial balance and the overall quality of the system.

The liberal position on choice is skeptical of marketplace analogies. Michael Alves, the consultant, points out that in the late 1950s and 1960s thousands of southern and northern school systems used "freedom of choice" and "open enrollment" plans as a way of perpetuating segregation under the pretext that blacks were "free" to enroll in any school where there was space. Liberals doubt that, as the free-market position implies, there is some Invisible Hand to assure that competition will work in the best interest of all students. Joe Nathan, who has been instrumental in promoting open enrollment in Minnesota but prefers the concept of controlled choice, cites the example of the price and quality of produce and vegetables in East Harlem and Westchester County. "What you get in East Harlem is more expensive and not nearly as good," he says, "because there are lots of reasons why running a grocery in a low-income area is more expensive. The same applies to schools. Trusting a free market alone is naive."

Albert Shanker of the American Federation of Teachers suggests that there is a fundamental difference between the goals of a free economy and a social service such as education. "In the economic system there may be unworthy buyers who are unwilling to pay the asking price. But in the education system, there are no unworthy seekers of knowledge," he says. "The economy moves toward its strength and nurtures those units most capable of producing goods and services for the benefit of the whole system. The educational system moves toward its weaker units and nurtures those least capable of functioning effectively, as a way of enhancing the total system. A market orientation is inappropriate in an educational situation, where mercy rather than fair price mediates relationships."

The all-important question becomes: What do you do with the unpopular schools, the ones that parents judge to be weak? The free-market approach implies some sort of academic triage. Just let them die. The liberal position, on the other hand, argues for some sort of control mechanism under which the district as a whole would intervene to improve these schools—and thus the overall system.

The failure to develop such controls has been a major weakness of magnet-school programs across the country. Magnets are what might be called uncontrolled choice. Schools are set up to specialize in certain fields, such as art or science, or to offer a particular style of teaching, such as open education. Donald Moore, executive director of Designs for Change, a research and advocacy organization in Chicago, along with Sue Davenport, studied the effects of creating a limited number of magnet schools in Boston, Chicago, New York, and Philadelphia. They found that a five-tiered system emerged in all cities except Boston, and they concluded that the magnets in these cities were used to foster "a new form of segregation by social class and on previous success in school." Middle-class families figured out the best schools and got their kids into them, leaving "the vast majority of families out in the cold." Says Moore,

"The idea of 'just let the market forces work and the system will take care of itself' will not work for these kids. Our evidence shows that choice plans need to be heavily regulated."

Charles Willie of Harvard, who has promoted controlled choice plans throughout the country, argues that the key to successful choice is to force everyone to make a choice by eliminating the neighborhood school. "When students are guaranteed attendance in specific schools because of their residence in specific neighborhoods, then educational interests are held hostage by real estate interests," he says. "This is inappropriate because a home and its value benefits a private group, while the school should serve a public good. Thus all of the people, regardless of their income, should have access to all of the schools." To assure this, you have to have a system in which every parent is *forced* to make a choice. "Unless everyone chooses, you have a system of choosers and non-choosers, and you cannot control for self-selection."

This is exactly what Cambridge did when it intervened to upgrade the programs at the Kennedy and Fitzgerald schools. In Cambridge, parental choice serves both as an opportunity for parents to seek out the educational settings that they believe will be most conducive to their children's growth and as an escape valve for those who are dissatisfied with the settings in which they find themselves. But it does this in such a way that the energy from those who do not get one of their top choices is captured and used to improve the overall quality of the system.

In recent months the politics of choice have become more complicated. The tidy alliance of liberals, conservatives, and populists working for choice within the public framework has been challenged by those at both ends of the political spectrum who have decided that the public system is beyond repair.

The most visible example is in Wisconsin, where Polly Williams, a Democratic state legislator and former welfare mother, has pushed through a voucher plan for Milwaukee schools with the support of Republican Governor Thompson. Under the plan, up to one thousand low-income students in Milwaukee are permitted to attend nonsectarian private schools. For each child who does this, the state puts up the private school tuition up to $2,500 and subtracts that amount from the budget of the Milwaukee public schools. The Circuit Court upheld the legality of the program because the

Wisconsin constitution does not expressly require public funds to go solely for public purposes, but the State Court of Appeals later ruled it unconstitutional on a legal technicality that is now being addressed. Opposition came from the state superintendent of schools and most organized education groups. "This is unrestrained and unregulated choice," said Robert Friebert, a lawyer representing the teachers union and other opponents. "There are no standards the private schools have to meet to get the money." Supporters, though, say that this is exactly the problem with the current school system that they are attempting to address. "We now have a formula to free the hostages," said Polly Williams. "The only time you're going to get some movement from any monopoly is if they're afraid they're going to lose something."

Similar cries can be heard elsewhere across the country. Minnesota already offers parents tax deductions of up to $1,000 toward private-school expenses other than religion classes and for certain public school programs that cost extra. The town of Epsom, New Hampshire, has authorized tax abatements for property owners who sponsor a high school student's education in a private school. The Board of Education in Detroit voted to hold hearings on a new charter that would enable private schools to become part of the public system, while twenty-seven Chicago parents have sued the State of Illinois demanding state-financed vouchers to spend at private and parochial schools. The new Bush plan supports this option.

A growing number of academics have begun to look for ways to restructure school systems so that the energies of private entrepreneurs can be unleashed within a public framework. Ted Kolderie of the Center for Policy Studies in St. Paul, Minnesota, wonders why school boards should have an exclusive right to operate publicly financed schools. He wants the state to be able to award "franchises" to businesses, colleges and universities, parents, teachers, and local organizations to run schools with public funds. The state would select among applicants, hold them accountable for results, and cancel the contracts of those who fail to meet agreed-upon performance standards.

In their controversial book *What Price Democracy? Politics, Markets and America's Schools* (Brookings Institution, 1990), John Chubb, of the Brookings Institution, and Terry Moe, a political science professor at Stanford, also advance a plan under which just about anyone would be free to start a school and have it chartered by the state in much the same way that the states now charter private schools. Students would receive vouchers—though that's not the word they use—to be cashed in at whatever school they selected. Children from disadvantaged areas or children with learning disabilities would carry larger scholarships, thus giving schools an incentive to take them. Transportation would be provided at public expense and parents would be assisted in making informed choices. Such a plan, the authors argue, would extend the concept of choice as it now exists and enable private schools to compete with public ones—but within the context of overall public control. "Public-school choice," says Chubb, "is merely a demand-side test. There's no choice on the supply side." Their plan is rooted in their conviction that "autonomy from bureaucratic influence is the strongest individual determinant of school effectiveness." The current system—read factory-model school—is built around control from on high. "The result is that schools are buried in policies, rules, and regulations that specify what they are supposed to be doing and how they are supposed to be doing it," they say. "The only way out is to embrace a new kind of system. It should give schools the legal authority to design their own programs, grant parents the ability to choose any public school, and fund those schools on the basis of their ability to attract students." The goal, they say, is neither to "privatize America's schools" nor to make them less democratic. "Governments would design and operate the system," they argue. "They would make policy decisions about issues from chartering criteria to making sure schools are funded equally. Public education would still be provided by the government—it would just be provided in a different way."

From the point of view of those seeking to promote parental choice within the public framework, the proliferation of plans such as Milwaukee's voucher scheme is a two-edged sword. On the one hand, vouchers reinforce the arguments of opponents who maintain that choice within the public framework is simply the first step toward the diverting of public funds to parochial and other private schools or otherwise undermining the public education system. "Choice is a smokescreen for diverting attention from problems that desperately need more government funds—such as Head

Start," said Gary Marx, the associate executive director of the American Association of School Administrators.

On the other hand, the sense of frustration, even desperation, about the quality of inner-city public schools articulated by Polly Williams and others should serve as a warning to those who are content with the status quo. Unless political and educational leaders find ways to radically transform the way public schools do business—through choice and other means—they will soon find themselves dealing with activists from both the right and left who are ready and willing to scrap the public school system entirely.

One difficulty with the choice debate thus far has been the political overkill of those who view it as a silver bullet for solving all educational problems. Some business leaders accuse the Bush administration of such overkill. "I think choice is a wonderful idea," said Owen B. Butler, chairman of the influential Committee for Economic Development. "But it's no cure-all."

While certainly no cure-all, choice can be a catalyst to promote other desirable values. Pressure to adjust to new parent demands can lead very quickly to shared decision making. Choice forces parental involvement in the school. It requires public schools to reexamine their agendas and to develop new approaches to learning. Choice repudiates the values of the factory-model school—a single, all-inclusive definition of educational quality, a standardized approach to schooling, a single way to organize schools—in favor of genuine diversity, empowerment of teachers, enhanced autonomy, and increased accountability.

Parental choice, though, is only one way in which schools are rethinking their traditional relationship to the communities they serve. Now it's time to look at other ways in which smart schools can forge new ties with their communities.

8.

LEARNING
COMMUNITIES

BY NOW a fundamental question has been raised in the minds of astute readers. It's fine to have an efficient, redesigned school, you say, one where democratic governance, active learning, flexible time, and personal attention are the norm. It's great to empower teachers and parents and to get students to take more responsibility for their own learning. But schools don't exist in a vacuum. How does a teacher engage a kid who comes to school hungry or battered? How do you establish respect for learning when pushers are selling crack down the street from the school? Redesigned schools may do fine if left to themselves, but outside forces can undo the work of the best of them. And the impact of those forces is stronger than ever.

The outside environment in which the factory-model school grew up was relatively stable. Families and churches were strong. There was no television. No one talked about the competing values of a "youth culture." Drugs were not the pervasive problem they are today. Perhaps most important, there was an implicit continuity between the school and other institutions, especially the family. In a very real sense schools functioned *in loco parentis* for that period of the week when students were in their care.

Unfortunately, that sort of stability is no longer out there. Sixty percent of today's students live in families where both parents—or the only parent—work. By 1995 two-thirds of all preschool children, and three out of four school-age youngsters, will have mothers in the labor force. Moreover, the deterioration of the family is so extreme that often there is nothing for which schools can stand *in loco*. Nearly half of all white children live with a divorced mother, and an even higher percentage of black children live with a mother who was never married. For Hispanics the latter proportion is one in three. Households headed by women have an average income of less than $12,000 a year. For many students, schools, for all practical purposes, *are* the family. Then there is the range of other social problems that impact directly on the functioning of schools. One in five children lives under the strain of poverty. The housing shortage is so acute that millions of students have no place to study, and even middle- and upper-middle-class students can come to school unprepared because of the stress their families are undergoing just to work and keep up. Inadequate urban transportation systems make it difficult for parents to become involved in their children's schools. In a country where 25 percent of pregnant women get no prenatal care, schools confront the problems resulting from underweight or crack babies. Social problems are, to be sure, nothing new. Poverty and latchkey children were not invented in the 1980s. But the problems are becoming more pervasive, and for the first time schools truly attempt to reach *all* children, even those caught in a web of social circumstances that makes them difficult to reach or teach.

There is another important way in which the relationship between schools and their environment has changed. The factory-model school was built on the assumption that since education was such a complicated enterprise, it should be left to trained professionals. Parents, by implication, should confine their role to supporting schools with fund-raising bake sales. "With the professionalization of teaching, and particularly of administration," wrote the late Lawrence A. Cremin, the Pulitzer prize-winning historian of American education, "the feeling developed that parents should be held at arm's length and that professionals should make the decisions about what education is best." As in other fields, that approach will no longer wash. Americans in the 1990s have come to distrust professionals in all fields, from medicine to politics. They are not only more willing to question the judgment of professionals but are demanding to play more of a role in decision making themselves. "People are recognizing that the notion that the school can be hermetically sealed and can do it without the parents is an illusion," says Henry Levin of Stanford.

Discussions of the relationship between public schools and their environment have all too often been muddied by two extreme positions. Some political and other leaders seem to view public schools as vehicles for single-handedly addressing every social malaise from racial injustice to the drug epidemic. Overwhelmed by the implication of such an assignment, educators respond by retreating to the opposite extreme. "Just leave us alone," they say, "so that we can do what we are supposed to do—teach children." The first position is clearly unrealistic. No single institution, least of all schools, is in a position to "solve all of society's problems." But the second position is a luxury educators can no longer afford. Schools may not be able to cure all social ills, but to succeed at all in their task of educating the next generation they must find ways of minimizing the negative impact of such problems on the teaching and learning process. To do this, they must find new allies and build new kinds of connections to the communities of which they are a part.

New relationships between schools and the surrounding environment have been seriously under way at least since the mid-1960s, when Congress launched Head Start and other enrichment programs for disadvantaged children and required parental involvement in programs. As discussed in chapter 4, the long-term benefits are now well documented. As important as it is, though, early-childhood education is only part of the answer. Young people must be protected after they leave such early-childhood programs and move on to regular public schools. To do this, schools are looking for new ways to address children's developmental needs, especially of poor and minority-group youngsters, and they are establishing new links both to families and to social service agencies in their communities.

The person who has given as much thought as anyone to these issues is James P. Comer, a psychiatrist who teaches at the Yale Medical School and serves on the staff of the university's Child Study Center. A short man with roundish face and an avuncular, coolly-charismatic manner, Comer, who is black, grew up in poverty in East Chicago, Indiana. Despite the hardships his family faced, his mother, a maid, was determined to get all five of her children through college—a goal that she achieved. Comer graduated from Howard University Medical School, and in 1960, as he was preparing to open his own practice in his hometown, he began to ponder the question of why he and his brothers and sisters had succeeded while most of his childhood friends were either dead or in jail. The answer, he decided, lay primarily in his mother's support but also in the fact that the other adults he knew were "locked into a conspiracy to see that I grew up a responsible person." Comer decided to devote his life to helping children whom society seemed the least willing to provide opportunities for success. "The education of 'at-risk' children is the most important task facing this nation," he said. "I wanted to give other low-income black children the same chance in life that I had." He decided that the public school was the best point of leverage for doing this and then, as he trained for psychiatry at Yale in the mid-1960s, began developing an approach to education that balances social and psychological needs with academic ones.

What has since come to be known as the Comer model or Comer process starts with the assumption that, as he and his brothers and sisters demonstrated, human beings thrive in supportive environments. The problem is that such environments are becoming increasingly rare. Before World War II, when the United States was a nation of small towns and rural areas, there was plenty of interaction between children and adults. Youngsters saw adults at work and in their neighborhoods, and young and old alike had a sense of belonging. "Even if you didn't have a good place, even if you had a low-status place, you had a real sense of place under those conditions, and there was a real sense of community," said Comer. "Everything that the child knew about what was right, wrong, good, and bad, came to him through those authority figures, and that gave them a great deal of power. Because of this interaction, the school was an actual place of the community, and there was an automatic transfer of authority from the home to the school." What so many of today's kids lack, he argues, is this "conspiracy of the entire community" resulting from contact with a variety of adults who can act as legitimate authority figures. "Without this sense of community, our youngsters today are under constant stress—overloaded with information but without models or tools to know how to act," he said. "They often act out in ways that lead to difficulty in school, particularly when school people aren't prepared to deal with the kinds of children with which they are confronted."

The problem of discontinuity is particularly serious for minority youngsters, especially African Americans, according to Comer. Slavery left a legacy of "forced dependency, inherent inferiority, and the conviction that they had no future—probably the three worst things you can impose on any group or individual," said Comer. These effects have been amplified by the devastating impact of urban poverty and the growing importance of education as a "ticket of admission to living-wage jobs." Since education, too, is a legacy, passed down generation to generation and making it easier for each new group of descendants to succeed, educational deprivation has damaged generations of minority youngsters. In 1968, backed by a grant from the Ford Foundation, Comer began working in two schools in New Haven, Connecticut. His strategy was to find ways to bolster the underdeveloped social and psychological needs of disadvantaged students as a precondition to effective academic training.

As Comer saw it, the factory-model school presented three obstacles to his strategy. First, the hierarchical structure made it impossible for them to respond to children's fundamental needs. "The teacher on the front line may see the problems but is powerless to change anything," he said. "Reading, writing, arithmetic, and science are delivered to students in much the same way as tires, windows, and doors are attached to the frame of an automobile on an assembly line." Such an approach, he says, takes no account of the developmental needs of individual children.

Second, there is a fundamental alienation between the world of inner-city children and the world of schools. Some inner-city students come to school without knowing numbers, colors, or even their last name. According to Comer, they lack well-developed body coordination and are not familiar with elementary social conventions, such as how to say "Good morning" or "Thank you." Comer recalled a recent trip to a supermarket where he observed a middle-class toddler discover the automatic door opener. "The parent paused to let him play with it and figure out how he could control the opening and closing of the door," he said. "The kid walked away with a big smile on his face—a real learning experience behind him. Later the same day I was at the airport and heard a low-income kid asking his mother as they went through the X-ray machine: 'What if I say I have a bomb?' The parent told him to shut up, and the kid skulked away. That was a learning experience missed." When they enter public schools, Comer says, "such kids are in foreign territory."

By the age of eight, Comer says, disadvantaged children are sophisticated enough to know that "these people" are different and that they do not belong. "There was never any intention in this society for blacks to participate in the mainstream," wrote Comer in his autobiography, *Maggie's American Dream: The Life and Times of a Black Family* (New American Library, 1988), recalling his own experience as an underclassman at Indiana University in the 1950s. "When I walked to class and crossed fraternity row on Jordan Street, I saw a great big invisible neon sign that read 'No Blacks Allowed.' Affluent students cruised the campus in cars. I had $5 a month as spending money." Moreover poor students are likely to live in neighborhoods where few adults have been success-ful either in school or in life. "Many students," he says, "never see an adult holding a regular job or watch their own parents being taken seriously by anyone in mainline institutions, including schools."

Finally, teachers are not trained to understand the cultural handicaps that poor children bring to school. "Most teachers have very little knowledge about child development, about its impor-tance, and the way to support it in school," says Comer. They have a difficult time relating to inner-city kids, and the children inter-pret their confusion as not caring. "A child whose development meshes with the mainstream values encountered at school will be prepared to achieve at the level of his or her ability. A bond devel-ops between the child and the teacher, who can now join in sup-porting the overall development of a child. A child from a poor, marginal family, in contrast, is likely to enter school without ade-quate preparation." Comer adds that expectations at home and at school are often at odds. "In some families a child who does not fight back will be punished," he said. "And yet the same behavior will get the child into trouble at school."

Comer's own moment of truth on this score came twenty years ago when, working as a child psychiatrist in a school in a low-income section of New Haven, teachers sent him a child who had recently been uprooted from a rural southern community. The child, terrified at his new urban environment, became hostile and bellig-erent. Comer explained to the staff that the child's response was "actually a quite healthy and realistic response to the situation he found himself in." It was the school that needed to change its way of dealing with the child, not the other way around, and to rethink the way it acclimated new children.

Comer set out to liberate the school environment from these obstacles. The basic message that he sought to convey to teachers and administrators in the schools where he worked was that learning involves more than native ability. Success in school is a product of overall development, made possible to a large extent by a child's ability to internalize the values and ways of significant adults. Since most youngsters lacked the psychological security that he and his siblings had known, schools had to provide it. "We had to create a school where people understood the developmental needs of the children and could establish a relationship between home and school that would enhance them," he recalled.

His first step was to chuck the traditional rigid, insensitive hierarchical management system and involve the entire community in the running of the schools. Comer schools—there are now more than one hundred of them around the country—are run by a "governing council" of teachers, counselors, and parents, headed by the principal. The second step was to bring parents actively into the life of the school and thus create a "shared sense of purpose between parents and staff." Parents are part of the governing council, but their participation in social events is equally important because this provides the opportunity for parents and teachers to interact in relaxed and positive ways where social differences can be minimized. Parents are also encouraged to become classroom assistants, tutors, or aides. "It's important for low-income youngsters to see their parents taken seriously by mainstream institutions," he said. The third and final step is to make this partnership more knowledgeable and effective by establishing a "mental health" team to assist the governing council in each school. The mental health team consists of guidance counselors, school psychologists, special-education teachers, nurses, and classroom teachers and meets regularly to discuss the developmental needs of individual children and how to combat problems.

One school that has implemented the Comer model over a period of time is the Columbia Park Elementary School in Landover, Maryland, a northeast suburb of Washington. Patricia Green, the principal, recalls her first day on the job in 1985. She pulled into the parking lot at the back of the school, where there was a huge dumpster, surrounded by rubber tires and other garbage, with a great big mattress hanging out of it. Dead trees lined the lot. Inside, the school was clean but stark. Instead of children's paintings, the halls were filled with faded pictures of the school in years gone by. But it was the windows that really got to the new principal. They were made of Plexiglas and over the years had become opaque. No one could see into the school, and no one could see out. "It was symbolic," said Green.

The first person to meet her at the door was the building supervisor, who stuck out his hand to her in welcome. It turned out that he cared about the school and had ideas about what to do to fix up the place, but no one had ever asked what he thought. Parents had had similar experiences. Green discovered that there had been a Parent-Teachers Association, at least on paper, but that it had no active members. Teachers explained to the principal that the parents didn't want to be involved, but parents told her a different tale. "They said they weren't wanted," she recalled. In their own way, teachers had also been neglected. They were short on supplies, yet Green discovered a bank account with unspent funds for just this purpose. The ultimate victims of this atmosphere, of course, were the children. A look at the records revealed that sizable numbers of elementary-age children, eighteen to thirty-two students, were being suspended from school every year.

Two other things happened during Green's first two years. First, Green heard James Comer give a speech. "What struck me was the way he talked about the development of children and the need to involve parents in the school," she said. She began the program with no additional funds. But then the second year the school was given extra funding to compensate for being racially unbalanced. So Green decided to use the additional funds to try out the Comer method, starting with greater parental involvement.

The principal invited parents to a meeting, which drew a standing-room-only crowd. That signaled to Green that parents were interested. She invited them to start working with her to make Columbia Park a better school. One of the first parents to sign up was Virginia Walker. For years she had been rebuffed in efforts to become involved in her children's school. "Did they need room mothers?" Walker would ask. "No," she was told. "Would they like help with the science fair?" "No, thank you, we have it covered." At that first meeting called by Green, Walker remembers being terrified. "There I was, dressed in jeans, sitting down with all those people who had four to six more years of education than I had," she said. At first she didn't say a word. But everyone in the room was invited to ask questions and brainstorm about how to improve the school. Walker felt strongly about the school's dismissal procedures. Younger children were let out first, which meant they milled about, sometimes frightened and crying, until their older siblings arrived to take them home. So Walker found the courage to stand up and ask why it was done this way. At first the staff became defensive and said, "We've always done it this way." The net result, though, was a decision to change the dismissal routine so that the older children are released first and leave as soon as their younger brothers and sisters come out of the building.

This seemingly trivial issue signaled to the parents that their opinions did matter. Walker and other parents started knocking on doors, visiting churches, and holding breakfasts and lunches at the school to get parents to meetings to talk about school matters. The school counselor went to local employers and asked the management to release parents from work to tutor in the school.

With parents now actively involved in the school, Green moved to set up the Comer-style "governing council." Columbia Park calls its council the SPMT, a.k.a. the School Planning and Management Team. Its members are the principal and representatives of groups with a stake in the school—teachers, parents, instructional aides, counselors, and representatives of the custodial and secretarial staffs. This team is charged with setting goals for the school, developing a plan to meet them, and providing ongoing assessment to see if the goals are being met.

At first the governing team addressed some easy problems. Parents were intimidated by the school handbook, a forty-five-page "Gospel According to Columbia Park" that was strong on preaching to parents but weak in specific information on such basic matters as the school schedule. The handbook was redesigned. Then the dead trees were cut down, and the teachers got the supplies they lacked— fans in the classroom for sweltering hot days, a new typewriter and copying machine, paper and supplies. New energy was infused into the PTA. Then the SPMT tackled the hard problems—such as reading scores, the math curriculum, and discipline.

Finally, the governing council put in place the most unusual part of the Comer model, the mental health team. In keeping with its penchant for unpronounceable acronyms, Columbia Park calls it the SSST, or Student Staff Services Team. The team is composed of a psychologist, a social worker, a special-education teacher, a reading teacher or speech-and-hearing therapist, a counselor, a community health nurse, parents, and the classroom teacher as well as the principal. They are, in a nutshell, child advocates who intervene in the school setting on the child's behalf. They work with individual teachers in identifying and preventing academic, disciplinary, emotional, family, and other sorts of problems. The team meets weekly and functions independently of the governing team, though one member of the mental health team serves on the governing group. As a member of the team, the school's social worker, Betty Young-Barkley, has the job of functioning as a liaison between a student's home and school and other community agencies. "Basically I find out why a child's not learning, then do what is necessary to mediate the situation," she explained. "I can then link the schools and social agencies together."

The working of the Comer process can be illustrated by the story of a first-grader whom we'll call Robert. A few years ago Robert's teacher advised John Haslinger, the guidance counselor at Columbia Park, that the youngster was having problems. Robert was aggressive toward other children, sometimes stabbing them in the ear with a pencil. He ran away from school and sometimes wet his pants. Haslinger began to observe the child and saw that he was using what he calls attention-getting devices. "He'd pour chocolate milk over his mashed potatoes at lunch and go 'Aaahhh,'" said Haslinger. "Childish misbehaviors, but we were clearly not getting through to him educationally, and he was falling behind." The teacher told the counselor she wasn't sure what was going on. "Is the child acting out in class to manipulate me?" she wondered. "Or is he trying to get attention? Is it attention from me or from the students?" Haslinger thought the child was having a hard time adjusting to school—something that is not unusual for first-graders. Sometimes, just by talking to them, he can identify their concerns and "get a quick turnaround." But it might also be that Robert was having troubles at home as well. So Haslinger called in Robert's mother for a chat with him and the teacher.

. The threesome decided that the reasons for Robert's acting out lay deeper than merely a desire for attention. "He felt inadequate and was retreating," said Haslinger. "He was saying, 'I am not going to try. I give up. It's no use. I always fail.' " More conferences with the mother followed. They talked about parenting styles and how Robert's mother could be more effective in enforcing discipline. "It's not that he wasn't being disciplined," said Haslinger. "It just wasn't working." The school put Robert on an "assertive discipline program," a form of behavior modification used by many of the Comer schools. The staff encouraged his mother to enter into a "contract" with Robert spelling out various rewards and punishments for good and bad behavior. Good behavior meant a trip to the park or the 7-Eleven. "Checks," for negative behavior, meant the loss of television or going to bed earlier. By late into the first grade Robert's bladder was under control, but he still continued to have difficulty paying attention. Clearly the behavior contracts were not doing the job.

At that point Robert's problems were referred to the SSST team, which met with Robert's mother. She seemed to underestimate the extent of her son's problems. "She was not buying into the suggested solutions," said Young-Barkley, the social worker. The team suggested some outside counseling, but the mother replied that she did not have the time. Then one day the team held a long conference with Robert and his mother. "We asked him to describe his behavior toward his mother," recalled Young-Barkley. "We talked about what we could do to bring him around. He was already on a behavior plan. We'd made modifications. What must we do? All of a sudden the youngster blurted out he wanted more time with a particular teacher—his homeroom teacher. He wanted more individual attention from her in class. It was a breakthrough. It was something the team had been missing, but it was something the child needed. So he got it."

Robert's mother asked the social worker to observe her child in class, which she did. The team arranged for Robert to be rewarded for positive behavior with the chance to do art on his own. His classroom behavior improved, and the teacher began working with his classmates to help them get along better with him. "Sometimes kids need to learn how to be a friend to other kids," said Young-Barkley, herself a former teacher. "This teacher was helping him be a better friend, and she was having other kids work with him in a cooperative way." The school upped its ante. The school staff started making phone calls to Robert's mother when he was good. "He loved getting a few words of praise from Mom," said Haslinger. "We worked hard for that. Sometimes it takes a while to figure out what a kid will work for. Almost any kid wants to make their family proud. Sometimes we just need to get that feeling across at home." Various members of the team continued to work with the mother, encouraging her to be affectionate and to reinforce positive acts while punishing negative ones. In essence the team was teaching parenting skills. "A lot of parents do things to tear down their child's sense of confidence," said Haslinger. "It's not huge abuse. But in this case Mom needed to let the kid know he had unconditional love, even when he misbehaved. She had to say, 'I love you' instead of 'You did it again; that's just the kind of person you are.' Parenting skills and childrearing are on-the-job training. You have to wait until a kid is grown to see if you are doing the job right. My role as someone in child development is to give parents guideposts." The beauty of the Comer process, to Haslinger's mind, is that the school works more closely with parents than it has in the past, and it means parents hear not just negative things about their child but positive ones as well. They are drawn into the problem. The school doesn't just solve it. "It's more effective, better for both of us," he said. "Nobody knows the child like the parents do. It's absurd to leave them out of the solutions."

With Robert the techniques began suddenly to take hold. Once he found success for a fairly long period of time he began to go two or three days without a troubling incident. At first, if he made it through half a day at school with no problems, his mom would get a phone call at lunchtime. When he made it through an afternoon, too, she got a call in the afternoon. Mom was coached on what to say: "I am proud of you. You are a good kid." "The kid needed to hear it," said Haslinger. "His drawings, for example, showed him as the devil with horns on his head. His self-esteem was in the basement. But after a couple of days of getting good calls, it nudged a doubt in his mind that maybe he was not worthless. And Mom was confirming it by saying, 'You are an okay guy. Just change a few things you are doing.' This gave him the confidence, finally, to go for a third day in a row with no problems. On the fourth day in a row, I'll never forget it, he came up to me and shouted, 'I am going to go for fifty days, then a hundred days.' His arm was raised in the air like a champion. And he did it!" said Haslinger. "He became a good kid, a success story. It's very gratifying."

As a result of the Comer process—with its emphasis on child development, parental involvement, and a team approach to problem solving—Robert went on to become a model student at Columbia Park. What would have happened to him otherwise? "He might have lucked into a mentor somewhere along the way, a football coach perhaps," said Haslinger. "But he would have been miserable all the way through school, and how much school would he have lost getting to that point, to turning himself around? It might not have been until he was flipping hamburgers later in life. But the Comer process shows you how to turn kids around early enough so they can still catch up educationally. This kid will put this memory behind him. There is no telling how far he can go."

To Young-Barkley the key element is that "conspiracy of the entire community" that Comer experienced as a boy and to which he attributes his own success. "My role was as liaison between home and school—to get everybody working with this kid, working for the same benefit," she said. "The Comer process means that everyone has the same goal—parents, the kid, teacher, other teachers, and everybody sees us working collectively. In this case there was a lot of talking, but we were all going in the same direction. We weren't at odds. We were all saying the same thing in the end and trying to be supportive. Nothing is guaranteed to work. If one thing doesn't work, do something else. The difference with Comer is that he has involved the parents more and has said that there are *significant others* in a child's life who should be consulted and involved. We haven't always done that. Everybody who can be of assistance should be of assistance, and we use that now. If a kid relates to a custodian, we involve the custodian. Whoever the kid relates to, that is what is important. You still work with the parent, and you work with all the other people."

The problems that the SSSTs deal with—and the insights they come up with to help solve them—vary widely. Pete, for example, was a youngster who was having a hard time in school. He was cross, anxious, and unable to concentrate. After members of the team observed him in his classroom, they decided that he was simply dealing with too many adults on a given day. "His day was too fragmented," said Young-Barkley. So his academic program was redesigned so that he did not have to change settings so often during the day. Then there was Jason, a kindergartner who was stumbling frequently in school and prompted teachers to wonder if he was having seizures. "No," said his mother. "Jason is just a little slow developmentally, like all our children at first." But Young-Barkley persisted and persuaded the mother to visit the school and observe her child with other children. Finally the mother took the child to a physician. The child did need medical attention and a prescription. "Even parents don't always see the problems," she said.

Not long ago a Columbia Park teacher noticed that Jack, a second-grader, was coming to school tired each morning. The child lived nine blocks from the school, normally within walking distance. Young-Barkley visited the mother and urged her to take him to the doctor. It turned out Jack had a health problem and has since missed a good deal of school. The social worker knew that the child would qualify for a special service in the school district for children with chronic health problems, so she arranged for a teacher to visit his home when he was sick and for transportation to the school when he was well enough to attend. "The child wanted to be in school," said Young-Barkley. "It's our job to get him there."

One of the things that makes such intervention possible is that, under the Comer approach, teachers become comfortable working with all children in a school, not just their own class. "With the team meetings there is an openness and sharing of problems, so teachers don't feel threatened," said Young-Barkley. "They know that just because they share a problem doesn't mean they aren't a good teacher. It's healthy. We educate youngsters collectively. Everybody in contact with a child has a role to play—everybody, including the custodian or the teacher. The youngsters look to all adults as people who are there for them. That makes the difference. The children's attitude is that the school is a place they want to be."

To Grace Knox, a fifth-grade teacher and twenty-year veteran at Columbia Park, having a team of experts at her disposal has been a godsend. When a child has trouble reading, she takes this problem to others on the team to see what she might do differently. Sometimes they suggest a different kind of testing or a modification in her reading instruction. Sometimes a child is referred, at their suggestion, to a tutoring program, or they suggest that she pair a child with another student or cut back on the number of written assignments. Because she can make use of this team of experts on a regular and systematic basis, Knox feels her own effectiveness has improved. "I feel more support," she said. "I feel free to call parents and ask for assistance where needed. There used to be times when I called parents and I felt threatened and assumed I wasn't going to get cooperation. I would make parents feel defensive, that I was criticizing their child. But now that parents are part of the picture, we keep them informed a lot more and provide positive communication weekly. Since parents feel good about what's going on in school, they don't hesitate to come in if there is a problem. Parents stand behind me."

Virginia Walker, the once-hesitant parent, knows the impact this had on her own children. She feels the Comer process changes not only the way parents and teachers relate to each other but the way children feel about themselves. Because they get lots of praise and old-fashioned discipline, they appear more secure, and their self-esteem is improved. Her daughter Dina would have been a problem in school, she feels, were it not for the Comer approach of putting parents on the team. "At first she was getting in trouble," said Walker. "She received no good positive response at school, which was making her worse. She was nasty with the teacher. But I wasn't aware of what was going on, except that she was in trouble. When Comer came in, I became involved. The teacher and I worked together on this child. She went on to the honor roll. Before, if she goofed up in school, she knew the home would never find out about it until she was bordering on suspension. But once they involved me, she knew the home and the school were working together." Walker's second child, Tina, was gifted and sensitive. But she was easily bored and came home from school crying. She wasn't a behavior problem, but she was having difficulties. With the Comer process the school came up with a plan to give Tina extra things to do. She helped the teacher, took extra programs. Walker feels that before the Comer process teachers could not have addressed her problem.

Today Columbia Park test scores are up, and there has been a steady increase in math and reading. Suspension of students is down to two or three a year. School attendance has improved. The school was recognized by the U.S. Department of Education for excellence, and a huge banner hangs in the school foyer announcing this achievement. And Walker, once terrified, now gives workshops around the county on parent involvement.

Jan Stocklinski, who directs the implementation of the Comer process for the Prince Georges County school district, sees its strength in the fact that it provides schools with a "structure" for handling complex situations. "There are lots of good things happening already in school, but schools don't have structured time to tie all the strings together," she says. "The old way in old schools was the principal would say, 'Now you do this and you do that.' With the Comer process, schools are a think tank. Everybody says, 'These are our children, not just the children of you, the principal.' The answers to problems come in the strength of many of us together." Another key to Comer's success is the way in which he improves the quality of relationships. "He teaches you to look at things with a no-fault approach instead of saying, 'This is your fault or your fault,' " said Green. "You strip away layers of alienation on both sides and start building instead of worrying about whose fault it is; everything we do is in the child's best interest."

The transition to the Comer process at Columbia Park and other Prince Georges County schools was by no means smooth. Many of the schools had physical needs that had to be met before anyone could focus on core educational problems. Some teachers disliked the program and went elsewhere. Perhaps most important, there was the sheer volume and magnitude of the problems facing the mental health teams. "It was like opening a dam," said Stocklinski. One result was that the SSST teams ended up getting pigeonholed into dealing with the special-education referrals and the behavior problems that teachers wanted taken out of their classrooms. The Comer staff kept insisting that troublesome students not be transferred out of the school and kept encouraging teachers to work together to help these children.

No experienced teacher was ever prepared for the Comer model in teacher-education courses, so retraining teachers became a major priority. Teachers took courses in child development so that when a problem arose, they could ask themselves, "Are we meeting this child's needs?" Many teachers began to infuse multicultural education into the curriculum, and there have been workshops and training programs on ways to involve black males in the school. Teachers at the William Wirt School took a crash course on adolescent growth and development so that they would better understand the growth of their children.

Likewise, Comer staff have been working with school psychologists and social workers to increase their knowledge of education or curriculum, how to teach thinking skills, and other educational matters. Young-Barkley, the social worker, is taking a class on "thinking skills" in children. The objective is to give both teachers and social workers overlapping training so that the social problems in a child's life can be addressed to improve the intellectual side.

Green has her master's degree in child growth and development and sees it as the job of the school to help children develop cognitively, socially, emotionally, and morally. To her that is what the Comer process enables schools to do. "It is their job to focus on child development," she says, "to appreciate the uniqueness of each child, and find ways in which that uniqueness grows and interfaces with society. It means meeting a youngster at any age and working with them, not so they will be the exact duplicate of another child, but so they can develop and grow and prosper with the school's support and guidance."

Comer's ideas are now catching on. The Comer process has already been adopted by more than one hundred schools in nine districts in eight states. The New Haven school system has expanded it to include all forty-two schools in the eighteen-thousand-pupil system. The Rockefeller Foundation will spend nearly $8 million over the next five years to help schools implement the Comer approach, with the major thrust in the District of Columbia and other large school systems. Southern Connecticut State University, a chief source of teachers for the New Haven schools, has revised much of its curriculum to include principles of the Comer program so that it can be easily replicated in other schools of education and school systems. A new institute, based at Yale, will train senior school officials in the workings of the Comer process so that they, in turn, can establish teams in their own districts. A series of "how to" videos is also being created to spread the word.

This expansion is being fueled by new evidence of its success. In 1981 a federal judge ordered schools in Benton Harbor, Michigan, to adopt Comer's School Development Program as a way of saving the rapidly disintegrating and racially troubled school district. The result was significant improvement in student performance and behavior. Suspensions in schools using the Comer approach dropped 8 percent while rising 34 percent in the district as a whole. Similarly, students in the Comer schools excelled in reading and mathematics. In reading, the average gain in the Comer schools equaled that of the district as a whole at the second-grade level. But at the fifth- and sixth-grade levels, the Comer schools, on the average, surpassed districtwide averages.

While Comer approaches the relationship between schools and their environment from a developmental and psychological point of view, others are taking more of a sociological approach. To them the key to protecting the educational enterprise from a hostile environment is to make the school into a center for child advocacy. Since traditional sources of support for the child—the family, the neighborhood, social and religious organizations, nutritional and health care programs—are either fragmented or do not exist at all, the school must step into the vacuum.

One such approach can be found at the Corporate Community School on the west side of Chicago. This school is the brainchild of Joe Kellman, a seventy-one-year-old businessman and philanthropist who dropped out of school at age fourteen to help his father run the family glass company, now a $100 million-a-year business. Kellman looks vaguely like a lean Albert Einstein with glasses. He possesses both a down-to-earth vocabulary and a sense of humor that once sustained him through his proudest accomplishment: a week of stand-up comedy in Cleveland backing up his friend Buddy Hackett. Twenty years ago Kellman became convinced that the country was, in his words, "going mad." "We're investing more money in prisons than in schools," he said. "If we don't figure out how to educate African Americans and Hispanics in our inner cities, then we can kiss our democratic society good-bye." His solution was to recruit business leaders willing to use their management expertise in the service of education and to develop models that could be replicated by public schools. Three years ago Kellman hit pay dirt when he enlisted Vernon R. Loucks, Jr., chairman of Baxter International Inc., to mobilize Sears, United Airlines, Quaker Oats, and other powerful Chicago businesses to create a tuition-free private school on the city's devastated west side. They came up with almost $3 million, and in August 1989 the Corporate Community School welcomed its first 150 children, chosen by lottery, into the spanking-clean classrooms of a former parochial school.

The executive-dominated board hired Elaine Mosley, a former elementary school principal in Oak Park, Illinois, to serve as "chief executive officer," a.k.a. principal, on a three-year contract. Her mandate was to provide quality education at the same cost per pupil as the Chicago public schools. She will be judged by how well students do on tests and other measures. "If she doesn't perform, she will be let go," Kellman said. The atmosphere that Mosley created is as gentle and child-centered as the management is hard-nosed and results-oriented. Parents can drop off their children as early as 7:00 A.M., pick them up as late as 7:00 P.M., and can stay at the school themselves to work on a high school equivalency diploma. The school runs year-round, with three weeks of summer vacation. Students as young as two are accepted. Teachers, who receive merit pay, work in teams.

The Corporate School has set itself up as the "hub"—the center in a network of social agencies. The network, at last count, includes approximately seventy organizations dealing with issues such as health, social services, recreation, and housing. The key player in this is the school nurse, who is known as a "Hub Coordinator." In most public schools the nurse, when there is one, is peripheral to a child's life. She—it seems it's always a she—spends at most one day a week at a school and handles the most critical of problems: checking for inoculations, reporting incidents of child abuse, referring the most severe learning problems to other programs or schools. At many schools daily problems and basic health issues go largely unattended, and the school stands isolated from the vast medical facilities available in this country.

At the Corporate School the nurse is a full-time member of the faculty. During the school's first year, Phyllis Pelt, a certified school nurse, made the role a highly visible one. Along with the rest of the staff she greets parents when they bring their students to school and when they pick them up—a requirement at the school for younger students. The point is to have the nurse get to know the parents as individuals, to establish rapport with them so that when she has a critical health issue to discuss with them, they will already know and trust her.

Pelt looks at the school as a consummate health professional. Every day she observes parents and students. She has trained teachers to spot possible health problems. Students might need glasses, a visit to the dentist, food, sleep, protection from sexual or emotional abuse, or just reassurance that they can sit through reading even with a case of the jitters. Pelt does not see health and wellness as a frill. "If a child has a health problem, it is a barrier to learning," she said. "Teachers can't help a child become a powerful learner if that child is constantly absent from school. Parents cannot focus on their child's education if they are cold, living in a house with no heat, or fearful with no locks on the doors."

At the Corporate School all staff members view themselves as the family's advocates—even, or perhaps especially, when a child's problem is rooted in his or her family. One day Pelt noticed that Andrea's mother, who drove her to school, sometimes seemed intoxicated. Andrea also had occasional bruises. So Pelt called the parent into her office. "You know," she said in her calm, soothing voice, "drinking is a health problem. And I noticed that when you came to school today, you had alcohol on your breath. It is not safe for you or your child if you are driving and you have been drinking. We're worried about you. Your child is depending on you, but you can't drive. Is there something we could do? Is there someone we can call?" The woman denied she had a problem, but the next day she had a niece bring the girl to school. Pelt saw that as a step in the right direction. The woman had realized she couldn't drive. The following day the mother called Pelt and said, "I had been drinking. I do have a problem." Pelt and the mother talked about it. The woman said she had been in Alcoholics Anonymous, but it didn't work. Then she moved and did not know whom to call. From her office Pelt helped the mother make the first call to AA and became her source of encouragement. One week went by, and the mother was bringing Andrea to school, sober. Another week went by. The mother continued her sobriety. Week after week she did not have a drink. "I am getting better now," she told the nurse in appreciation.

Pelt knows that abuse is likely to occur after a holiday or

weekend. She monitors attendance because that is how the school believes it is likely to find out what is going on. By 9:30 A.M. the school has made contact with the family of an absent child to find out why the child is not in school. The school started parental stress classes and then follow-up parental support groups. All classes for parents are offered in two shifts, one during the day, one in the evening. There are also school family meetings. At first Pelt used little enticements to get parents into the school on a regular basis. First-aid kits, donated by a corporation, were handed out at one meeting after a talk on first aid. She offered classes with catchy titles: "Fire and Teeth," for example. How are they related? "You can't ignore either fire safety or your teeth," she explained. A foundation donated fire detectors for the parents. Pelt established a partnership with the University of Illinois Dental School to check the teeth of all students and their parents, and she discovered that a quarter of the children had more than three cavities. She arranged for a corporation to donate the $1,000 eye-screening machine so that she could test everyone's eyes. She discovered one nine-year-old child's parent had arranged for him to be absent from school three years in a row when eyes were tested to avoid having to pay for glasses. The child could not see the printed page. Pelt contacted a local optometrist who gave families a "two-for-one" deal.

Pelt notes that such practices are already recommendations of the American School Health Association. The American Dental Society, for example, suggests that everyone brush their teeth three times a day. Yet, she asks, how many schools have students brush their teeth after breakfast or lunch? At the Corporate School students do so after every lunch. The school banned sugar snacks—it was harder on the teachers than on the children—and urged parents to stop buying soft drinks for their families at home. Pelt substituted stickers to be used as bribes and yogurt, cream cheese, and apple cider as snacks. She noted that the American Medical Association strongly recommends six glasses of water a day. But at many schools, she notes, the drinking fountains don't work. At the Corporate School she made water a priority. Everyone takes water breaks.

If a child has miscellaneous aches and pains, Pelt has a motto: "There Is No Secondary Gain to Being Sick at School." She checks out a child thoroughly and takes the child's temperature and some-times discovers the child is just afraid of sitting through reading. At a typical school the child is likely to be sent home and miss half a day of school. Once Pelt determines the root of the stomachache, she sits with the child in class until the child feels comfortable about remaining there. "Students learn to control their anxiety so they can focus on learning," she states.

Most of this is common sense, Pelt points out, and is actually an attempt to make use of existing resources in a community. In many cases parents do not know how to access the resources available to them. She helps parents get information about food stamps, for example, or medical facilities and insurance. The school can be the hub of information for them. "If students have drugs out of their homes, food in their stomachs, their basic med-ical needs attended to, they are not preoccupied in school," said Pelt. "It frees their minds to get the information they need about reading, writing, and arithmetic. You eliminate their barriers to learning. That should be one of the school's main jobs. It is a ho-listic approach to education."

This school year Pelt turned her job at the Corporate School over to a new nurse, Mary Banks, and the school continues to refine its mission as a "hub" in a network of social agencies. Meanwhile, Pelt now works in a public school district closer to her home.

Nor is it just the inner-city schools that feel the ill effects of problems plaguing America's youth. For example, at affluent Penn High School in Mishawaka, Indiana, with its mixture of rural and suburban students, the demand for social services and counseling assistance is high. "We are going out to the school system and doing family counseling on alcoholism and other problems," said A. Dean Speicher, superintendent of schools of the Penn-Harris-Madison School Corporation and a former president of the American Asso-ciation of School Administrators. "We've bought services from them, and they are part of our staff in schools." Students at the high-tech school have complex and deep social and psychological needs that may not be obvious to those around them. "Five years ago we didn't have much interaction, or we probably weren't very sen-sitive to services that were available to our community in terms of social agencies," said Speicher. "Now we have major partnerships and coalitions with all kinds of social agencies. Our district doesn't get much state money, because the perception is that we don't have kids 'at risk.' But as a matter of fact, I know a lot of affluent kids who are at risk for a whole set of different reasons than poor kids. Thus, we are building all kinds of relationships with family counseling centers. It is not just for kids, but families. That's the wave of the future."

One person who has advanced the idea nationwide of public schools as centers of services to families is Edward Zigler, a professor of psychology at Yale University, who was a founder of Head Start and has labored for many years as an advocate of the rights of young children. Like his faculty colleague, James Comer, Zigler is troubled by the impact of outside forces on schools, especially those that undermine students' families. His solution is to use schools not only for teaching but also as centers for preschool education, day care, parent education, family support counseling, and other social services designed to bolster family life. "The three major influences on a child's growth and development are the family, the school, and the youngster's child-care system," he said. "How well a child does in school depends on the child-care system in the five years before school." Zigler's goal is to make the school, *qua* institution, an integrating force in the community—especially for its own students and teachers. He calls his model Schools of the Twenty-first Century.

Implicit in Zigler's approach is a fundamental assumption: Just because something is located in a school building does not mean that the public school system has to control it. This is an important affirmation—one with a long political history. For many years the teachers unions battled with the day-care community over preschool education. It was a battle for political control, but also one with philosophical overtones. Was early-childhood education an upward extension of the family or a downward extension of schooling? Each side accused the other of shortsightedness and naïveté. The child-development specialists argued that day care should be viewed as an upward extension of the family and that, put in the hands of elementary school teachers, it would be turned into kindergarten for three-year-olds. Schoolteachers, they said, are not likely to respect the importance of unstructured play and other developmental needs of young children. Educators, however, replied that putting a preschool or latchkey program in a school building does not mean that it becomes just another pedagogical enterprise. That battle has now largely been resolved, with both sides acknowledging that they can work together without having to control everything.

One of the first of Zigler's Schools of the Twenty-first Century is the Dr. Ramon Emeterio Betances School, located in a tough downtown section near the state capitol in Hartford, Connecticut. The school is open thirteen hours a day, providing before- and after-school day care for the children of working parents. Its Family Resource Center runs a full-day child-care program for three- and four-year-olds and in Saturday workshops trains women to provide day care in their own homes for younger children. Others give childrearing advice to new parents. The center also offers counseling and referral services to families and will soon begin programs in teenage pregnancy prevention and adult education.

The principal of Betances is Edna Negron, a former specialist in bilingual education who is constantly reminded, in big ways and little, of the social burdens that her students bear. Talking with a visitor in her office, she heard the sound of a child crying and paused to listen. "It was a sad cry, not an 'I'm in danger—help me' cry," she remarked. "It's important to learn to tell the cries apart." The reasons for the help-me cries are not hard to find. "We have children from severely limited environments. They see an awful lot in terms of drugs and crime and abuse," she said. "Before day care, I had latchkey kids with keys around their necks going home to the most dangerous neighborhoods in the city. We have children of addicts who are essentially disturbed at birth and unable to bond with anyone. The first thing we have to address is trust." Then there are the deprivations stemming from poverty that complicate learning. "Physical exercise, the development of large and small motor skills, is important for reading and writing," said Negron. "But we have had fifth- and sixth-graders who couldn't jump rope, and when the phys-ed teacher tried to start a soccer league, he had kids who couldn't run and kick at the same time." Cultural stimulation is another problem. "Families don't talk to their children," said Negron. "We have kids who arrive at kindergarten unable to put together a sentence."

It is 7:30 A.M., more than an hour before school begins, when Joshua Rodriguez, six, arrives with his sister, Bianca, three, at his side. Joshua heads for the child center on the school's ground floor, where he plays with friends. Bianca sits at a table coloring pictures. Bianca will stay all day. Joshua, a first-grader, goes to classes but returns to the center when school ends at 3:00 P.M. Bianca is handing out paper towels to other three- and four-year-olds, who wash their hands before eating a breakfast of cereal, milk, and juice. "Sit in a circle," she says to the others as a teacher assistant counts out eight towels. One by one the children wash their hands and then eat breakfast in a spacious, carpeted room, where walls are lined with brightly colored posters of numbers, colors, and shapes. Bianca, a tiny girl with deep brown eyes and black hair pulled into a ponytail, is dressed up for school. Their mother, Carmen Rodriguez, who is divorced and has a full-time job at the Connecticut Natural Gas Company, picks them up at 5:00 P.M. She says it is comforting to know her children are safe at a school right down the street from where she lives. "This is the school for her," she says. "She wants to come on Saturday and Sunday." Parents pay anywhere from nothing to $98 a week for the day care, depending on family size and income.

The day care center is run by La Casa de Puerto Rico, a community agency. It enrolls nineteen preschoolers and twenty-five school-age children and has a waiting list. More than just a baby-sitting service, it provides stimulation, exercise, and socialization that help prepare children for school. "Without Betances, I would take them to a baby-sitter or a relative or someone, but they probably would watch TV all day or sleep a lot," said Rodriguez. To Zigler, linking public schools to day care is not only an efficient use of public schools and a sensible response to the growing need for day care but an educational necessity. "Children who grow and thrive in good-quality care-giving settings are likely to become productive members of society," he said. "It is in the nation's self-interest to make sure that every child receives good child care as well as a good education. We are losing a generation of our children. I can guarantee you if a child has had five lousy years of child care, that child will not be ready for school."

Laura Lundgren-D'Oleo was in charge of a program that benefited even younger children—offering childrearing advice to first-time parents. "A lot of parents just wing it," she commented one day as she drove to visit Kimberly Long, the mother of a twenty-two-month-old son and a two-month-old daughter. Long, twenty-four, lives with Leonard Hicks, the children's father. She heard about the program from a nurse at Hartford Hospital, where her daughter was born prematurely. In a tiny third-floor apartment in a run-down neighborhood in Hartford's North End, Long proudly held her daughter on her lap, telling Lundgren-D'Oleo that Takeisha was gaining weight and recovering from a cold. She also told the worker that her son, Franklin, still tested her patience sometimes, though she was learning how to deal with him. Sometimes, she said, she asked Franklin to help care for his new sister. "When you ask him to get a diaper and powder, that's perfect for him because it's building self-esteem," Lundgren-D'Oleo said. Franklin, wearing a New York Yankees cap cocked back on his head, scooted across the floor on a plastic fire truck and spilled a bag of chips. His mother reacted calmly. "Now slow down so you don't hurt yourself," she said. Long said Lundgren-D'Oleo had become a friend. "She's been teaching me how to relate to him. I felt like anything he did wrong, I was supposed to holler and scream and spank him. I might have been going about it wrong." The cries of a baby in another apartment could be heard as Lundgren-D'Oleo left. As she drove back to Betances, she commented, "This is really something a lot of parents could use."

Betances also functions in an advocacy role. Take, for example, the case of a first-grade boy who had difficulty adjusting to school and often misbehaved in class. "We thought he was learning-disabled," said Negron. "He couldn't focus. He couldn't function." Then one day he came to school with bruises, and the principal suspected parental abuse. After meeting with the boy's mother, along with a social worker and a nurse, Negron learned that the boy's father had struck him. She also learned that the father, who was unemployed, was undergoing treatment for paranoid schizophrenia. "The mom broke down, and she asked for help," Negron said. By placing her first-grade son, her third-grade son, and her preschool daughter in Betances's day-care program, the woman was able to obtain a full-time job. In addition the Family Resource Center put her in touch with a psychologist, who counseled the family. "The change was dramatic in the kids and in her," Negron said. "It kept the family together. This center is a godsend."

The call to the psychologist was just one example of an estimated 150 referrals made by the Family Resource Center during its first year, according to Carmen DeRusha of La Casa de Puerto Rico. Many of the referrals are for day-care programs for children less than three years old, too young for its own program. Staff members answer questions and make referrals on issues such as child-custody cases, rent assistance, housing, and child-support payments. Because everyone in the office speaks Spanish, the center has been used increasingly by the large Puerto Rican population in the neighborhoods around Betances. "Word of mouth is starting to work," said DeRusha. "People call places they feel familiar with. Sometimes they call the school because they know Betances has something for the family."

Connecticut was the first state to link schools to social services in 1987, when it enacted legislation setting up pilot schools in North Branford and Killingly as well as Hartford. In 1984 Missouri became the first state to mandate that every district offer a program of parenting education to the families of infants and preschoolers. A follow-up study found that at the end of the first grade, children involved in Missouri's pilot project scored significantly higher on reading and math tests than a comparison group and had parents who were more involved in their education.

Since then, thirty-two states have launched similar efforts, most of them on a smaller scale. Individual schools are using Zigler's approach in Colorado, North Carolina, and Wyoming. Arkansas, like Missouri, has created a program to help parents prepare youngsters for learning before they reach school age. South Carolina and California have adopted policies of reaching out to parents once their children begin school. Like Connecticut, New York is experimenting with efforts to place comprehensive services for families within school buildings. As part of its omnibus school reform package (see chapter 9), Kentucky has begun setting up a Family Resource Center at or near every elementary school with 20 percent or more poor students and a Youth Service Center at every middle and high school. Within six years, officials expect to have nearly five hundred such centers.

Other states are arriving at similar programs from a very different direction. In recent years health and social service providers across the country have begun looking for ways to coordinate their efforts. They find that, especially in severely disadvantaged urban and rural areas, children and families frequently have multiple problems. Alcoholism or drug addiction can go hand in hand with homelessness or child abuse. Addressing multiple problems is difficult, though, because services tend to be specialized and fragmented, with each agency concentrating on a single problem. So the new trend is to organize services around individuals and families rather than around symptoms. It is known as "service integration" or, more colloquially, "one-stop shopping." In dealing with children, the most logical place to locate the services is in schools—which is exactly what New Jersey has been doing for the last three years under its innovative New Jersey School-Based Youth Services Program. "One of the last, the only, institutions now standing in some of these communities is schools," said Edward J. Tetelman of the State Department of Human Services, who created the program. "That's where families and children and youth gather, and it's the correct place for us to be in order to give them access to needed services."

So far the state has set up twenty-nine one-stop-shopping schools, each of which offers a full package of health, mental health, employment, recreational, substance abuse, and family counseling services in or near the school. One-third of the programs are under primary control of the local Board of Education; the other two-thirds are under a nonprofit organization in the community. "It's generally easier if the school is not the lead agency," said Roberta Knowlton of the State Department of Human Services, which has put $6.5 million into the project. "Boards of education are under such pressure that it is hard to keep the funds separate. If the nonprofit is in charge, the program comes as a gift to the schools."

One of the school-run programs is located at Plainfield High School in Plainfield, an urban area with high rates of teenage pregnancy and other problems. The program, which is sponsored by several foundations and local corporations, offers a huge array of services, including one for teenage mothers. At 7:45 each weekday morning, junior and senior girls descend from school buses with their infants and toddlers and head for a nursery on the ground floor. While the young mothers attend classes—regular courses plus one in parenting and child development—their offspring play, sing, sleep, and eat in the nursery. The mothers are assigned mentors, many of whom are employees of American Telephone and Telegraph, which provided many of them with summer jobs. Over the last two years, only one of thirty-four students in the program has had a second child. "We are not grooming them to be day-care providers," said Yvonne Duncan, director of the program.

On the fourth floor of the high school is the program's main office, which includes several counseling rooms and a large recreation room know as "The Place." The walls are lined with posters, such as a picture of a high school boy dressed in a track uniform with the inscription, "If you really want to see how fast he can run, tell him you're pregnant." Students drop by during lunch or other free time to play ping-pong, shoot pool, watch TV, or simply hang out. Counselors are on duty until 8:00 P.M. every school day, and they make it their job not only to be available for students who want to discuss a problem but to spot those who seem to need help. That's what happened in the case of a girl whom we'll call Annette. One of her friends confided to a counselor that Annette was planning to run away from home. The counselor, a social worker, approached the girl and said, "Let's talk." He found out that Annette had been raped by her sister's boyfriend two weeks previously and that her stepfather was abusing her mother and "sexually teasing" the girl. The counselor convinced family members to come by, and a team of counselors, psychiatrists, and social workers met with the family and got the stepfather to pledge to stop abusing Annette and her mother. The counselors met with Annette three or four times a week, and with their support she stayed in school, graduated, and won a scholarship to a nursing college. When that college folded, they helped her find another one. The Place has also been the base for a mentoring program that offered tutoring after school and on Saturdays to students who had missed so much school time that they were in danger of failing. "Over the last two years, fifty-nine students have graduated who otherwise would have failed to get a diploma," said Knowlton. Locating social services in one-stop-shopping schools has presented numerous practical problems. Rules on confidentiality restrict educators and social-services workers from passing on information about students that they might find helpful, and turf battles are common. The day-care center at Plainfield High School had to spend more than it wanted to transport the mothers and children because the Board of Education demanded an expensive school bus rather than a van. But such problems can be worked out over time.

The convergence of two sets of needs—those of social-service providers to coordinate their efforts and of educators to protect the teachers and learning enterprise from a hostile environment—is a powerful force. Kentucky and Iowa have established programs modeled on New Jersey's, and two federal departments, Education, and Health and Human Services, are sponsoring joint research on the one-stop-shopping school. "Among the things that students lack today are adults with the time to talk to them when they are confused about relationships with a friend or how to deal with the drug dealer on their street," said Knowlton. "Schools are safe places where adults can be available and where services can be provided without a stigma."

Research supports the obvious. In a 1987 synthesis of research on the topic, Anne T. Henderson, an associate with the National Committee for Citizens in Education, cited forty-nine studies showing a positive correlation between family-school collaboration and gains in student achievement. Students in schools that maintain frequent contact with their communities outperform those in other schools, and students who are failing in school improve dramatically when parents are called in for help.

To Negron of the Betances School, linking schools with a system of support for families is not only good for the community but constitutes a way to build on the latent strengths of her students. "When I first took over this school, I cried every night," she said. "I don't cry anymore—not because I cried myself out but because I realize that these kids have amazing strengths. Despite everything, they manage magnificently. As a country we can't afford to lose them."

The message of all this is clear: If kids are coming to school hungry, you'd better feed them, or you're not going to be able to teach anything. If parents are not telling their kids to do homework, you'd better find a way of involving parents in their kids' education. If you have kids who have no knowledge of or connection to the world of work, then you'd better talk to the businesses. It's no longer a sign of weakness for schools to admit that they don't have all the answers. Whatever the problem is, there is most likely some sort of external institution out there that will help solve it. The school-as-coach looks for every resource it can get. It is, after all, a learning community.

But there's a *quid pro quo* that comes along with the use of public resources: accountability in how they are used. Devising new forms of accountability is the final missing piece in the creation of smart schools, as we see in Kentucky.

9.

HOLDING FEET
TO THE FIRE

IN THE SPRING OF 1989 the nine justices of the Supreme
Court of Kentucky took a hard look at the way the commonwealth
was running its schools.

What they saw did not make them happy.

The justices found a school system that ranked near the bottom
nationally "in virtually every category that is used to evaluate
educational performance." They discovered that one out of three
adults in Kentucky is a high school dropout and that today's high
school students are following in their footsteps at the same rate.
The justices compared Kentucky with its eight neighboring states
and found that the Bluegrass State was seventh in teacher salaries,
sixth in per-pupil expenditures, and seventh in the number of teachers for every student.

Everyone had assumed that the case before the court, brought
by a coalition of sixty-six financially strapped school districts, was
a garden-variety "school finance reform" action aimed at reducing
the vast disparities in how much rich and poor districts spend on
their children. In Kentucky these disparities ranged from $1,800
per pupil in the poorest district to $4,200 per pupil in the wealth-
iest. As expected, the court, in its 7-to-2 decision, ordered the General Assembly to devise a more equitable system of paying for public
education.

Then came the bombshell!

Instead of merely ordering lawmakers to come up with a more
equitable way of paying for schools, the court, in a decision written
by Chief Justice Robert Stephens, ruled that "Kentucky's *entire
system* of common schools is unconstitutional." The court gave the
legislature until April 15, 1990, to scrap the existing structure and
to come up with "a new system of common schools in the Common-

wealth." Judge Stephens emphasized that when the majority said
"*entire system*," it meant just that. Each and every law and regulation "creating, implementing and financing" public education in
Kentucky had to go. So did the State Education Department, as
then organized, as well as all procedures for creating local school
districts and school boards. The decision, he wrote, "covers school
construction and maintenance, teacher certification—the whole
gamut of the common school system in Kentucky."

By the time the 138 dazed members of the Kentucky General
Assembly headed for home in April, they had complied with the
court's mandate. In the most sweeping educational reform ever
undertaken by a state legislature, the lawmakers designed a more
equitable system of distributing state aid to public schools and
enacted a $1 billion tax increase to pay for it. They endorsed a new
set of educational targets for public schools and ordered a new State
Education Department, whose job was to *help* local school districts
meet these targets, not boss them around. Along the way the politicians eliminated grade levels for the first three years of primary
education and set up a system of carrots and sticks—including financial bonuses and threats of dismissal for teachers and
administrators—to encourage schools to do better. "It's the first
time any state has gone back to the drawing board and rebuilt its
entire education system from scratch," commented Frank Newman,
president of the Education Commission of the States.

More important than the scope of the change, though, is the
fact that Kentucky has begun to fill in the "missing link" of school
restructuring accountability.

The school-reform efforts described in previous chapters are
aimed at overhauling a factory-model school system that is top-
heavy, calcified by regulation and bureaucracy, and accountable
only to its own procedures. The recurrent leitmotivs are decentralization, freedom, empowerment of stakeholders, ownership, and taking charge. In a word, they aim at creating a *deregulated* public
school system. That's all well and good. It's important to democratize
the running of schools, have happy teachers, relax time constraints,
develop authentic tests, and give parents a role in selecting schools
for their children. But such changes are not ends in themselves. It
does no good to deregulate the system unless deregulation results in
more student learning. And it would be irresponsible from a public-

policy standpoint to permit deregulation without some mechanism to assure parents, taxpayers, and others that increased learning is in fact taking place.

Much of what has been discussed in earlier chapters can be viewed as efforts to provide such assurance. Shared decision making, for example, makes principals more sensitive to the views of teachers and forces schools to be more sensitive to the wishes of parents and the community at large. The concept of student-as-worker implies a new form of student accountability based on assuming responsibility for making educational choices rather than simply parroting what the teacher says. Parental choice makes educators more accountable to the needs of families.

The Kentucky Supreme Court decision in the case, called *Rose v. The Council for Better Education*, takes on landmark status because it represents the first time that a court has ruled that a state's system of public education is unconstitutional because of outcomes—or the lack thereof. In the past, courts looked at the fairness and reasonableness of what went *into* the system. Did every child have access to a school? Was there adequate funding? Were teachers properly trained and certified? The Kentucky court broke with that tradition and rejected that logic. Inputs in rules and regulations are fine, it said, but the bottom line is output. Are students learning what they need to know? In the final analysis all that really counts is whether or not students get the "adequate" education to which they are constitutionally entitled. Whether they knew it or not, Justice Stephens and his colleagues had latched onto what is emerging as a whole new definition of education.

It used to be that when you walked into a classroom and saw a teacher standing in front of a class talking, you could assume that education was taking place. Education was *teaching*. Under the new definition, education is *learning*. Sy Fliegel, one of the architects of the parental-choice plan in District 4 in New York City, likes to illustrate the point this way: "I taught my son to swim," he says, "but every time he gets in the water he sinks to the bottom."

The traditional identification of education with teaching has deep roots in the factory model. "Millions of people's careers hinged on the belief that what they did in school each day constituted education, that what was spent on their salaries was purchasing learning and other desirable results, and that the greater the sums expended, the grander the education that would follow," wrote Checker Finn in the education journal *Phi Delta Kappan*. Such assumptions were natural ones, given the factory-model school's orientation toward process and bureaucracy. But now a new value system is beginning to make itself felt. *Rose v. The Council for Better Education* represents the first repudiation from the judicial point of view of values and principles underlying the factory-model school. Under the new definition of education, said Finn, "education is the result achieved, the learning that takes place when the process has been effective."

Put these two ideas together—deregulation of the system and a focus on results—and you have the makings of a very different accountability system for American public schools. Educators cannot enjoy the fruits of deregulation without ensuring that the ultimate purpose of public schools is being accomplished. The multibillion-dollar savings-and-loan scandal has treated the United States to a lesson in the perils of unbridled deregulation. The other side of the deregulation coin is having a way to hold people's feet to the fire. You cannot have *yin* without *yang*. When it comes to the redesigning of American public schools, you cannot have freedom without accountability.

Seen in its broadest terms, the movement to overhaul the basic structure of American public education is thus the search for new ways of doing three things: first, establishing goals and standards of learning that will equip American young people to function as workers, citizens, and civilized human beings in the twenty-first century; second, freeing up students, teachers, administrators, parents, and others with a stake in the system to be as creative and effective as possible; and third, developing a system of accountability that assesses results in a way that circles back to the original goals—a system that rewards those who succeed and intervenes with those who do not.

As the failures of the factory-model school become more apparent, politicians have begun offering educators a new deal that goes along the following lines: "We, the policymakers, are prepared to give you, the educators, more pay and more autonomy. We will free you up to run schools in the fashion that you, as professionals, believe best. But you have to understand that there is a price to be paid for that. You will get those things on the condition that you will accept much higher standards for professional competence, include parents and other concerned citizens, and be willing to take responsibility for the outcomes." Every one of the reform efforts described in the previous eight chapters will go for naught unless this deal gets struck. That's exactly what Kentucky has set out to do.

The goal-setting part of the new equation actually had its roots in the 1987 gubernatorial race in which Wallace G. Wilkinson, a millionaire textbook publisher, running as a Democrat, fought a successful uphill battle to win the state's highest office. Improving Kentucky's school system was a pivotal part of his campaign; Wilkinson proposed a package of measures that would decentralize schools and reward and punish teachers on the basis of how well their students did on state tests. His plan passed the Senate by a 2-to-1 margin but was dead on arrival at the House, where it never even reached a vote.

Unrepentant, Wilkinson figured that even though his school-reform schemes had gone nowhere, it would not hurt for everyone at least to know what it was that schools were supposed to be doing. With the blessing of legislative leaders, the governor issued an executive order in February 1989 creating the Council on School Performance Standards. The council, whose members included teachers, school administrators, business executives, members of the state board of education, and political appointees, was given two assignments. First, it was charged with finding out what Kentuckians wanted their children to know and be able to do after twelve years of school. To do so, the council held focus groups of parents, recent graduates, employers, and others. It also enlisted the University of Kentucky to survey six hundred randomly selected citizens and interview two hundred members of various interest groups. Second, it was charged with suggesting how the state might determine whether these goals were being met.

In its report, released in September 1989, the council laid out some general principles about what schools should be teaching. "Kentuckians," it said, "expect high school graduates to be able to perform tasks that require an excellent command of basic communication and computational skills." They regard traditional academic content, such as history and science, not as an end in itself but as a means to practical skills, such as solving problems, getting along with people, keeping a job, and managing household finances. "In other words," the council concluded, "Kentuckians want graduates to be able to *use* their education in real-life situations." The council listed six specific goals for Kentucky schools. Every graduate, it said, should possess basic language and math skills; know how to apply core academic concepts to real-life situations; be a self-sufficient individual; know how to function as a responsible member of a family and a work group, and in other social settings; be able to think and solve problems; and possess the ability to integrate knowledge gained from various sources and become a lifelong learner. By no coincidence, the council's six goals looked suspiciously similar to the seven "capacities" that the Kentucky Supreme Court had already called for in its landmark decision. For example, the court called for "sufficient oral and written communication skills to enable students to function in a complex and rapidly changing situation" and "sufficient self-knowledge and knowledge of his or her mental and physical wellness." The council cross-indexed its six "goals" with the court's seven "capacities."

While the council was completing its work, the General Assembly was setting up a twenty-two-member Education Reform Task Force to oversee compliance with the court's mandates. As a means of ensuring eventual passage of a school-reform bill, its members included the leadership of both houses as well as representatives of the governor. Deliberately excluded were educators and members of the legislature's education committees other than the chairmen. "We figured that these people were part of the problem," said Jack Foster, the governor's chief education adviser. "They were the ones who created the old system." One of the task force's first acts was formally to endorse the goals for Kentucky schools drawn up by the council—an action that was taken in part at the urging of David Hornbeck, a former superintendent of schools in Maryland who had been brought in as a consultant and was the principal architect of the omnibus reform. "The assumption at the outset was that if the goals were drawn up by Kentuckians, then they probably weren't any good," said one political insider. "It took an outsider to convince them that they were terrific."

With a new set of goals in place the task force, working through its three subcommittees, turned to the task of deregulating Kentucky's schools. Working with Hornbeck and other consultants, the task force for all practical purposes embraced every one of the major ideas underlying the reforms described in the previous eight chapters of this book, starting with a new definition of the role of the State Education Department. The purpose of state education officials in Frankfort is not to tell local school districts how to go about their business. Their role is to set learning goals, assist schools who ask for help in meeting them, and then reward those who succeed and discipline those who do not.

Thus, June 30, 1991, was designated as the magic day on which the existing state education bureaucracy would self-destruct. The following morning, phoenixlike, a new, more flexible, less centralized State Education Department would rise from the ashes—one with greatly diminished regulatory authority in instructional matters. The new department had some marching orders. It was charged with implementing a five-year plan developed by a new Council for Education Technology to improve the use of technology and to link school districts electronically with each other and with the new department in Frankfort. It was instructed to set up a network of family resource centers and youth service centers near schools in disadvantaged areas. The Council on Performance Standards was reconstituted—with new members—and given until December 1991 to translate the six broad goals into specific student performance targets for each subject and grade. It, too, would then self-destruct and turn goal setting over to the new department. The new bureaucracy was also instructed to develop a new curriculum framework for Kentucky schools by July 1993. This framework must include concrete suggestions on teaching techniques, assessment devices, quality textbooks, and other teaching materials, uses of school time, and how to involve the local community in schools. But in keeping with the spirit of deregulation, no school district was obliged to follow the new framework!

The revolutionary plan adopted by the General Assembly did not limit decentralization to the relationship between the state and local school districts. Under the legislation every one of the commonwealth's 177 school districts was required to designate by the fall of 1991 at least one school that would operate on the basis of shared decision making. It also stipulated that by 1995 each district must surrender control of local school budgets and educational programs to management teams in each building made up of three teachers, two parents, and the principal—or some multiple thereof. Once again, though, schools that were successfully meeting their assigned goals could apply for waivers from this, or any other, requirement, and the department would be obligated to grant them. The only exceptions are waivers for regulations relating to health, safety, civil rights, or required by federal law.

One of the most revealing aspects of Kentucky's reform effort was the nature of the political struggle that surrounded it. As one might expect, most of the horse trading revolved around fiscal matters such as the new formulas for distributing state aid to poor school districts. Conspicuously missing, though, was a concern that local school boards were being stripped of virtually all their control over curriculums, textbooks, and other educational decisions. Instead lobbyists for the Kentucky School Boards Association concentrated their resources on a futile battle to prevent the enactment of antinepotism provisions that bar them from putting relatives on the school payroll. "It's a metaphor for the way the old system works," said Jack Foster, the governor's education aide. "People care more about controlling schools than controlling education."

With goals defined and the framework for a deregulated system of public education in place, the task force in Kentucky then turned to the all-important task of building accountability into an entire state system.

The General Assembly in Kentucky framed the accountability issue in terms of the new results-oriented definition of education discussed above. "In the past, universal education meant universal *opportunity*—not universal *achievement*," said Foster. "Schools were expected to sift and sort out the unmotivated and poorly performing students and favor those with some promise of academic excellence. In fact the academic failure of a certain percentage of students was to be expected. Now Kentucky expects a high level of achievement of *all* students, and schools will be held accountable for meeting this expectation."

The new system works as follows: The redesigned State Education Department will set specific goals for educational improvement for every school, and each school's success will be determined every two years, in part by the performance of its fourth-, eighth-, and twelfth-grade students. The goals will be framed in terms of the proportion of its students who attain a specified level of academic proficiency and meet other standards dealing with qualities such as citizenship and personal self-sufficiency. Schools will be expected to reduce the proportion not meeting this standard by a certain percentage each year. Schools will also be judged by other criteria, such as the number of students who stay in school and the success of graduates in getting jobs and staying in college. The statistical base is being established in 1991, with the first goals set for 1993.

A system of carrots and sticks is also being put in place to reward those who meet their goals and punish those who do not. The carrots come in the form of financial rewards. Schools that show steady improvement will receive cash awards to be used as the majority of faculty in the school determine. Carrots are handed out when the number of students performing surpasses the threshold set for the school by at least 1 percent.

The sticks are wielded in a somewhat more complicated fashion. If the proportion of students who attain the expected level of performance either declines or fails to improve between 1991 and 1992, the school will be given two years to meet the goal. The State Education Department will provide them with whatever help they request in doing so. If by 1994 the school has either lost ground or not improved sufficiently, a set of sanctions is triggered, including possible designation as a "school in crisis." At that point a team of "distinguished Kentucky educators"—professional peers selected on one-year terms for such assignments—will be sent in to try to turn the school around. When schools are so designated, parents get the right to request transfer to another school of the superintendent's choice, and the faculty and administrators in the school will become subject to transfer or dismissal based on outside evaluation. After two years the school can be closed. The designation "Kentucky Distinguished Educator" will be given to the outstanding certified educators willing to assist the Department of Education in research projects and staff training and to accept assignments in schools or districts "in crisis." They will serve on one-year sabbaticals, receiving $250 as an honorarium when selected and a 50 percent salary supplement when working in a troubled school. While final testing procedures are being worked out, an interim program will be launched in the 1991–92 school year to establish baselines for the first biennial assessment of schools in 1993–94. Implicit in the plan is what Foster calls a shift from a "production" to a "professional" model. "We are saying that we will let you practice your profession in as unconstrained a manner as possible, but we will also hold you responsible for the results you achieve," he said.

Still unresolved is the pivotal issue of how to measure how much students are learning—and thus whether schools and school districts are meeting their stipulated goals. In its original report the Council on School Performance Standards spelled out some of the practical means by which its six goals should be evaluated. Reading and math skills, for example, should be assessed by exposing students to "lifelike" problems such as reading a manual, writing a business letter, or calculating the cost of a loan. Personal self-sufficiency might be evaluated by self-reporting, simulated activities, or by teacher observation of how the student conducts himself or herself. The ability to integrate knowledge might be evaluated by giving students new information, such as an article describing a new development in the automobile industry or a collection of artifacts from an Indian burial ground, and then asking them, either individually or in groups, to make connections with "previously learned knowledge and knowledge in other fields." In other words, Kentucky will embrace the "authentic" means of testing described in chapter 5.

The job of developing a battery of authentic testing devices has been given to Roger Pankratz, a science educator on leave from Western Kentucky University who was named executive director of the council. The State Education Department has been given until 1995 to get the system up and running. Private test developers, under a contract with the state, will develop performance tests over a four-year period. These tests are to follow prototypes developed by the council and adopted by the state board by the end of 1991.

Kentucky is also working on new ways of reporting results to the public. Instead of determining what numerical score students can obtain on a nationally normed test—something that insures that at least one-half the students will fail—the focus will be on determining how many students can function at what level. "We are now in a world where 'quality' has come to mean 'zero defects,' " says Foster. "We want assurance that every student is learning at the highest level of which they are capable. Another principle is that all students will be expected to perform any and all of the assessment tasks. Each school board must make daily and weekly assessments of student progress and regularly report this progress to students and parents according to local board policy."

Built into the system now being designed is the assumption that Kentucky teachers will "teach to the test." Since the state assessments will mirror regular class assessments, says Foster, "there is no need for concern about cheating or test security." Preparing for the state test is the same as preparing for daily classroom exercises. "In effect, the assessment tasks become the new curriculum," says Foster, "so they must be as rich and complex as the learning outcomes they purport to document." Other measures of accountability are designed to keep these learning goals in focus. State officials will look at attendance, retention, and graduation rates so as to keep schools from raising test scores by holding students back or forcing low-scoring students to drop out.

As a way of keeping the assessment process scandal-free, the Education Reform Act also creates an Office of Educational Accountability as an independent arm of the legislature. Its function will be to monitor the education system, review school finances, verify the accuracy of school district and state performances, and investigate wrongdoing.

By all accounts the first year of Kentucky's reform plan went well. Many school districts raised local tax rates and received corresponding increases in state funds. *Education Week* reported that by April, 93 of the 177 districts had already designated at least one school for shared decision making. Preschool programs and community service centers were proliferating, and many educators who were initally skeptical had begun to boast of results.

Kentucky is still working out the practical problems of implementing its new accountability system, but aspects of its conceptual framework—setting statewide standards and goals, deregulating the system, and holding schools accountable in ways that circle back to the goals—are already being taken up by other states. Simultaneously with Kentucky, South Carolina, for example, enacted a new deregulation plan that rewards schools with good records by freeing them from state regulations governing such matters as staffing, class scheduling, and class structure. Also, principals in such schools no longer need to be certified as principals, and teachers—except those working with handicapped students—do not have to be certified in the subject areas in which they teach. Virginia has moved to transform its State Department of Education from a regulatory agency to a consulting service for districts. The new department will set general goals regarding what students should know and be able to do and then provide support to local districts in meeting these goals. In Washington, under an effort called "Schools for the Twenty-first Century," the state is working with twenty-one schools to waive state regulations, provide additional funds, and allow local school officials to develop their own educational programs. Legislators there are also considering a proposal from Governor Booth Gardner that would eliminate most state-imposed standards and requirements, such as those mandating the number and types of courses needed for graduation. Instead, a new statewide commission would establish performance standards that students would be required to meet, and state officials, using portfolios, projects, and other new assessment devices, would administer examinations to both elementary and high school students.

In moving toward a radically deregulated system, Kentucky is bucking a national trend. Most Americans think of education in this country as a local enterprise, run by locally elected school boards and supported by local taxes. But the last twenty years has brought a major shift in control from the local to the state level. Largely in response to suits challenging the use of the property tax to pay for schools, states have taken more and more control of the financing of public education. Over the last two decades the percentage of school dollars coming from state treasuries jumped from less than 40 to more than 50 percent. Centralizing tendencies were then accelerated by the school-reform efforts of the 1980s. Pressured by business leaders and others to improve the quality of schools, governors and state legislators did what politicians usually do in such situations: They imposed thousands of new rules and regulations, tests, and reporting assignments. The regulations now repealed in Kentucky, for example, included those spelling out the precise number of minutes that teachers must devote to each academic subject each day. Kentucky teachers had been known to interrupt a heated literary discussion because they hadn't done that day's twelve minutes of health education yet. The trend toward centralization is, of course, hardly surprising, for it reflects the prevailing factory model of schooling. The problem is that top-down reforms have the effect of reinforcing the worst aspects of the system they seek to improve.

There is, of course, a certain paradox in all this. The judicial system and the Commonwealth of Kentucky have, in effect, used their *centralized* authority to *decentralize* the system. But given the fact that the Constitution of the United States places responsibility for public education squarely in the hands of the various states, the paradox is one that is likely to become increasingly familiar. When the Minnesota legislature passed that state's parental-choice programs, the lawmakers were essentially saying: We will improve public education by delegating some of our control to parents and students at the grass-roots level.

No one should underestimate the wider implications of the stance that Kentucky took. The legislation specifically calls for shared decision making and, in the case of failing schools, a form of parental choice. But winning carrots and avoiding sticks will require many more changes in how schools operate. It will force teachers to make students take more responsibility for their own learning and encourage them to try proven new techniques, such as cooperative learning. Curriculums will become more focused, and since they will be asked about the performance of every student, teachers will become more innovative and responsive to individual needs. In short, like parental choice, Kentucky's new accountability system is likely to be a catalyst for bringing about all of the changes discussed in previous chapters.

What will it take to get other states to follow Kentucky's lead? That's the topic of our last chapter.

10.

CREATING SMART SCHOOLS: POLITICAL IMPERATIVES

THUS ENDS our journey. It was a fascinating excursion, one that began in Florida, took us to classrooms in Massachusetts, Connecticut, Illinois, Missouri, and Minnesota, across the country to California and Washington, and finally back to the statehouse in Frankfort, Kentucky.

We began with the premise that the factory model of public education—with its top-down governance, its passion for standardization and passivity, its inflexible sense of time, and its lack of any real accountability—can no longer serve the country's educational needs. The factory model may have done the job in simpler times, when schools could take for granted the support of cohesive family and social structures and when the economy did not require large numbers of highly educated workers. But those days are long gone.

The other part of our premise was that somewhere in this vast land someone is taking every one of the values and structures of the factory-model school and turning them on their head. We set out to find these educational pioneers. We saw educators decentralizing school systems, empowering teachers and parents, rethinking the relation of time and learning, and creating new ways of measuring learning. We met parents and students who were choosing their own public schools, and legislators coming up with new ways of holding schools accountable to students, parents, and taxpayers. In short we have seen most of the elements that must go into the creation of smart schools.

The problem, of course, is that most of these educational visionaries are working in isolation. Each has focused on one or two of the structures of public schools that must be overhauled. But no one has put together a whole package. It's as if a dozen people were trying to modernize an old car. One person is streamlining the hood. Another is converting the engine to fuel injection. Still others are working on the wheels or finding a place for air bags. But we still haven't reached the point where all these changes are put together so that we can say we have a new car. We've seen most of the elements that must go into smart schools. But how do we put enough of the pieces together so that we can say we finally have a totally different system of public education? No one has yet taken a Ted Sizer classroom, put it in a decentralized school system, loaded it up with new technologies, made teachers responsible for student progress, measured this progress with authentic tests, brought social-service agencies into the school, and then given parents the choice of whether this is what they want in the first place.

The astute reader has already noted that the process of combining two or more of the elements of smart schools is already well under way. While each of the preceding chapters focused on a particular aspect of restructuring, many of the schools were, in fact, experimenting with more than one. Indeed, there seems to be a symbiosis in the restructuring of schools, with certain changes flowing from others as surely as the sunrise follows the sunset. One of the themes that runs through all of the preceding chapters is *empowerment*—the empowerment of teachers through shared decision making, of students by giving them a more active role in their own learning, of parents through choice. But empowerment cannot be confined to only one set of players. Dade County quickly discovered that once you embrace the concept of empowering stakeholders and delegate decision making to teachers, there is no philosophical reason not to empower parents as well and give them a role in the cadres. As a matter of fact, it becomes a political impossibility not to do so. Jim Streible's efforts to get his students to take more responsibility for their own learning was protected by the political umbrella of Fairdale's shared decision making. His efforts also hinged on the use of authentic tests. Teachers and school officials in Cambridge found that giving teachers a say in instructional policy is essential to the success of parental choice. Where else would the schools get the ideas to respond to parental needs? Decentralization is also the key to Kentucky's new approach to accountability, for teachers are not likely to be willing to accept responsibility for student achievement unless they have some control over what transpires in the classroom. By allowing high school students to take their state per-pupil fund with them when they enrolled in college courses, Minnesota was implicitly challenging the traditional time sequence, which says that college is preceded by four years of high school. Bringing parents into the running of schools is central to James Comer's efforts to build new bridges to the community. Technology, we saw, is important, not only as a powerful learning and teaching tool in itself but as a catalyst to force other changes. Put powerful computers in the hands of the students, and teachers are forced to abandon their traditional authoritarian posture and take on the new role of coach and mentor.

The question then becomes, How do we speed up the process? What will it take to encourage more districts to start thinking in terms of smart schools and to spur those districts that have already bought into one or two elements of them to try others as well?

The first requirement is a *vision*—a sense on the part of the American public that it is possible to have a school system that differs in virtually every fundamental respect from the one that is now failing us. The major purpose of this book is to contribute to the emergence of this vision of smart schools. The sheer diversity of the new approaches described in previous pages should lend confidence that we are talking about a realistic scenario for the future, not a fantasy. But at this point, with school restructuring still in its infancy, it is too early to say with any degree of precision what a system of smart schools will look like. We are all "looking through a glass darkly." But with most of the elements in place somewhere, it is only a matter of time until we see it "face to face."

The one thing we do know is that there is no single model for smart schools. Each of the previous chapters focused on one of the elements of smart schools. But collectively, they constitute a list of ingredients, not a recipe. No single ingredient can make a meal, and different cooks have their own ways of creating the same meal. This point is extremely important, for the last thing that we need is another Frederick Taylor laying out an updated "one best system" for solving our current educational woes. The redesigning of American public education is a process to be pursued, not a project to be completed. Ted Sizer likes to say that his Coalition of Essential Schools is selling "ideas, not models." "We believe that good people with the right idea can fashion a school that will meet the particular needs of their community," he said. American public education has had enough saviors peddling elixirs that will, all by themselves, transform schools—teaching machines, phonics, black English, "teacher-proof" curriculums, computer-assisted instruction. Fortunately, given the diversity of the examples we have cited in previous chapters, this does not seem to be a problem. Teachers, administrators, and political leaders are following widely different paths to the redesigning of public education. They are also bringing different political and philosophical strategies to the task of restructuring schools.

As a graduate student in Geneva many years ago, I took part in numerous lively political discussions, mostly in French, involving students from around the world. Among them were African students, some from former French colonies, some from former British ones. It soon occurred to a German friend and myself that the two groups of African students argued in very different ways. The French-speaking Africans usually started with a broad principle and then, when pressed, looked for specific examples. They were, in a word, Cartesians. Those brought up in English-speaking schools, on the other hand, tended to begin their argument with specifics and then grope their way toward generalities. Call them Lockeans. My friend and I devised a game. Could we, based on the logic used by our fellow students from Africa, determine whether they were from French or British school systems? We became pretty good at it.

Similar differences of approach can be observed in efforts to redesign public schools. Some reformers are Cartesians, approaching problems from the top down. They start with the system as a whole and seek to create the right environment for learning to take place. Paradoxically, Dade County used this top-down approach to decentralize its school system and create a new sense of professionalism among teachers and administrators. The Kentucky legislature used centralized authority to deregulate education in that state. Parental choice in Cambridge and Minnesota is also Cartesian in that it relies on outside pressure on the system to encourage teachers to make the kind of adjustments that will enhance student learning. Other efforts are Lockean, or bottom up. Ted Sizer, for example, starts at the most elemental level of education: the relationship between student and teacher. His assumption is that if we can strengthen that relationship, then the larger structures will fall into place. Parental choice evolved in District 4 in New York City in bottom-up fashion because, in contrast to choice plans elsewhere, it grew out of efforts by teachers to create small new models of education in the form of minischools.

Both the top-down and the bottom-up approaches have their risks. For example, there is no automatic assurance that decentralizing a school system, whether by legislative fiat or through grassroots political agitation, will result in significant improvements. A governing board dominated by teachers can be just as tyrannical as old-style administrators. The Rochester, New York, school system, which has moved heavily toward shared decision making, learned the dangers of what Peter McWalters, the former superintendent, calls the new orthodoxy, in which elected steering committees start behaving like factory-model principals. "If an idea doesn't come from someone at the table, it gets shot down," he said. This happened in the case of Nancy Sunberg, the district's "Teacher of the Year." She and several teachers from other schools developed a proposal called First Class. Their idea was to mix regular and special-education students in the same classroom and bring in an additional teaching aide. She could not get the proposal accepted by her own school's governing team, and other schools could not be found that were willing to try it out. McWalters came to their rescue with district funds. The best that can be said is that giving all of a school's constituents a voice in decision making enables some good things to happen that in the past were impossible. Similarly, as Ted Sizer discovered, there is no assurance that a well-run classroom where students take charge of their learning can survive without political protection. That's one reason why he made his unlikely alliance with the Education Commission of the States and why he and his staff have recently begun conversations with James Comer and his colleagues about developing some joint projects. For more than two decades Comer focused on the developmental needs of disadvantaged students and on ways of bringing parents and teachers into the governance of schools, always working under the assumption that, once everyone was primed for achievement, teachers would know how to make the appropriate changes in their teaching style. But he found that this was not the case. Comer found that he can benefit from Sizer's pedagogical model—student as worker, teacher as coach—just as Sizer can benefit fom Comer's help in understanding child development and in building bridges to the community. "We are all aware of gaps in our own approach that others can fill," said Sizer. In short, the overhauling of American public schools requires both top-down and bottom-up approaches. Smart schools will emerge full-blown only if some people work on the systemic issues while others start in the classroom and work up. They need to meet in the middle, like the workers building the tunnel under the English Channel.

Schools and school systems also bring different cultures, traditions, and political conditions to the process of creating smart schools. Shared decision making and teacher "professionalism" became the wedge in Dade County largely because of the district's solid tradition of cooperation between the school board and the teachers union. It was the logical point of entry. In Los Angeles, where board-union relations were hostile, the same strategy would have been impossible; school-based management was imposed on a reluctant board through labor negotiations. It is no coincidence that it was Minnesota, with its strong populist political tradition and a governor who was a political product of this tradition, that approached reform through parental choice. In Chicago, where the political atmosphere is highly charged, the decentralization of schools came about because parents, teachers, community representatives, and business people formed a coalition that worked with the state legislature. In the absence of such a broad outside political coalition, it is doubtful that any major redesign of schools would have survived.

Let there be no illusions about the enormity of the task of implementing the vision of smart schools. We are talking about the *total* overhaul of a $220 billion-a-year system of education that had remained essentially unchanged in its fundamental structures since the end of the nineteenth century. At issue is nothing less than a *cultural transformation* of American public schools. Systemic reform requires a whole new value system, one that promotes freedom, diversity, and professionalism. It entails the redefining of relationships between students and teachers, administrators and faculties, parents and schools, school systems and political authorities. It means new symbols of success, symbols revolving around what students accomplish, not what authorities prescribe. It requires abandoning the long-standing assumption that the central activity of education is teaching and reorienting all policy making and activities around a new benchmark: student learning.

Leaders who have helped bring about changes of similar magnitude in other institutions also describe their work in terms of "cultural" changes. That's the way leaders of major American corporations talk about their own reform efforts. If you had visited a Ford Motor Company stamping plant in Dearborn, Michigan, ten years ago, you would have seen a small army of workers picking up one side of a heavy piece of steel and maneuvering it under a giant press that transformed it into a door or a fender. At that time, if something happened to the stamping machine, the workers would most likely have called an engineer to report the problem and then sat down for a smoke, presumably glad to have a break in the routine. Today you do not see a small army of workers. Instead a single hourly worker walks around a highly automated machine holding a clipboard, taking readings from computer screens, and referring in conversation to "my machine." It is, in a sense, "his" machine, because he has the authority to determine the best rate at which it will turn out car doors at any particular moment. When something goes wrong, his first act is to peruse his computer screens and see what he can do to correct the problem. Only then would it occur to him to call in the engineer.

This is an example of a cultural change because the worker is the *same person* who, a decade ago, would have sat down and watched someone else try to solve his problem. He has to be the same person because Ford has, for all practical purposes, not hired any new hourly workers in ten years! It laid off tens of thousands of workers and then, after setting out to create a new corporate culture around the idea of "quality," hired some of them back. Donald Petersen, Ford's chairman during most of the period, has a speech in which he refers to the "total transformation of the company"— "literally rethinking, redirecting and reshaping almost every aspect" of the giant automaker. "For management, this new culture meant recognizing that the responsibility for a job well done must be shared by all employees," he said. "Teamwork inspires a 'culture of responsibility.' It fosters a commitment to a mutual goal—in our case superb quality."

The emergence of smart schools requires a parallel shift. The outdated values of the factory-model school—centralization, standardization, fixed schedules, and accountability based on following rules—are giving way to the new values of decentralization, respect for diversity, an emphasis on learning, and accountability based on results. School administrators accustomed to ruling by fiat must learn to become agenda setters and mobilizers of consensus. Teachers, like the worker in the Ford stamping plant, must become part of the decision-making process and, by implication, accept responsibility for the consequences of the decisions they help make. Scheduling policies that build failure into the system because everyone has the same amount of "seat time" must give way to policies that focus on getting *all* students, whatever their learning style, to a satisfactory level. And, of course, the amount of actual learning that students do must become the criterion on which educational professionals, administrators, and teachers alike are held accountable.

The questions that immediately come to mind are: How do you bring about such a fundamental change in the attitudes and values of administrators, teachers, and everyone else associated with the running of public schools? How do you train people to create and run smart schools?

In previous chapters we saw how the Dade County schools underestimated the amount of training that would be required to make school-based management and shared decision making work. That school system now has a training program for future principals that makes clear that anyone hoping to advance up the administrative ladder in Dade County must demonstrate effectiveness in managing a decentralized system. Many districts run future administrators through the training programs of local corporations, where such techniques are becoming routine. We saw how Vermont poured most of its $450,000 budget for new assessment devices into teacher training. Kentucky's new school reform program has training components built in at all levels, including a professional standards board, made up primarily of teachers, responsible for the training and certification of teachers. Yet according to Linda Darling-Hammond, the dean of the School of Education at Harvard University, restructured schools spend one-half of 1 percent on staff development, whereas restructured corporations spend 15 to 20 percent of their revenues on staff development. "The situation of teacher training in the United States is desperate," she said.

Convincing teachers to assert themselves after years of being told to be quiet, take orders, and leave their ideas at the schoolhouse door, though, is going to be far more difficult than equipping principals with a new administrative style or showing parents how to run a meeting or read a budget. In the case of teachers, we're talking about altering a public image—indeed, a self-image—that is deeply rooted in social and educational tradition. Changing this image may be the single most difficult part of the needed cultural transformation.

For as long as anyone can remember, Americans have had a low image of the teaching profession. In 1776 the Maryland *Journal* reported that a ship had arrived in Baltimore from Belfast and Cork with a cargo that included "various Irish commodities, among which are beef, pork, potatoes and schoolmasters." Things weren't much better in 1824, when James Gordon Carter, writing about schools in Massachusetts, said that "if a young man be moral enough to keep out of state prison, he will find no difficulty in getting approbation as a schoolmaster." The first American schoolmasters were men who doubled as town criers or church-bell ringers to make ends meet. By the mid–nineteenth century, teaching had become a "women's profession," a development that assured continued low pay and solidified the popular conviction that teaching was something "anyone can do." Because most young women taught for only a few years before leaving to marry and raise families, training was necessarily brief and limited to passing on a few "norms." Hence the term *normal school* for early teacher-training institutions. Teachers in this country continue to lack the status of their counterparts in other countries, such as Japan. There the teacher is *sensei*, the one who has "gone before," and is paid about as much as an engineer.

Such a humble view of teachers is of course built into the factory model of schooling. "In the bureaucratic model, teachers are viewed as functionaries rather than as well-trained and highly skilled professionals," says Linda Darling-Hammond. "Little investment is made in teacher preparation, induction, or professional development." That's why novices can be treated in the same way as veterans. "In the bureaucratic conception of teaching, teachers do not need to be highly knowledgeable about learning theory and pedagogy, cognitive science and child development, curriculum and assessment," she said. "Teachers do not plan or evaluate their own work; they merely perform it."

If anything, the overall picture is getting worse. In its report "The Condition of Teaching, 1990," the Carnegie Foundation for the Advancement of Teaching found that despite the school-reform efforts of recent years, the nation's teachers "see themselves less involved in key school decisions, find working conditions unsatisfactory, and give the reform movement itself low marks." In 1989 only 55 percent of teachers said that they were satisfied with the control they have over their professional lives, down from 75 percent in 1987. Seventy-one percent said they were "not at all" or only "slightly" involved in setting student promotion and retention policies, and 35 percent said they were not at all or only slightly involved in shaping curriculum in the school. "The conclusion is clear," said Ernest Boyer, president of the foundation. "Improved working conditions are essential if we hope to attract and hold outstanding teachers. They must be *regarded* as professionals, *treated* as professionals, and *consider themselves* to be professionals. Unless we create an environment in the schools—and most especially in the larger community—that sustains such an attitude, we cannot expect improvements to occur."

Obviously much of the responsibility for transforming the nature of the teaching force lies within college and university schools of education. They are the ones charged with turning out future teachers who understand the new professionalism, who are prepared for differentiated staffing arrangements, who are willing to accept the responsibility for making decisions on educational policy, and who are willing to be judged on the basis of how much their students learn. Indeed, the original intention was to have a chapter in this book describing a school of education that has begun to redesign itself along such lines. Unfortunately such a school does not exist. Teacher education is the big black hole in the movement to create smart schools.

Much has been written about the abysmal quality of schools of education in this country. We are all familiar with the stories of dull methods courses and faculty members who fled the elementary and secondary school classroom twenty years ago and, thankfully, have never returned. Suffice it to say that schools of education are failing because they, too, are products of the factory model of education—authoritarian, dogmatic, and *boring, boring, boring.* In other fields, such as law or medicine, the faculty of the professional schools are major change agents. Not so in education.

While it is impossible to point to a school of education that has made the switch from the factory model to smart schools, we can certainly speculate on what one would look like. If the new designs for public school that we have been describing are sound, then the same principles used to teach little kids should also be applicable to training grown-ups who want to be teachers. Faculty members at schools of education must become conversant with—and committed to—the values and methods of smart schools. They must abandon what John Goodlad describes as the prevailing "technocratic" view of teacher education, one that focuses on "what works," in favor of a more reflective approach that thinks of teachers as professional educators, thoughtful and competent practitioners of the art of teaching. Moreover, faculty members must themselves become exemplars of these values and methods. Within schools of education, professors must function as coaches rather than lecturers, and the future teachers must become workers who take control of their own learning. A new accountability system must assure that grades and credentials are based not only on accumulated credits and "seat time" but on demonstrated ability to function in the classroom.

There is some reason for hope that in the not-too-distant future schools of education will get on the restructuring bandwagon. In April 1990 the Holmes Group, an organization of the education schools in ninety-seven public and private universities, issued a report entitled "Tomorrow's Schools" that laid out a plan for "professional development schools" in which college faculty members and schoolteachers would work together to teach the next generation of teachers and to conduct applied research on teaching and learning. The University of Maine, for example, has a new program under which new teachers do their training in public schools under school and university faculty members.

While schools of education are still groping their way toward understanding the ingredients that go into smart schools, some hint of what must eventually come may be seen in new approaches to the so-called in-service training of teachers already on the job. The traditional pattern of such training is for districts to hire education professors or other "experts" to come in and run workshops on anything from the latest theory on teaching reading to multicultural education. Several years ago, leaders of the Pittsburgh school system decided to break with this system of outside experts by letting teachers help each other. They took Schenley High School, which had been closed, and reopened it as a demonstration high school. A staff of master teachers was recruited and given the dual task of operating a regular school and helping colleagues improve their skills. Every teacher in Pittsburgh was given a six-month paid sabbatical to refresh and retool himself or herself by working alongside talented colleagues.

The Jefferson County school system in Kentucky took Schenley one step farther with its Gheens Academy in Louisville. Gheens, which takes it name from the local foundation that helped set it up, is located in a former elementary school that has been renovated to reflect a sense of professionalism. "Most in-service training takes place in spaces that revert to adults after three thirty P.M.," said Terry Brooks, director of the center. "We've tried to create a place that says, 'You're human, and you're a professional.' We've created informal conversational areas where teachers can come early, stay late, and share ideas. We have coffee and soft drinks and don't charge for them." In order to encourage collegiality, Gheens emphasizes school team participation in projects rather than traditional training approaches that emphasize individual participation. Like Schenley, Gheens draws upon teachers to work with colleagues, but with an important difference: The teachers who come for training set the agenda. "There are a lot of well-paid gurus going around the country saying they have *the* method for saving schools," says Brooks. "We try to avoid having the answers before the questions are asked." In other words, at Gheens the teachers are the workers. "We've taken Ted Sizer's notion and applied it to big people," said Brooks. "We reject the idea that someone in the central office knows what you need to be a good teacher. Our job is to be a broker, to find the people who can help you solve some problem that you define."

Pressure on schools of education to change their ways is likely to come from the new National Board for Professional Teaching Standards, which in 1993 will begin issuing the country's first *na-*

tional teaching certificates. Under the existing system, each state issues teaching certificates to graduates of education programs recognized by the state education department. The underlying assumption is that, if the candidate has the correct diploma, he or she must be qualified. This is, of course, yet another example of process-oriented accountability; what counts is seat time, not demonstrated ability! The new credential—board-certified teacher—is unique in three ways. First, it will be national and thus immune from state-level political squabbling. Second, it is optional. It is available only to experienced teachers who seek an additional credential testifying to their professional expertise, in much the same way that physicians, already licensed, seek recognition by specialty boards. Finally, it will be awarded only to teachers who have *demonstrated* their knowledge and teaching competence through written examinations, videotapes, classroom observation, interviews, and other means still being developed.

The National Board, which by its constitution must consist of a majority of practicing teachers, is, arguably, the first formal new structure to be introduced into public education since the early part of the twentieth century. Its principal goal is to restructure public school teaching around a new set of professional standards. The board assumes the existence of a body of professional knowledge that can be codified and transmitted to new practitioners, and it encourages a variety of teaching roles. Board-certified teachers will take on additional tasks, such as serving as mentors to younger colleagues, and a mechanism will at last be in place to pay some teachers more than others. Moreover, it rejects the image of the teacher as someone who simply carries out orders. It sees the teacher as an "educational decision maker," someone who joins with the principal and other colleagues in designing curriculums and other policies. The hope is that once there is a critical mass of board-certified teachers, local schools will begin competing for the services of this new pedagogic elite, thus pushing up salaries, attracting highly competent people into the field, and at last putting to rest the image of teachers as latter-day Ichabod Cranes. Perhaps most important, schools of education whose graduates have difficulty passing the board examinations may be embarrassed into reforming themselves.

There is, of course, an element of chicken-and-egg in all this talk of teacher professionalism. As Marc Tucker of the National Center on Education and the Economy put it, "You can't improve schools without good teachers, but you can't get good teachers unless you treat them as professionals." And at the present time there aren't that many schools that offer this sort of working environment. The National Board comes at the problem from both directions: holding out a new ideal for current and future teachers but also insisting that this ideal be reflected in actual working situations.

The political roadblocks standing in the way of solving such problems are numerous and formidable, starting with the first obstacle, sheer inertia. No institution changes without outside pressure, least of all American public schools. Earlier chapters in this book have described how efforts to do such things as give teachers new authority to make educational decisions, bring parents into the high school, and introduce new technology encountered resistance simply because that's not the way things have always been done. But in the case of schools, this normal human resistance to change is magnified by the bureaucratic weight of the factory-model school system and the nature of educational politics. For one thing, it is by no means clear that many, much less most, teachers *want* to change their role from dispensers of information to coaches or mentors, and they know from experience that they can probably succeed in sitting out what looks like the latest educational fad to come down the pike. Adam Urbanski, president of the Rochester, New York, Teachers Association, estimated that only about 60 percent of his members are strong supporters of efforts to give them a greater role in decision making in return for higher pay and greater accountability. That narrow margin helps explain why the proposed historic contract between that city's school board and teachers union—one that would have tied pay raises directly to job performance through a new evaluation system—became bogged down in a protracted political squabble.

Overt opposition can also be expected from the middle-level managers whose primary function—passing instruction down from on high and reporting back up a compliance—disappears under a decentralized management system. That's been the experience in every major corporation that attempted to decentralize. That was the case in Dade County and in Rochester, where the administrators association went so far as to sue the school district, unsuccessfully, on the ground that allowing master teachers to serve as mentors to fellow teachers usurped their own administrative prerogatives. In Los Angeles, school administrators, worried that they were losing power to teachers under decentralization, organized themselves into a collective bargaining unit. Similar opposition is voiced to parental choice from those whose professional lives are complicated by such a change. Writing in *Education Week*, Dennis L. Evans, a high school principal in Newport Beach, California, questioned whether most parents are prepared to make "substantive decisions" on matters such as the most appropriate form of teaching for their children and whether managerial techniques born in corporate America can be appropriately applied to public education. "For every success story in the business world, we can also point to an Edsel, an Eastern or a Lincoln Savings," he wrote. "If we are so enamored of the corporate model, then perhaps we should consider a Chrysler-type bailout for our schools. Give the schools everything they need financially, and then see if they can 'turn a profit.' "

Thomas B. Timar, a professor of education at the University of California at Riverside, points out that in urban school districts the task is complicated by political balkanization. "In urban districts neither the union nor the school board controls schools," he says. "Instead, various groups compete over issues. Unions generally want to control such items as staff development, merit pay, and career ladders. Administrators want to control finance, resource allocation, and personnel decisions. Other groups control special education. Still others control bilingual and compensatory education or education for the gifted and talented." A similar pattern exists at the state level. "Interest groups, particularly single-issue interest groups, have proliferated, while formal patterns of authority have waned," he says. "The 'iron triangles' of educational politics—schools of education, state education departments, and National Education Association affiliates—that prevailed until the mid-1960s have given way to more porous systems. Finding the center of control over schools in order to create a more hospitable policy environment for restructuring is like 'nailing Jell-O to a wall.' " Timar concludes that "an integrated response to restructuring is not likely to occur without a basic redefinition of the roles and responsibilities of just about every party connected with schools: teachers, administrators, professional organizations, policymakers, parents, students, and colleges and universities." In other words, a cultural change.

The forces of school restructuring need political allies. There was a time when parents might have provided the necessary support, but with the aging of the population, the proportion of voters who have children in public schools—and thus a direct stake in their quality—is declining. Moreover, a growing proportion of such parents either are economically disadvantaged or belong to racial or ethnic groups that lack political clout. Powerful new change agents are needed. The most obvious candidates are the two major recipients of the graduates of public schools: institutions of higher education and employers.

The first of these, colleges and universities, were major players the last time school reform became a major national issue, following the launching of Sputnik by the Soviet Union in October 1957. Faculty members from major universities eagerly plunged into the job of designing new approaches to the teaching of physics, biology, and other sciences at the secondary level, and summer workshops on college campuses provided nurture and inspiration for a whole generation of high school science teachers. This outpouring of interest in school reform also yielded, for better or for worse, the "new math."

This time around, however, colleges and universities were slow to climb aboard the school reform bandwagon. One reason may be that, in contrast to the post-Sputnik era, there are few simple and clear-cut jobs to be done, such as writing a new physics curriculum. The post-Sputnik reform movement focused primarily on science, math, and foreign languages at the high school level, and the goal was to turn out a small core of graduates who were highly competent in these fields. The reforms of the 1990s, though, are aimed at improving academic performance in *all* grades, *all* subjects, and on the part of *all* students. It is a far more daunting task, one that does not hold natural appeal to an academic culture that does not encourage risk-taking. The challenge of redesigning public education looks intractable; better to stick to deconstructing texts and building resumes and leave uncharted social change to others. Another difficulty is that the logical contact point between public schools and universities is the schools of education, which, as we discussed earlier, are, on the whole, part of the problem. There are some conspicuous exceptions, such as Boston University's ten-year commitment to operate and overhaul the schools in nearby Chelsea. But by and large there are few schools of education whose faculty members possess either the understanding, the expertise, or the will to become that heavily involved in the underlying problems of public schools.

Fortunately, this aloofness has begun to disappear. College officials have begun to recognize that, given the current demographics of the school-age population, they have a major stake in improving the quality of elementary and secondary schools. Either public schools get better, or colleges and universities will face the choice of either lowering their standards or getting smaller. It's that simple. As a result, we are now witnessing the growth of what have come to be known as "partnerships" between schools and colleges. A recent study by the American Association for Higher Education identified more than fourteen hundred such programs. It found that partnerships exist in every state, target all grade levels, and involve every type of postsecondary institution, from public community colleges to private research universities. In some cases, colleges and universities offer services directly to students, such as bringing them to their campuses for enrichment work on Saturdays or during the summer or organizing mentoring programs to encourage middle-school students to pursue college preparatory courses once they move on to high schools. Other partnerships focus on improving the professional knowledge of teachers, while still others are aimed at improving curriculums and teaching materials. A few—but still *very* few—institutions have set out to promote school restructuring. The University of Houston, for example, has mobilized faculty members from its business school to encourage the development of school-based management in the Houston Independent School District.

The other ally with enlightened self-interest in improving public schools is the business community. While higher education was still tiptoeing around the issue, many business leaders had already set out to narrow the gap between the skills of today's graduates and the demands of tomorrow's jobs. One of the most visible is David Kearns, who as chairman of Xerox Corporation led his own organization through an elaborate restructuring process and co-authored a book on the subject with Denis P. Doyle, *Winning the Brain Race* (ICS Press 1988).

The alliance between business and the schools is developing at all levels—local, state, and national. Relationships typically begin with an "adopt-a-school" program under which a company establishes a relationship with a specific school. Employees volunteer to serve as tutors or mentors, and the firm comes up with funds to fix the backboard that breaks on the eve of the big game or to send the senior class to Washington, D.C. Such activities constitute a good way for two alien institutions to get to know each other, but while playing sugar daddy may bring delight to the heart of the corporate public relations director, it is not going to produce significant improvements in how much students learn. At that point, companies either back off or decide to become involved on a deeper level.

The range of activities on this deeper level is as varied as the schools and companies involved. AT&T, for example, sponsors a Hispanic Mother-Daughter Program in Phoenix aimed at increasing the educational aspirations of disadvantaged eighth-grade girls by bringing them and their mothers onto the campus of Arizona State University. Honeywell, Inc., which has been instrumental in organizing prenatal-care programs aimed at cutting down the high infant mortality rate and problems of low birth weight in its home city of Minneapolis, has now gone one step further and turned over six thousand square feet on the first floor of its headquarters to a public school for teenage mothers and teenage girls who are expecting.

Companies that are serious about school reform soon come to understand the need for fundamental changes in the way public education is organized. In Boston the Private Industry Council struck a deal with the Boston School Committee (the local school board) under which the school system would work to improve schools and the business community would, in return, promise to arrange either a job or further education to every high school graduate. The Council soon discovered, though, that its members were more successful in meeting their hiring goals than the School Committee was in delivering on its half of the bargain. Reading scores edged up slightly, but dropout levels jumped 10 percent, to an appalling 46 percent of all students. So in 1988, when it was time to renew what was known as the Boston Compact, the business community laid out new terms for a continued relationship. In essence, they said: "We know something about management, and we see our job as sharing that knowledge with you. We insist that you decentralize your management structure." After some bitter negotiations between the School Committee and the Boston Teachers' Union, Boston schools embraced school-based management and a new accountability system that measures individual school performance.

Corporations have also banded together at the statewide level. Not long ago the Lincoln National Corporation, a major insurance company and the largest single employer in Fort Wayne, Indiana, interviewed three thousand candidates for entry-level clerical jobs and discovered, to its horror, that more than half were so lacking in basic employment skills—reading, basic math, writing a cover letter, communicating with other people—that they could not even take the firm's preemployment test. Ian Rolland, Lincoln's chief executive officer, responded in two ways. First, he scrapped plans to construct a $60 million office building that the city had hoped would be a catalyst for rebuilding the downtown business area. "We couldn't be assured that we could attract enough qualified people," said Roland. Then he joined with fifteen other leaders of Indiana corporations to form an organization called COMMIT aimed at improving the state's public schools. The agenda includes giving teachers a greater role in decision making, abolishing rules and regulations that stifle creativity, and setting up programs to assure that first-graders arrive ready for academic work. Another statewide group, the Minnesota Business Partnership, an organization of eighty-seven corporations, was a prime force in getting that state's legislature to approve parental choice.

On the national level, the Business Roundtable, made up of the chief executives of the top two hundred corporations, has launched a ten-year campaign to promote "systemic" change in public education. The organization has drawn up a list of nine "Essential Components of a Successful Education System" that its staff and that of member corporations are working to implement across the country. The so-called Nine Points embrace most of the changes described in previous chapters: decentralization, performance-based assessment, high-quality preschool programs, greater use of technology, a system of rewards and punishments, and the locating of health and other services in schools in order to "reduce significant barriers to learning." The Roundtable has built alliances with governors, teachers unions, and other business groups, such as the National Alliance of Business, in a push to get these principles enacted as operative public policy in all fifty states. One technique has been to conduct a "gap analysis" to measure a state's education policies and programs against the Nine Points, identify the discrepancies and then figure out how to bring the two into line. John Akers, the chairman of IBM who served as the first chairman of the Roundtable's education task force, explained that he and his fellow corporate leaders were acting out of enlightened self-interest. "American business leaders have a vital stake in raising the quality of America's public schools," he said, emphasizing that this can be accomplished only by altering the entire system. "The school reforms of the 1980s failed because they tried to take a nineteenth-century institution and make it work for the twentieth century," he added. "By contrast, the Nine Points represent a plan for going back to square one and rethinking every aspect of the way we organize and run schools—from the way we manage districts, schools, and classrooms to the way we use time, measure student achievement, and hold educators accountable." One stipulation of the Roundtable effort is that anyone who wants to join them must buy into the whole package. "The Nine Points is not a list of options from which to pick and choose," said Akers. "It is a package that, to be effective at all, must be implemented in its entirety."

There are, however, some troubling aspects to business involvement in the redesigning of American public schools. For one thing, business has traditionally shown a short attention span when it comes to matters like school reform. More important, it is unclear that, as a whole, the American business community understands the need for restructuring even in its own backyard. The bipartisan Commission on the Skills of the American Workforce, cochaired by two former U.S. labor secretaries, William E. Brock III and F. Ray Marshall, recently conducted a major cross-cultural study of industrial practices and concluded that most American companies continue to rely "on an outdated system in which a small educated and highly trained elite directs the activity of another three-quarters of our workers with minimal skills."

Of the $30 billion that business spends on employee training, only 7 percent reaches frontline workers. Rather than increase productivity through fundamental improvements, the vast majority of businesses have relied on cutting wages or "outsourcing" work to Third World countries, a tendency that has kept hourly wages of American workers 15 percent behind the pace of inflation in the last decade. The commission's report, written by Ira Magaziner and entitled "America's Choice: High Skills or Low Wages," warned that such head-in-the-sand thinking was an invitation to national disaster, both economically and socially. "If productivity continues to falter," it said, "we can expect one of two futures. Either the top 30 percent of our population will grow wealthier while the bottom 70 percent becomes progressively poorer, or we will all slide into relative poverty together."

Not surprisingly, most of the interest in school reform on the part of American business has come from the 5 percent of industries that have undergone restructuring themselves, and some of these have come up with ingenious approaches. RJR Nabisco, for example, has begun handing out $30 million in grants to schools willing to do what is routine in the business world but against the instincts and acculturation of most educators: take risks. "We want to fund the china-breakers," says Louis Gerstner, RJR Nabisco's chairman. "The biggest risk in education is not taking them."

Another needed ingredient for the creation of smart schools is effective political leadership of a special sort. The effort to redesign American public schools has progressed in ways that might be compared to the civil rights movement of the 1960s. At that time people in communities all around the country decided for a variety of reasons, local or otherwise, that there was an urgent social problem that needed to be addressed. There were, to be sure, highly visible national leaders such as the Rev. Martin Luther King, Jr., but the leadership as a whole was broad, diffuse, and stylistically varied. The National Association for the Advancement of Colored People has little in common with militant groups such as the Congress on Racial Equality, beyond a broad commitment to certain basic social and political goals. Often the leaders were running to keep up with the led. The movement to restructure public schools has followed a similar scenario. It is, first of all, a "movement"—one that grew out of the concerns of citizens in thousands of communities across the country that schools as currently organized are not serving the needs of either their children or the nation. Ideas were fed by innovators such as Ted Sizer and James Comer, and financial support came from regional and national foundations. But the implementation of new ideas has relied largely on the skill and dedication of teachers, school administrators, parents, and others in individual schools and local districts.

As the preceding chapters have shown, these grass-roots efforts have matured to the point where it is now possible to begin thinking about how to pull them together and create whole new systems of smart schools. Kentucky did this on its own, and since early 1991 the major foundations that have been bankrolling individual reform efforts—Rockefeller, Ford, MacArthur, Pew, and the like—have begun wondering out loud whether the time has come for them to stop putting their money on individual horses and begin funding projects that would combine the ideas of several of the reformers. The National Center on Education and the Economy, whose 1986 report, "A Nation Prepared: Teachers for the 21st Century," was one of the first to call for a package of structural changes, has organized a dozen reform-minded states and local districts into a National Alliance for Restructuring Education. The point is to identify common concerns, swap lessons they have learned, and bring in outside experts to conduct research on how to solve common problems. For example, most districts found that the all-important first step of identifying common goals turned out to be far more difficult than they expected. "There's no tradition for this sort of thing," said Marc Tucker, president of the Center. So the Alliance came up with a series of techniques for tapping into a variety of constituencies such as telephone polls, community-wide forums, and focus groups with students, business leaders, and local colleges and universities.

The most effective leadership so far has come from state governors, both individually and collectively. The current school reform movement first began developing in the late 1970s and early 1980s in Sunbelt states like North and South Carolina whose economies had been prospering because of cheap labor. Their governors, though, were wise enough to realize that this was not a permanent condition, that the cheap labor was only stopping in their states temporarily until it bounced to some place like the Caribbean or Thailand or South Korea. They realized that the future prosperity of their states required better public schools and, backed by business interests, took steps to improve them. By the mid-1980s school reform had become a major focus of the National Governors' Association, which formally embraced the notion that incremental changes in the current system of public education—the tightening measures advocated by "A Nation at Risk"—were no longer sufficient. In 1989, the NGA published a report entitled "Time for Results" laying out a comprehensive strategy for the restructuring of American public schools. The agenda included school-based management, parental choice, and accountability based on outcomes rather than following rules. The governors have continued to make restructuring a major topic of their meetings, and the association has published yearly reports on what has been done to realize the goals they espoused.

Political leadership at the national level has been a different story. Ronald Reagan's first secretary of education, T. H. Bell, played an important role by appointing the National Commission on Excellence in Education and generating the 1983 report "A Nation at Risk." This document was pivotal because it thrust the deficiencies of American public education onto the national political stage. The problem was that Bell's successor during the second Reagan administration, William J. Bennett, either failed to understand the underlying structural nature of these deficiencies or chose to ignore them in order to pursue other political agendas. Bennett's successor, Lauro V. Cavazos, demonstrated an intellectual understanding of the problem but never developed an effective program for addressing it.

The political situation changed abruptly with the inauguration of George Bush in January 1989. Apparently sensing—quite correctly—that the quality of schools was an issue with considerable grass-roots appeal, Bush as a candidate declared his intention to be "the education president." In September 1989 he convened the country's governors for an "education summit" on the campus of the University of Virginia in Charlottesville. It was only the third time that a president had called the governors together to discuss a single issue (Theodore Roosevelt did it on the environment and Franklin Roosevelt on the economy). Building on the work already done by the National Governors' Association, the president and his guests drafted a set of six national goals for American public schools by the year 2000 and established a National Education Goals Panel to monitor progress toward them. The goals were: All children will start school ready to learn; the high school graduation rate will rise to 90 percent; students will demonstrate competency in challenging subject matter; American students will be first in the world in science and mathematics achievement; every adult American will be literate; and every school will be free of drugs and violence.

In the months that followed, the White House did little to push the "education president" theme. This puzzled many observers, for it seemed tailor-made for a Republican president who needed a good, low-cost domestic political issue to exploit. Few people were arguing that the federal government should pour tens of billions of new dollars into public education, much less take over the running of 16,000 local districts. To the contrary, much could be achieved if the president simply used his bully pulpit to define the stake that the country has in good schools, highlight the structural nature of the problem, and use the resources of the Department of Education to encourage and coordinate the efforts of those working at the state and local level. Major new federal spending could be confined primarily to traditional programs such as Head Start. Politically such an approach had the appeal of preempting what has traditionally been considered "a Democratic issue."

By April 1991 such thinking had apparently filtered into the White House. By then Lamar Alexander, a widely respected former governor of Tennessee who had been an early advocate of school-reform in his own state and was a major architect of the policies of the National Governors' Association, had succeeded Cavazos as secretary of education. Working with the White House domestic policy staff, he put together a political strategy that dramatically altered the politics of school reform.

The Bush plan, entitled "America 2000" and rolled out with great fanfare by the president at a White House briefing, broke with the past in a significant way. Whereas the political strategies of "A Nation at Risk" were based on the assumption that the current system could be improved, the new strategy called for far-reaching changes. "To those who want to see real improvement in American education, I say: There will be no renaissance without revolution," he said. "For the sake of the future, of our children and our nation, we must transform America's schools. The days of the status quo are over."

"America 2000" was built on three pillars, starting with the development of new models of "break-the-mold" schools. Paul O'Neill, the CEO of Alcoa, was enlisted to form a nonprofit New American Schools Development Corporation to raise as much as $150 million in private contributions to be passed on to teams with proposals for new school designs. The plan also called for the creation of 535 "New American Schools," one in each congressional district and two more for each state by 1996. The president would ask Congress to appropriate at least $1 million for each school, which would then become self-supporting with public or private funds, and local communities seeking designation as an "America 2000 Community" would apply for funds to build their won "break-the-mold" schools. The contest for the initial round of grants of $500,000 to $3,000,000 by the New American Schools Development Corporation was a resounding success, drawing 686 proposals from organizations as diverse as General Motors, the San Diego Board of Education, the Smithsonian Institution, and the YMCA. On the other hand, Congress reacted coolly to the idea of paying for a new school in every district, and many corporate leaders resented being asked to contribute to the new corporation. Most argued that they were already investing heavily in their own school improvement efforts, and some expressed fears of being drawn into a partisan effort, especially during an election year.

Secondly, to no one's surprise, Bush also enthusiastically embraced the idea of giving parents choice of which school their children will attend. To the consternation of many, though, he went on to encourage states and local districts to change their rules so that parents could apply tax dollars to send their children to either public or private schools. He also called for a change in federal policy so that, in states that have adopted choice programs, federal Chapter I benefits for disadvantaged students could follow individual children out of the public system into any nonpublic school they selected. This posture represented a reversal of the previous policy of limiting choice to the public framework and thus promised to complicate the building of alliances working toward the realization of smart schools.

Finally, the Bush plan pushes hard for the creation of a national system for assessing how much students know. He called for the drawing up of national standards defining what all American students should know in five subjects—mathematics, science, English, history, and geography—and the establishment of voluntary American Achievement Tests geared to these standards for students in the fourth, eighth, and twelfth grades. The Bush proposal for testing follows the general lines of a project jointly organized by the National Center on Education and the Economy in Rochester and the Learning Research and Development Center at the University of Pittsburgh. Backed by $2.45 million in foundation grants to cover the first eighteen months, the New Standards Project aims at developing a series of assessments based on portfolios and other new measuring devices. The tests would be based on a highly publicized "syllabus" of what students should know and be able to do in each subject, developed by teachers in these subjects. The program could vary from state to state, and an independent "national education standards board" would decide whether each state's program met a predetermined national standard. "The object is not to sort students out, but rather to create a system designed in the expectation that all students, sooner or later, would meet a high standard and pass the exams," said Marc Tucker of the National Center.

Among the various pieces of "America 2000" the proposal for a system of national assessment has struck the most responsive chord, primarily because it echoes a recent, and fundamental, change in public attitudes toward standards and assessment. Unlike virtually every other industrialized country, the United States has never had either a formal set of expectations for its public schools or a national system for benchmarking the achievement of every student. Instead, the defining of standards has been left willy-nilly to the publishers of textbooks and standardized tests. We measure student performance by whatever it is that can be machine-scored on a standardized test, which is to say that our expectations are minimal and confined primarily to the recall of factual information and other low-order skills. Calls for national testing or a national curriculum have been roundly rejected on the ground that they would undermine local control of schools.

Growing public awareness of the stake that the country as a whole has in the success of our 16,000 local school districts has now led to a sea change in public attitudes toward national standards and assessment. In 1989 the Gallup Poll, in its annual survey for the education journal *Phi Delta Kappan*, found that 77 percent of Americans favor national high school graduation examinations, and 69 percent support the use of a standardized national curriculum. "For the first time in our history, Americans appear to be more concerned about national outcomes than about local school control," said Ernest Boyer of the Carnegie Foundation for the Advancement of Teaching, "and they're demanding evidence that our huge, 200 billion dollar annual investment in public education is paying off."

The political process of drawing up national standards for educational outcomes and devising a national system for measuring the performance of individual students, schools and school systems against these standards is well underway. It began at the Education Summit in Charlottesville in 1989, when the president and the governors agreed to work toward the six national goals for education, including higher academic performance. Then Congress set up a National Council on Education Standards and Testing to study whether it was feasible to set up a national system of academic expectations and assessment. In January 1992 the thirty-two member council issued a report answering "yes" on both counts and proposing a new governance structure to oversee the new system, including a twenty-one-member council of educators, public officials, and representatives of the general public. The proposal remains controversial. Critics argue that the federal government should not be telling local districts what to do and warn that, if history is any guide, some sort of Gresham's Law will set in, and any such tests are likely to gravitate to some sort of lowest common denominator and oversimplify complex learning processes. There are also issues of fairness and equity. What about students in struggling and underfunded schools? Is it fair to hold them responsible to new and higher standards? Proponents reply that the proposed system is "national" rather than "federal"; that is, it reflects the consensus of professional groups such as the National Council of Teachers of Mathematics, not the will of a government agency.

They agree that assessment based on an updated version of existing multiple-choice tests would be worse than no system at all, but they point out that the proposal calls for a "system" of assessments, not a national test, and that the technical difficulties can be overcome if political leaders give designers enough time. As for the fairness issue, they argue that national standards will be a force for equity because it will make it clear to all for the first time where inequities exist and where resources to correct them must be targeted.

The debate over national standards and assessment is important because it goes to the heart of the struggle for systemic change. The adminstration's "America 2000" plan presents a good-news/not-so-good-news scenario. The good—actually, very good—news is that the president of the United States has proclaimed that *comprehensive* and *structural* changes in our system of elementary and secondary education are a national priority. Moreover, he has set in motion a series of forces that are likely to keep the need for such changes on the national political agenda. The not-so-good news is that while the Bush plan talks a lot about successful new schools, it does not say much about a successful new *system of education*. It talks about creating new American schools, but there is no mention of state boards of education, school districts, school boards, or superintendents. There is nothing in the administration's thinking that addresses the need for a new outcome-based system of public accountability, nor is there any talk of a "safety net" for students who, for reasons beyond their control, fall through the cracks. Indeed, the emphasis on vouchers suggests an unspoken agenda that these structures are not needed. What looks at first glance like a comprehensive Cartesian scheme to drag American public schools from the nineteenth into the twenty-first century is actually very bottom-up and Lockean. Individual smart schools cannot survive for very long unless they have company. Exceptional schools must work in a regular system. "Bush has proposed a giant demonstration project and a new examination system," said David Hornbeck, the consultant to Kentucky. "It's fine to generate a lot more Comers and Levins or Sizers, but there is no vehicle to organize them into a system other than choice, which is not a powerful vehicle. The president is feeding the bottom up. But we need both."

Proponents of national standards and assessments argue that such a system would be a positive force for systemic change. The problem is essentially strategic: How do you move from a list of desired structural changes to a totally changed system? How does a school system that has its hands on several pieces of the elephant—say, school-based management, parental choice, and portfolio assessments—develop a strategy for integrating the missing pieces? If there is common agreement as to the goals of education and accountability based on measured student performance, then a system of standards and assessments would provide a benchmark against which virtually all important education policies would be measured. Susan Fuhrman, director of the Policy Center of the Eagleton Institute of Politics at Rutgers University, points out that at the present time most education policy is "characterized by contradiction and ambiguity." For example, state laws require special education students to be pulled out of classes, while teachers and administrators work for continuity and stability. English teachers stress the understanding of literature while state tests measure spelling. A system of common standards and assessments would bring coherence not only to curriculums and teaching but to structural issues as well. Decisions about which textbook to use, which teacher training program to fund, how to organize the school day, and so forth would all be made with reference—explicit or implicit—to whether a particular choice will lead to the desired student performance.

One perennial issue, of course, is money, a topic that has taken on a greater and greater urgency as states and local school districts face budget crises driven by the recession. Where will the funds come from to finance investments in not only new tests but technology, the retraining of teachers and administrators, parent information centers, and other elements of restructured schools? Reformers argue that, once up and running, such schools may be more efficient than current ones. But even if that is true, the transition costs for retooling our schools are real and considerable. Achieving the first of the six goals that came out of Charlottesville—adequate preschool programs for all children—is itself a big-ticket item.

As in other issues surrounding the redesign of American public education, the solution lies in how one frames the issue. During the 1980s spending on education increased by 33 percent after inflation. Though it is true that the schools have taken on major new responsibilities, such as the education of handicapped students, no one would seriously argue that the quality of education in this country has increased by one-third during this period. School officials and union leaders argue that to improve schools, states and local communities must spend more money on education. Skeptics reply by asking what schools have done with the gigantic increases they have already received. And so the argument goes round and round.

The basic premise of this book—that the current system of public education has been stretched to the limits—leads to the assumption that pouring more money into the factory model of schooling is, for the most part, foolish. It does no more good to spend more money on teacher talk than it does to increase the amount of time that students have to sit in class listening to it. Such reasoning underlies taxpayer revolts against higher taxes for schools in states like Nebraska and Oklahoma. On the other hand, there is reason to believe that spending more money on restructured schools will pay off in terms of increased performance. Numerous politicians, including Democrats such as Governor Bill Clinton of Arkansas, argue that the American people are willing to spend more for public education. "All they want," he says, "is some assurance that they will not be pouring money down a bottomless hole."

There are some signs that time may be running out on those seeking to create smart schools within the existing public framework. One must not forget that the current system of public education is by no means carved in stone. Other democratic nations have, in fact, created quite different ones. Holland, for example, has three separate systems. Britain has moved in the same direction by allowing groups of parents to "opt out" of the public system, establish their own schools, and receive public funds. Some in this country have already given up on the possibility of overhauling the factory-model public schools—witness the Milwaukee attempts at a voucher plan for poor students, the home schooling movement, and Chelsea's willingness to turn its schools over to Boston University. With its emphasis on vouchers and its focus on restructured schools rather than on redesigned systems, President Bush's "America 2000" plan gives practical as well as spiritual support to those looking beyond the public school system. In an interview with the author, Lamar Alexander, the secretary of education, made it clear that the administration is operating with a new definition of public education. "So far, when we think of putting public and education together, we only think of schools operated by local schools districts," he said. "We don't think of schools operated by anyone else. And I think we need to begin thinking of that." Sophisticated union leaders understand this threat, which is why some of them have been at the forefront of structural changes. "This is our last chance to make public schools work," says Pat Tornillo, the union chief in Dade County.

In its simplest form, the challenge confronting American public education is to do on a national scale what Kentucky is doing on the state level—establish goals, deregulate the system, and produce new forms of accountability. We must take this principle and apply it to the way states relate to Washington, districts to their states, schools to their districts, teachers to their schools, and students to their teachers. As Terry Brooks of Gheens in Louisville puts it, "What we need to do is centralize the troublemaking and decentralize the solutions. Leaders should be in the business of selling problems, not solutions. If the dropout rate is a problem, get teachers and principals to agree and to invest in some solutions."

In "Time for Results," the National Governors' Association endorsed the all-important link between goals and an output-based system of accountability and, in effect, offered educators and the public a deal: We'll get off your back if you agree to be held accountable for results. Lamar Alexander, then the governor of Tennessee, put it succinctly: "The kind of horse-trading we're talking about will change dramatically the way most American schools work. First, the governors want to help establish clear goals, and better report cards, ways to measure what students know and can do. Then, we're ready to give up a lot of state regulatory control— even to fight for changes in the law to make that happen—if schools and school districts will be accountable for the results. We invite educators to show us where less regulation makes the most sense. These changes will require more rewards for success and consequences for failure for teachers, school leaders, schools, and school

SMART SCHOOLS, SMART KIDS

districts. It will mean giving parents more choice of the public schools their children attend as one way of assuring parents of higher quality without heavy-handed state control."

In the final analysis, the success of the movement to redesign American public education will depend on whether the American public can come to understand the urgency of the situation. George Bush has articulated the national "stake" in what a decentralized system accomplishes. Cecil Daniels, Jim Streible, Mary Lou Mc-Grath, Mark Share, and the hundreds of other local teachers and school officials involved at the grass-roots level in the reform efforts described in this book understand it. So do many elected officials and other leaders. "For the first time, all the power brokers are saying that the school system is no good," suggested Frank Newman, president of the Education Commission of the States. Among the power brokers he referred to are the nation's governors who wrote, "If our standard of living is to be maintained, if the growth of a permanent underclass is to be averted, if democracy is to function effectively into the next century, our schools must graduate the vast majority of their students with achievement levels long thought possible for only the privileged few."

In 1983, shortly after the publication of "A Nation at Risk," I made a trip to Japan to look at its schools in behalf of *The New York Times*. At the time, numerous reports had heralded the successes of Japanese schools. My goal was to determine what the Japanese had figured out about education that had somehow eluded American educators and what secrets we might appropriate. The answer, of course, was that there were no such secrets. The culture of Japan is so different from ours that what works there has little chance of working in the United States. Japan is a homogeneous culture, one where conformity to social custom is not only a fact of life but a social ideal. The Japanese people agree not only on the importance of education, both for individuals and for the nation, but on the nature of education. Education is essentially the transmitting of knowledge from the teacher to the student. As a result, Japan operates a highly efficient, centralized system of education that violates many of the tenets that American educators hold dear. For example, most classes have forty-five students. The United States, by contrast, is a heterogeneous nation, one where public education is a local enterprise and whose citizens disagree vigorously over the nature of education.

One thing that we must learn from Japan, though, is the importance of education. Japan is a collection of islands, cumulatively the size of California, two-thirds of it uninhabitable, with a population slightly more than half that of America crammed into this space—and with no natural resources. Ever since the Meiji Restoration about the time of our Civil War, and especially since World War II, the Japanese have realized that, as a nation, they must live by their wits, by what comes out of their heads. They have nothing else going for them. The United States, on the other hand, has always had vast natural resources—oil, coal, timber, farmland. We could always be a little sloppy about our educational system because we had other resources to fall back on. But now, as everyone knows, the ecological frontier has closed. As the Japanese have long understood, we must now live by our wits.

There is evidence that Americans want good schools and are willing to pay for them. There is evidence that the systemic reform of American schools is underway. The only issue is whether it will happen fast enough to prevent us from becoming a second-rate industrial power and a socially polarized nation. In the final analysis, what is at stake in the movement to replace the factory-model school with smart schools is not only the quality of education that we seek for our children but also the kind of nation they will inherit.

Appendix: Resource Guide
to Smart Schools

O NE "authentic" test for *Smart Schools, Smart Kids* is whether it inspires readers to become involved in creating smart schools in their own local communities. Here are some resources—by no means inclusive—to help readers get started.

CHAPTER 1. THE LEARNING CRISIS

"A Nation at Risk: The Imperative for Education Reform," published in 1983, is an important historical document. For a free copy write the National Commission on Excellence in Education, U.S. Government Printing Office, Washington, DC 20402.

Two recent reports spell out the economic and social cases for school improvement:

- "America's Choice: High Skills or Low Wages," the report of the Commission on the Skills of the American Workforce, published in June 1990, is available from the National Center on Education and the Economy, P.O. Box 10670, Rochester, NY 14610; $18.
- "Investing in Our Children: Business and the Public Schools," published by the Committee for Economic Development, can be obtained from the CED, Distribution Division, 477 Madison Avenue, New York, NY 10022; $9.50 prepaid plus $1.05 shipping.

CHAPTER 2. SMART SCHOOLS

The National Committee for Citizens in Education, a parent advocacy group, has two recent technical manuals about school-based management and shared decision making:

■ "School-Based Improvement, a Manual for Training School Councils" by Barbara J. Hansen and Carl L. Marburger (1989); $39.95.
■ "A Workbook on Parent Involvement for District Leaders" by Anne T. Henderson and Carl L. Marburger (1990); $39.95. Write the NCCE at 10840 Little Patuxent Parkway, Suite 301, Columbia, MD 21044.

The *School-Based Management Forum Newsletter* is a monthly publication that monitors current trends and offers practical advice. It is published by the National Clearinghouse on School-Based Management, P.O. Box 948, Westbury, NY 11590; $89 a year. Ask for a free sample copy.

For those wanting more information about specific cities, try the following:

■ The Dade County public schools offer a free packet on their experience, including reprints of articles, evaluation reports, and descriptions of their new Satellite Learning Centers. Write Frank R. Petruzielo, Assistant Superintendent, Bureau of Professionalization, 1450 N.E. Second Avenue, Room 421, Miami, FL 33132.
■ The Hammond, Indiana, story is described in "Expanding the Teacher's Role: Hammond's School Improvement Process" by Jill Casner-Lotto, in the January 1988 *Phi Delta Kappan,* a monthly education journal available in most public and school libraries.
■ Chicago's *Catalyst: Voices of Chicago School Reform* is published ten times a year by the Community Renewal Society, 332 South Michigan Avenue, Chicago, IL 60604; annual subscription: $10.

CHAPTER 3.   SMART CLASSROOMS

For a look at the state of teachers and teaching in America, see "The Condition of Teaching: A State-By-State Analysis, 1990," published by the Carnegie Foundation for the Advancement of Teaching. Copies are available from the Princeton University Press, 3175 Princeton Pike, Lawrenceville, NJ 08648; $12 prepaid.

The Coalition of Essential Schools has a free packet of information about its activities. Write Brown University, 1 Davol

Square, Providence, RI 02903. For information about Re:Learning: From Schoolhouse to Statehouse, write the Education Commission of the States, 707 Seventeenth Street, Suite 2700, Denver, CO 80202-3427.

The Cooperative Learning Center at the University of Minnesota will send general information about cooperative learning and the work of the Johnson brothers. Write Cooperative Learning Center, University of Minnesota, 202 Pattee Hall, 150 Pillsbury Drive, S.E., Minneapolis, MN 55455.

CHAPTER 4. RESETTING THE CLOCK

The national organization tracking the growing trend toward year-round education is the National Association for Year-Round Education, P.O. Box 11386, San Diego, CA 92111. Ask for "The Seventeenth National Reference Directory of Year-Round Education Programs for the 1990–91 School Year," a sixty-one-page directory; $10. Also ask for "The National Association for Year-Round Education: A Historical Perspective" by Don Glines and James Bingle, a forty-five-page booklet; $5. The association also publishes a newsletter, available to members, called *The Year Rounder*.

The Accelerated School project is now a national program operating in several states. For more information, write the project at the Center for Educational Research at Stanford (CERAS), CERAS Building, Stanford University, Stanford, CA 94305. For "An Overview of the Missouri Accelerated Schools Project," write Joan Solomon, Project Director, Director of Urban Education, Department of Elementary and Secondary Education, P.O. Box 480, Jefferson City, MO 65102.

CHAPTER 5. BEYOND TESTING

Need a little CLASS? That's the acronym for the Center on Learning, Assessment, and School Structure headed by Grant Wiggins and Holly Houston, two nationally known assessment experts. CLASS will send *Smart Schools, Smart Kids* readers a portfolio (naturally) of sample assessments and articles on assessment. Write CLASS, 39 Main Street, Geneseo, NY 14454; $5.

Portfolio News, edited by Winfield Cooper, is a new newsletter tracking alternative forms of assessment throughout the country. For a subscription write *Portfolio News*, c/o San Dieguito Union High School District, 710 Encinitas Boulevard, Encinitas, CA 92024; $25 a year.

"Beyond Standardized Testing: Assessing Authentic Academic Achievement" by Doug Archbald and Fred Newmann (1988) provides a seventy-six-page framework for thinking about assessment and reviews the uses of standardized tests and alternatives. It is available from the National Association of Secondary School Principals, 1904 Association Drive, Reston, VA 22091; $8, ask for item number 2108808.

For details on how Vermont is changing the nature of its testing contact W. Ross Brewer, Director of Planning, Department of Education, 120 State Street, Montpelier, VT 05620, and ask for the free "Vermont's Packet on the Student Assessment Program."

CHAPTER 6.   NEW TECHNOLOGIES

One national education group that follows the efforts at implementing technology in the schools is the National School Board Association, which publishes an annual report called "The Electronic School"; $10, updated every fall. It also publishes "Bridging the Learning Gap: Selecting and Implementing an Integrated Learning System"; $125, which includes a fifteen-minute videotape and guidebook. Write NSBA, 1680 Duke Street, Alexandria, VA 22314.

To see how Silverdale, Washington, is planning for the future, ask for a copy of "Strategy 2020," a booklet on technology; $6.50. If you prefer the high-tech approach, ask for the video, "Schools for the 21st Century"; $5. Write Central Kitsap School District, c/o Warren Olson, P.O. Box 8, Silverdale, WA 98383.

CHAPTER 7.   THE LAST MONOPOLY

The federal government has established a hot line to answer questions about school choice. Call the Center for Choice in Education at

1-800-442-PICK for information about choice programs, 9:00 A.M. to 5:00 P.M. eastern time Monday through Friday.

A recent thirty-two-page handbook, "Public School Choice: An Equal Chance for All?," is available from the National Committee for Citizens in Education, 10840 Little Patuxent Parkway, Suite 301, Columbia, MD 21044.

Two recent collections of essays on a variety of political and educational perspectives:

■ *Public Schools by Choice* by Joe Nathan (Free Spirit Press, 1990); $7.95 plus postage and handling.
■ *Choice in Education* by William Lowe Boyd and Herbert J. Walberg (McCutchan, 1990).

Two books that look at the choice issue from the point of view of teachers and other educators:

■ *Politics, Markets and America's Schools: The Fallacies of Private School Choice* by Albert Shanker, president of the American Federation of Teachers, and Bella Rosenberg, assistant to the president of AFT, raises questions to ask choice advocates. It is available from the American Federation of Teachers, 555 New Jersey Avenue, N.W., Washington, DC 20001; $29.00, ask for item number 100.
■ Keith Geiger, president of the National Education Association, has written a book with Ruth Randall, former Minnesota State Commissioner of Education, called *School Choice: Issues and Answers*. It is available from the National Educational Service, 1821 West Third Street, P.O. Box 8, Bloomington, IN 47402; $21.95.

The theory of controlled choice and a description of the Boston experience can be found in a chapter called "Choice, Decentralization, and Desegregation" by Michael Alves and Charles V. Willie in Volume II of *Choice and Control in American Education,* edited by John Witte and William Clune (Falmer Press, 1991). "Access to Opportunity" describes the experiences of Minnesota students in four statewide school choice programs in 1989–90. It is by Joe Nathan and Wayne Jennings and is available from the

Center for School Change, Hubert M. Humphrey Institute of Public Affairs, University of Minnesota, Minneapolis, MN 55455; $7.50.

CHAPTER 8. LEARNING COMMUNITIES

To learn more about James Comer's program, write the School Development Program, Child Study Center, 230 South Frontage Road, P.O. Box 3333, New Haven, CT 06510-8009. A video about the Comer process will be available soon.

An information packet about Edward Zigler's Schools of the Twenty-first Century can be obtained by writing the Bush Center in Child Development and Social Policy, Yale University, 11A Yale Station, New Haven, CT 06520-7447. The packet is free and includes reprints of articles about the program, as well as a booklet, "The School of the Twenty-first Century," that describes programs in different cities.

CHAPTER 9. HOLDING FEET TO THE FIRE

For a look at how one state is overhauling its education system, write the Kentucky Education Reform Task Force, Office of Communications, Kentucky Department of Education, Capital Plaza Tower, Frankfort, KY 40601.

CHAPTER 10. CREATING SMART SCHOOLS: POLITICAL IMPERATIVES

The nation's governors are issuing ongoing reports on education; "Time for Results" is their 1991 report. For a copy, write the National Governors' Association, Publications, 444 North Capitol Street, Suite 250, Washington, DC 20001-1572; $12.95 prepaid.

Another report that lays out a more comprehensive plan for reform is "A Nation Prepared: Teachers for the 21st Century," a report of the Taskforce on Teaching as a Profession for the Carnegie Forum on Education and the Economy, published in 1986. For a copy, write the National Center on Education and the Economy, P.O. Box 10670, Rochester, NY 14610; $9.95.

You'll find more than one thousand college-school connections in the *National Directory of School-College Partnerships: Current Models and Practices* by Franklin P. Wilbur, Leo M. Lambert, and M. Jean Young (1990), published by the American Association for Higher Education. Write to AAHE Publications, One DuPont Circle, Suite 600, Washington, DC 20036; $13.95 plus $2 postage and handling.

A FINAL WORD

Building coalitions is important. For information on a variety of grass-roots organizations, strategies, and resources, contact the National Committee for Citizens in Education, 10840 Little Patuxent Parkway, Suite 301, Columbia, MD 21044. This organization provides reports, books, and information on a range of topics about schools. NCCE operates ACCESS, a computerized information bank; to use it, call 1-800-NET-WORK. Also ask for a copy of *NET-WORK for Public Schools,* a twenty-four-page magazine published six times a year; free with membership, otherwise $12 a year. For a free catalogue of other publications and a copy of the newsletter *Network,* call 1-800-NET-WORK (301-997-9300 in Maryland) between 10:00 A.M. and 5:00 P.M. eastern time, Monday through Friday. A Spanish-speaking counselor is available from noon to 5:00 P.M.

"Essential Components of a Successful Education System" is a pamphlet available from the Business Roundtable that lays out a nine-point overall plan for school restructuring. Write: The Business Roundtable, 200 Park Avenue, Suite 2222, New York, NY 10166; free.

Finally, for a look inside the educational establishment—organizations, journals, research—the Educational Resources Information Center sponsors clearinghouses on a variety of topics. Contact ERIC, U.S. Department of Education, Office of Educational Research and Improvement, Washington, DC 20208-1235, or call 1-800-USE-ERIC. There is also "A Parent's Guide to the ERIC Database," available from the Educational Resources Information

Center, ERIC Clearinghouse on Rural Education and Small Schools, P.O. Box 1348, Charleston, WV 25325; 1-800-624-9120.

To track general trends in education and news about school reform efforts, see *Education Week*, a Washington-based newspaper published forty weeks a year by Editorial Projects in Education, Inc.; write *Education Week*, P.O. Box 2083, Marion, OH 43305; $49 a year.

INDEX